D1164691

LEADERS OF PHILOSOPHY

ARISTOTLE

ARISTOTLE

by

G. R. G. MURE, M.A. (OXON.)

Fellow and Tutor of Merton College, Oxford

NEW YORK
OXFORD UNIVERSITY PRESS
1932

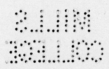

PRINTED IN GREAT BRITAIN

ΤΟ ΠΑΛΑΙ ΤΕ ΚΑΙ ΝΥΝ ΚΑΙ ΑΕΙ ΖΗΤΟΥΜΕΝΟΝ ΚΑΙ ΑΕΙ
ΑΠΟΡΟΥΜΕΝΟΝ, ΤΙ ΤΟ ΟΝ

'The eternal question : What is Being ?'

ARISTOTLE, *Met.* 1028^{b}2-4.

CONTENTS

CONTENTS

PREFACE

I DO not know what would be the ideal form of a short book on Aristotle, and I cannot hope that my selections and emphases will satisfy all the readers of this most imperfect work. I have in the main followed Aristotle's own order of exposition, which is roughly reflected by the order of the treatises in our *Corpus Aristotelicum*. But I have made an important exception by treating the logical doctrines last instead of first. For, however the matter may have appeared to Aristotle and to his students at the Lyceum, I do not think his logic becomes intelligible to the modern reader until the general character of the Aristotelian universe is understood. Lack of space has inevitably given my exposition a dogmatic appearance, which conceals many doubts on the part of its author. I can only ask the reader to treat my interpretations as no more than the best suggestions which I have to offer. I have quoted no Greek without translating it, and for that purpose I have taken the Oxford translations as a basis. But I have not scrupled to alter their renderings when I thought I must. I have felt it necessary in Part I to give an account of Platonism which may seem too detailed and too loosely connected with my main theme. But I do not think that Aristotle can be understood unless Plato is first presented as something more than a mere source of his pupil's philosophy. I could include in Part III only the merest fragment of a vast subject-matter, and that has not saved me from having to touch upon topics with which I am most incompetent to deal. I have included a rather long account of Professor Jaeger's views, not because I regard his method of approach as any substitute for close study of the actual philosophic content of the treatises (nor, I am sure, does he), but because, right or wrong, they call attention to a neglected problem, which no Aristotelian can henceforward ignore.

Professor Joachim, who has taught me almost all I know

ix

of Aristotle, has put me yet deeper in his debt by reading this book in MS. His very valuable comments have not only saved me from many mistakes, but also, I hope, enabled me to set some points in a clearer light. I have received great assistance from discussions with Professor J. A. Smith, and he has been kind enough to express in writing for me his views on some of my difficulties. Lastly, I count myself most fortunate to have had the general advice of an Editor who is himself a distinguished Aristotelian scholar.

THE *CORPUS ARISTOTELICUM*[1] WITH LIST OF ABBREVIATIONS USED

LOGIC (the *Organon*)

Categoriae	Cat.
De Interpretatione	Int.
Analytica Priora	An. Pr.
Analytica Posteriora	An. Post.
Topica	Top.
De Sophisticis Elenchis	SE

NATURAL SCIENCE

Physica	Ph.
De Caelo	Cael.
De Generatione et Corruptione	GC
Meteorologica	Meteor.
De Anima	An.
De Sensu et Sensibili[2]	Sen.
De Memoria et Reminiscentia	Mem.
De Somno	Somn.
De Somniis	Somni.

[1] The fragments of the dialogues, etc., and all certainly spurious works are excluded from this list. The authenticity of Meteor. and MA is questionable, though their doctrine is Aristotelian. Where page and line are cited, the reference is to the Berlin Academy edition.

[2] This and the eight following treatises are usually grouped under the title *Parva Naturalia*.

De Divinatione per Somnum
De Longitudine et Brevitate Vitae
De Juventute et Senectute[1] . . Juv.
De Vita et Morte
De Respiratione
Historia Animalium . . . HA
De Partibus Animalium . . . PA
De Motu Animalium . . . MA
De Incessu Animalium
De Generatione Animalium . . GA

FIRST PHILOSOPHY

Metaphysica . . . . Met.

PRACTICAL SCIENCE

Ethica Nicomachea . . . EN
Ethica Eudemia . . . . EE
Politica . . . . . Pol.
Atheniensium Respublica
Rhetorica . . . . . Rh.
De Poetica . . . . . Poet.

[1] An editorial title for the first two chapters of *De Vita*. It does not represent their contents.

PART I
THE HERITAGE OF ARISTOTLE

I

ARISTOTLE'S LIFE AND PROBLEM

I

IN 399 B.C. Socrates talked for the last time with his friends, and died a martyr's death. About twelve years later Plato, long sickened of Athenian politics, founded the Academy, and transplanted to within its walls the ripening seed of philosophy which Socrates had sown in the open market-place of Athens.

By 367 the Mediterranean peoples knew that a fresh intellectual world was being conquered. A group of brilliant specialists, particularly mathematicians, had joined Plato, and men of action were constantly leaving the Academy to practise as politicians the principles which they had learnt as Plato's pupils. For its curriculum, closely reflected in Plato's *Republic* (see p. 40), was organised on the assumption that a strict scientific training is the best education for practical life. Plato too, like Socrates, had the gift of attracting youth, and young men of varied ambitions flocked to join the first of all universities.

In this year Plato himself, though sixty years of age, was in Sicily, trying to make a philosopher-king of the young Dionysius II, who had just become tyrant of Syracuse. During his absence Aristotle of Stagira in Chalcidice, the seventeen-year-old son of one Nicomachus, physician to Amyntas II of Macedonia, joined the Academy.

For the twenty years during which Aristotle remained an Academician there is little evidence. Plato is said to

3

have called him "the reader" and "the mind of the School." Tales of insolent behaviour to his master are amply disproved by the courteous, if uncompromising, tone in which he expresses disagreement with Plato in his writings. From these we can also safely infer that he absorbed knowledge with unexampled energy and versatility, but that he leaned rather to natural science than to mathematics. Paternal influence may account for his special interest in zoology.

On Plato's death in 347 his nephew Speusippus became head of the Academy. Aristotle, a Greek but not an Athenian, could hardly have succeeded Plato, and he was probably out of sympathy with the direction in which Speusippus was developing Platonism. Moreover the threat of Macedonian domination was already looming—it was the year of the fall of Olynthus—and Aristotle was probably unpopular from his Macedonian connexion. In any case, he migrated with Xenocrates to the court of Hermias, the enlightened tyrant of Assos and Atarneus in the Troad, who may himself have been educated at the Academy. Hermias gave him his niece, Pythias, in marriage, and, joined by several other Platonists, he worked there for three years. He and his wife then moved to Mitylene in Lesbos, probably induced to do so by Theophrastus, once Aristotle's fellow-student and subsequently his successor.

In 343 he was asked by Philip of Macedon to become tutor to his son Alexander, who was aged thirteen. Hermias at the time was intriguing with Philip against Persia—he was in fact two years later treacherously captured and tortured to death by the Persians—and the invitation may have been due to him. We know no details of this romantic connexion, but Aristotle acquired enough political influence to intercede on behalf of Athens, Stagira, and Eresus, the native city of Theophrastus, who was still his companion at the court of Pella. No doubt political philosophy occupied much of his time. He is known to have written works for Alexander on Monarchy and on Colonies, which do not survive. Aristotle had been brought up in the shadow of the Macedonian monarchy, and was hence perhaps not wholly wedded to the city-state ideal. We may suppose that he hoped in Alexander to discover the Platonic philosopher-king in a fresh form ; the man of genius who would Hellenise the whole civilised world, even if he should revolutionise its political structure. But to the temperament of an Alexander the heroic legend of Greece made more appeal than did her intellectual heritage. From Alexander's subsequent career and from the silence of history the inference is that Aristotle inspired respect, but exercised an influence over his pupil even less permanent than Plato had exerted upon Dionysius. Alexander became regent for his father in 340, and Aristotle probably spent the next five years at Stagira.

In 335 he returned to Athens and founded the Lyceum in some buildings which he rented close to the temple of the Lyceian Apollo. From some covered walks in the gardens his followers acquired the name of Peripatetics. Alexander, who had now for a year been king of Macedon, is said to have contributed handsomely to the foundation, but he was himself preparing to conquer the East in a spirit hardly consonant with the Hellenism which Aristotle had no doubt tried to inspire.

For twelve years the output of the Lyceum was enormous. Its work was much more professional and specialist than that of the Academy, which soon stood by its side an overshadowed rival. Plato had professed contempt for the written word as a dead thing, incapable of answering questions (cf. *Phaedrus*, 257c ff.). He had done his best to give it life by writing in dialogue form, and philosophy was still so young that he needed to introduce as speakers only the men of his own and of Socrates' time. The

B

detailed memory and the lively but critical imagination of a great artist enabled him to portray them conversing with Socrates as if they were still alive, and his sense that he was Socrates' true inheritor allowed him to develop their conversation towards conclusions of his own. But Aristotle had no such gift, and philosophy had already a past. As the school under his influence extended the huge range of its activity, its students had to collect records of fact and of the theories of men long dead. Not for nothing had Plato called him " the reader." The amassing of a great library of MSS. marks the foundation of the Lyceum as the beginning of learning in the modern sense of the term. Aristotle himself, whose power of work has no parallel, systematised his own notes into something like an encyclopedia of the sciences. No doubt he often embodied the results of others, but the treatises bear the stamp of a single master mind. During this period Aristotle lost his wife, who left him a daughter called after her mother. He took a mistress, Herpyllis, a Stagirite, who bore him a son, Nicomachus.

In 323 Alexander died at Babylon. Aristotle was at once in a dangerous position. He had come to Athens when the sack of Thebes was exciting strong anti-Macedonian feeling. He was the intimate friend of Antipater, whom Alexander had left as regent during his Asiatic campaigns. Only a year before his death Alexander had insulted the Greek world by sending a herald to the Olympic Games to command the recall of all banished citizens on pain of instant invasion ; and the herald was Nicanor, son of Aristotle's guardian Proxenus, and adopted by Aristotle. A charge of impiety was trumped up—the Academy and the school of Isocrates may have had a hand in it. Aristotle, " lest," as he is supposed to have said, " the Athenians should sin twice against philosophy," left the headship of the school to Theophrastus and retired to Chalcis, where Macedonian influence was paramount.

There a year later he died from chronic indigestion, probably aggravated by overwork.

Gossip attributes to Aristotle a bald head and thin legs, small eyes and a lisp ; but he is said to have dressed smartly. His reputed statues are less unflattering. We are told also of a mocking tongue and a ready wit, and, less plausibly, of a dissolute life. The man who wrote that " Most men are timid in danger and corruptible " (Rh. 1382^{b}4), had doubtless no great opinion of common humanity. But well as he knew the world, he can have left himself little time to indulge in its vices. His ethical teaching is neither cynical nor ascetic, and we may suppose that he himself made that proper and necessary use of the pleasures of sense which he enjoins. His will bears witness to a kindly nature. The executor is Antipater. He leaves the greater part of a considerable sum of money to Nicanor, who is to become guardian to Nicomachus and to marry the young Pythias when she is of age. He frees many of his slaves, and provides against the rest being sold. For Herpyllis he provides amply, mentioning her with affection. But, when he dies, the bones of Pythias are to be moved to his own place of burial.

2

" Becoming is for the sake of substance, not substance for the sake of becoming " (PA 640^{a}18, GA 778^{b}5). A conception of substance, or the real, as the goal towards which develops a potential being that, save as ultimately realised, is neither real nor intelligible, dominates the whole course of Aristotle's speculation. Follow him as he applies it in every sphere which he investigates ; watch it grow from this initial abstract formula into a concrete universe of thought ; and you may hope to grasp the essential meaning of his philosophy. Use this conception again to relate him to his predecessors, and you do precisely what he himself does in the first book of his *Metaphysics* ; extend it beyond him in a history of Aristotelianism, and still you will be applying what he must have recognised as his own critical method.

This programme—though the last part of it is somewhat beyond our scope—has its difficulties. The history of philosphy, like philosophy itself—if they be not identical—is always a verdict given on insufficient evidence. The historian can depict little more than a formal pattern, an abstract scheme of ordered stages, upon a limited canvas. To closer scrutiny much that he has made to appear irrelevant and accidental stands out with an obvious vitality, falsifying the picture, convicting him of a false a priorism, exposing his generalisations as purely empirical. The pre-Socratics, it is true, only survive in fragments ; and for the most part our knowledge of them has passed through the medium of history. Socrates himself we cannot wholly distinguish and separate from the pupil who immortalised him. But the dialogues of Plato, who least of all thinkers claimed finality, have yet, not only as works of art but as " visions of all time and all Being," a deathless individual quality, mocking ironically the industrious historian. Men have lived and died contented to be Platonists, two thousand years after Plato.

Aristotle presents the same problem, and a fresh one as well. Had none of his writings been young with that immortal youth which asks no maturity, he would not have cast his spell upon the middle ages. But, besides this, Aristotle does not offer a single and consistent interpretation of his own formula. Men are both less and more than movements, and the historian must accept his limitation. He can only try to hold a balance between losing the individual thinker in an interrelated whole, and letting the triumphs of " creative " thought stand out in isolated, and therefore partially irrational, perfection. His best hope of success is to remember that he can never quite succeed, and to supplement generalisation with quotation. And the exponent of Aristotle may find further consolation in the fact that it is this very difficulty which is reflected in Aristotle's own struggle with the problem of substance. We shall hold, then, to our programme, though space will confine our account of Aristotle's predecessors to a mini- mum relevant to our main theme.

To Aristotle, as I have already suggested, every philo- sopher of an earlier generation is important as a lisping Aristotelian. " Greatness of soul," we are told in the *Ethics*, " deserves and demands great things " (EN 1123b2), and there is much justice in Aristotle's claim to inherit the accumulated wisdom of nearly three centuries. Despite some omission and wrong emphasis he is no bad historian of Greek thought, at any rate from Thales of Miletus to Socrates ; and for that period he will provide us with most of what we need. On the other hand, a frequent obscurity in his treatment of Plato, a too literal interpreta- tion of myth, and an occasional lack of sympathy, have left his commentators a problem not easy of solution. We will follow Aristotle, therefore, until he speaks of his master, and then sketch for ourselves very briefly a few essential features of Plato's teaching. But first we must give a rather more concrete, though still far from precise, meaning to the formula which introduced this discussion.

That whatever can be known by man—who as such is rational—must in some sense *be*, and must owe its being to a cause, and that whatever *is* can be in some measure known by man, Plato taught and Aristotle assumed ; nor did either of them question that ultimately goodness, in a broad sense of value or excellence, is this cause, nor that knowledge is desired by man for its own sake. The universe, however—at least in part and in so far as it is perceptible by the senses—is a universe of change. But if the being of a thing is also change—if it, seemingly, both *is* and *is not*—what is it ? How can we know it ?

Aristotle answers that change too is not irrational nor uncaused. In all its forms—in substantial change (the process, for example, of which the termini are birth and death) and also in the less radical alterations of quality, bulk, or even spatial position—change passes always to or from a climax ; it is never mere flux but always either ebb or flow, anabolic or catabolic, a doing or an undoing. And it is this tide taken at its height which reveals what the developing thing is. At this climax the thing is realised (*is* ἐνεργεία, " in a state of actuality ") ; then only it possesses its own full nature and excellence, and is at once real and intelligible. Before and after this zenith it *is* only potentially (*is* δυνάμει, " in potentiality ") ; its full nature is beyond or behind it ; it is neither fully real nor fully intelligible.

So far we have viewed the developing thing dynamically. But we can also arrest it at any stage of its continuous development, and take the tide in cross-section. Then, if we look forward to the " end," we must say that the thing *is* only potentially ; but if we look back across the course already traversed, we can say that at least in relation to its previous potential stages the thing *is* in actuality. Thus the thing is actualised relatively at any stage, but not completely save at its culmination or end ; and according to the direction in which we look, we may say that it *is*, or again that it *is not*. To take a common illustration of Aristotle's which, as we shall see, seemed to him less artificial than perhaps it does to us :—Bronze that the sculptor is fashioning is mere potency and promise of the statue to be ; but already in bronze simpler physical elements are actualised.

If we now concentrate solely on the cross-section we have taken, and analyse the developing thing statically in terms of its composition, we shall find that it is a concrete (σύνολον) of matter (ὕλη) and form (εἶδος). Matter and form are in fact the respective static equivalents of potentiality and actuality. They are consequently, like the latter, a pair of terms purely relative to one another. For Aristotle means by matter not a kind of " stuff "— perhaps opposed to mind—but the materials of which a thing is composed. Correspondingly by form—though often in speaking of physical things he couples it with the term μορφή, shape—he means structure, or structural principle. Yet in saying that form is structure we must remember that only so far as the concrete of matter and form is not in possession of its own full nature, so far as it *is* only potentially, only so far does form appear as a structure imposed upon a matter in some degree alien and indifferent. So far as the concrete is something actualised, it *is* form. Matter stands out as a positive constituent (a positive complement of the form) within the concrete, only so far as the latter is still something potential : in relation to the yet unrealised climax the matter of the concrete is the measure of its failure to become form. And even this apparently positive and constitutive character which matter bears is due to form. For that which at any given stage of development we see as matter becoming actualised—or, we may now say, " in-formed "—is, relatively to its past stages, already in-formed matter. The bronze which is matter to the sculptor is already a structure in-forming the simpler elements that go to compose it.[1]

For its ambiguous nature as both a positive constituent and a measure of failure to be form, Aristotle calls matter " a cause both of being and not-being " (Cael. 283ᵇ5). Usually he speaks of matter as " recipient " of form, or as the " substratum " (ὑποκείμενον) out of which the formed thing develops and into which it passes away—*i.e.* the potential element which persists and is present at every stage, dwindling as the thing develops, increasing as it dissolves. He adds that a thing comes to be also out of

[1] Modern physics seems to be re-discovering this conception of matter.

its " privation " (στέρησις), and " privation " in its most strict sense means the absence of a character from a subject which is by nature such as to possess it. That is in fact to say that the substratum, though numerically one, contains two moments : (a) the substratum proper, the positive element which persists through the change ; and (b) the negative element—the determinate absence or not-being of the form—which throughout the course of the change is being replaced by its contrary. The bronze statue, for instance, comes to be out of the unshaped bronze : (a) out of bronze as the positive persistent ; (b) also, though only incidentally, out of the privation or determinate not-being of shape as out of its contrary. In short privation—the shadow, as it were, which form casts before it, or leaves behind it—is really matter so far as matter *is not*, or is *merely* potentially.[1]

We have then two analyses of the developing thing, the one dynamic the other static ; and their intimate union will become clearer still if we add that ἐνέργεια, so far translated " actuality," can, where the full nature of the subject of change consists in active function, be rendered also and more significantly " activity."[2] It now remains to show how this process is rational ; in virtue, that is, of what kind of cause or reason the developing thing can at once *be* and be understood.

The Aristotelian αἰτία, commonly translated " cause,"

---

[1] The same bronze can of course take various shapes. The matter of natural change is characterised by a far more precisely determinate privation of the form which it is destined to subserve ; see Chapters V–VII.

[2] In Met. VIII Aristotle makes what is in effect a distinction between (1) ἐνέργεια as actualisation of matter or potentiality, and (2) ἐνέργεια as active putting forth of power ; *e.g.* the sculptor's activity would be ἐνέργεια in the second sense ; the bronze, as he shaped it, would be in transition towards ἐνέργεια in the first sense. But there is no real difference of principle ; both are cases of actualisation. Accordingly in this book I have usually translated δύναμις " potentiality," though in some contexts " power " or " potency " might have rendered the term more exactly.

is a notion far wider than any familiar usage of the English term. It presents a fresh analysis of the situation in four aspects, three of which correspond to form and actuality or activity, and one to matter. (1) The formal cause is the form itself ; for it is *qua* form and in virtue of form that the thing possesses its full and intelligible being. Aristotle often calls a thing's formal cause the τί ἦν εἶναι of it, the " what it was[1] for it to be," or, as it is usually rendered, its " essence." The final cause (2) is form, but form operating on the developing thing *a fronte* as its yet unrealised " end " (τέλος). It is the οὗ ἕνεκα καὶ τἀγαθόν (" that for the sake of which, *i.e.* the good ") of the development. The efficient cause (3) is again the form, but as operative *a tergo*. It is the answer to the question τί πρῶτον ἐκίνησε ; " what initiated the development ? " Form appears as the efficient cause in different ways, but efficient and final causes are generally found together. The originative source initiating the development—ultimately, of course, the form—is proximately a temporally prior manifestation of the end or τέλος. Examples from spheres which it will concern us later to differentiate, are : the conscious but ideally conceived end of the sculptor or of the moral agent, which is the *prius* of their activity ; the adult animal which initiates in the sexual act a process of development of which embryo and adult are the termini. (4) The material cause is matter as the substratum out of which the thing comes to be ; *e.g.* the sculptor's bronze—a passive but necessary condition of development.

Diremption of the form into formal, final, and efficient causes which do not wholly coalesce, and the corresponding prominence of matter, are of course the measure, wherever they are found, of imperfection and unreality.

This causal analysis is the foundation of Aristotle's theory of knowledge. " We think we know when we know

---

[1] The so-called " philosophic " imperfect tense, used to express timeless being.

the cause " (An. Post. 94ᵃ20), and that is, primarily, when we grasp the form as a definition—a λόγος or " defining formula."[1]

But here emerge difficulties which at present we can only state. The object of a perfect knowledge must be fully actualised form, Being self-subsistent and self-caused, an object of intelligence and not of sense ; and that, as our introductory formula hinted, Aristotle commonly entitles substance. But can the ambiguous " developing thing " of our analyses claim any such title? If it was a singular individual which developed, this even at its climax—as an adult animal, for example—still visibly contains matter, and " the cause both of being and not-being " can hardly be what " we know when we know the cause." Matter is perceptible to sense and, as such, is opaque to knowledge. The defining λόγος which knowledge requires is universal, and the singular individual is just what defies definition.

Can we, on the other hand, identify the developing thing with the genus, or better, the species, which as actualised it exemplifies ? That is at least something intelligible and not, as such, perceptible to sense. We might argue that we can only define the singular in terms of its specific character ; therefore this character is its real nature, its τί ἦν εἶναι. Yet surely substance must be individual, even if its individuality be not that of the perceptible singular ?

Are there, then, degrees of substance, and is genuine substance to be found elsewhere than in this realm of " developing things " ? But that way lies a total divorce of substance and becoming.

Aristotle strove continually with the problem of substance, and we have dimly foreshadowed some of his

---

[1] So closely does Aristotle link knowledge and its object that λόγος in one of its many significantly related meanings is an actual synonym of form.

attempted lines of solution.   Yet the fourfold causal analysis is the permanent centre of his philosophy and the crucial test to which he brings the metaphysic of his predecessors.[1]

[1] For a detailed account of it, cp. Ph. II, 3, and Met. V, 2.

II

THALES TO SOCRATES

I

In man's delighted exercise of his senses—sight especially —for their own sake, Aristotle finds proof that " all men by nature desire to know."[1]

When the struggle for bare existence has yielded him a necessary minimum of security and comfort, man has leisure to wonder at the world. First he makes a myth, a " composite of wonders,"[2] which still is more of a question than an answer ; then he begins to philosophise, to be in earnest with the problem of what ultimately *is*.

The primitive monists of Miletus readily fit into Aristotle's scheme. " Of the first philosophers," he says, " most thought the principles which were of the nature of matter to be the only principles of all things ; that of which all things that are consist, and from which they first come to be, and into which they are finally resolved (the substance remaining, but changing in its modifications)—this is what they call element and principle of things, and therefore they think nothing is ever generated or destroyed, since this sort of entity is always conserved " (Met. 983b6 ff.). . . . Thales,[3] the first founder of this school, says the principle is water (for which reason he declared that the earth rests on water), getting the notion

[1] The first words of Met. I. This account is based chiefly on Met. I and Burnet, *Early Greek Philosophy*, and *Greek Philosophy, Thales to Plato*. My debt to Burnet's work in this chapter is too great for detailed acknowledgement.

[2] Cp. Met. 982b19.   [3] *Floruit* 565 B.C.

perhaps from seeing that the nutriment of all things is moist, and that heat itself is generated from the moist and kept alive by it (and that from which they come to be is the principle of all things) " (*ibid.*, 20 ff.). . . . " Anaximenes . . . makes air prior to water, and the most primary of the simple bodies. . . . Heraclitus of Ephesus says this of fire " (*ibid.*, 984ᵃ5 ff.).

Aristotle means in fact that these early Ionians selected some one of its *prima facie* pervasive constituents from the world of popular thought as their answer to the problem of what ultimately *is*. They took the " substratum " of change, that from which a thing comes to be and into which it dissolves, not as its residue of potency dwindling as it actualises, increasing as it perishes, but as the permanent underlying and explaining change ; as a full reality and not as a privation of form.

And Aristotle on the whole seems to be right, though the Milesians may perhaps have so far refined upon the popular elements as to conceive water, air, and fire rather as intermediate liquid or gaseous states of matter.[1] The " Boundless " which Anaximander,[2] the immediate successor of Thales, substitutes for water, though a promising adventure beyond the *prima facie* deliverance of sense-perception, was evidently a positive material substance quantitatively infinite, not a ὕλη indeterminate in quality.

2

In supplement of Aristotle we may say that the next stage is the reaction of Parmenides against the Ionian point of view. In the hands of Heraclitus this had developed in startling fashion. Anaximenes had explained

---

[1] Aristotle remarks in 989ᵃ5 ff. that no monist has taken earth as the primary substance, probably because the coarseness of its particles made it unsuitable.

[2] *Floruit* 570 B.C. ; not here mentioned by Aristotle.

change as rarefaction and condensation of air : Anaximander had talked of the " separating out of opposites " (probably earth, air, fire, and water) from the Boundless, and called their return to it " a reparation for injustice." To Heraclitus the world is " an ever living fire " : its reality consists precisely in the tension of the opposites which pass into one another in an eternal process of combustion. Hence his fire is the ceaseless flux which tradition associates with his name ; the eternal substratum of change has become change itself.

Parmenides of Elea replied with a dialectical argument : It is the same thing which can be thought and which can *be*, and therefore what cannot be thought cannot *be*. Now what *is* cannot come to be from nothing, for there is no nothing ; nor from something, for there *is* nothing but what *is*. Parmenides maintained in short that change is unthinkable ; therefore the world—what *is*—is one and not also many, a single, solid, immovable plenum ; and the whole shifting kaleidoscope of the perceptible world is illusion.

3

Aristotle shows more interest in the pluralism which arose to meet Parmenides' reduction of monism to absurdity.

To escape the charge of deriving change *ex nihilo*, Empedocles of Agrigentum[1] posited earth, air, fire and water as primary substances, and added two further principles, Love and Strife ; and in his cosmos Love unites and Strife divides the four elements in alternate cycles. To Aristotle this pluralism heralds the efficient cause. " It became obvious," he says, " that even if things come to be from one or more elements, yet the substratum itself does not make itself change—something else must initiate the movement " (*ibid.*, 984[a]19 ff.). Accordingly

---

[1] *Floruit* 455 B.C. His point of view is markedly, if not always consciously, biological.

Aristotle regards Love and Strife as a pair of efficient
causes, though he considers Empedocles' use of them both
inadequate and inconsistent. He is, however, unduly
optimistic :[1] Empedocles in fact treats Love and Strife
merely as respectively a synthesising and a solvent material
body.

Anaxagoras of Clazomenae[2] seems to have posited as
original substances the hot, the cold, the fluid, and the
dry.[3] All things were originally together in a mass, the
least portion of which contained all four. Then by separation and mixture were formed the various compound
bodies—primarily earth, air, fire and water—which were
characterised by the proportion in them of the hot, the
cold, the fluid and the dry. Aristotle borrowed a good deal
from Anaxagoras for himself, but he is here concerned with
the fact that Anaxagoras introduced Reason ($\nu o\hat{\upsilon}s$)—
though as a clumsy and incompetently used *deus ex
machina*—as the source of this mingling and decomposition.
" When one man said that Reason was present—as in
animals so throughout nature—as the cause of the world
and of all its order, he seemed by contrast with his predecessors like a sober man compared with idle babblers "
(*ibid.*, 984^{b}15 ff.). Again Aristotle's view is anachronistic ;
for the $\nu o\hat{\upsilon}s$ of Anaxagoras, source of motion and of
knowledge in us, the sole unmixed element, which enters
the animate to give it mastery over the inanimate, is a
mere fluid, " the thinnest of all things."

The Atomists, Leucippus and the later Democritus,
applied the pluralist solution directly to the Parmenidean
one. To find room primarily for motion and thereby for

---

[1] He is even ready to see in Love and Strife a vague anticipation of
the final cause (985^{a}7 ff.), and in Empedocles' statement that bone exists
by virtue of the ratio in it, a hint of the formal cause as structural
principle.

[2] Born 500 B.C., but wrote later than Empedocles.

[3] See Burnet, *Early Greek Philosophy*, §§ 127–31, and Giussani's
edition of Lucretius (1896, vol. ii, pp. 147–50). No one has interpreted
Anaxagoras' theory of matter so as to harmonise all the fragments.

all forms of change, they multiplied (or divided) the Eleatic plenum so that it became a universe of solid impenetrable atoms whirling in all directions in empty space. These atoms, though all smaller than the *minimum visibile*, differ in size and shape, and the arrangement they assume when they group themselves is the basis of all differentiation in things. Now our only surviving fragment of Leucippus states that " Nothing happens for no reason, but all things for a λόγος and of necessity," and we might have expected Aristotle to attribute to him some rudiment of formal cause. In fact, however, he regards the Atomists as generating the world from two material principles, plenum and void, and complains that they do not explain how their vortex movement occurs. He does nevertheless attribute to Democritus some interest in definition.

4

It is common to call the early Ionian philosophers " physicists," but though this development from Thales to Democritus is the first chapter in the history of modern science, not one of them was a man of science in any sense which opposes science to philosophy. The pre-Socratics make no conscious abstraction from the full nature of what *is*. Not only do they envisage no group of special sciences such as physics, chemistry and biology, but their theology, when it appears, is usually pantheistic. They react from the personifications of myth to a materialist metaphysic : the Gods and Mind find no place in their world save as matter. If we persist in regarding them from a modern point of view, " cosmologist " and not " physicist " would be the better term. Though we have no space to describe their quaint pronouncements upon the nature of the heavens and the earth, it is here that their main problem lies : the ultimate nature of a cosmos is the goal of all their inquiries.

c

It is well to bear this in mind when we come to consider the school of thought which originates in the semi-religious society founded by Pythagoras of Samos in Crotona soon after 532 B.C.

The disciples of Pythagoras exerted on two centuries of Greek philosophy an influence hard to trace in detail. Their teaching seems to have been mainly oral, and Aristotle's account of it is practically void of chronology. " The Pythagoreans devoted themselves to mathematics. They were the first to advance this study, and having been brought up in it, they thought its principles were the principles of all things. Since of these principles numbers are by nature the first, and in numbers they seemed to see many analogues of the things that are and come to be (more easily than in fire, earth and water)—such and such a modification of numbers being justice, another being soul or reason, another opportunity, and similarly almost all other things being dependent upon numbers ; since again they saw that the attributes and the ratios of the musical scales were expressible in numbers ; since, in short, all other things seemed in their whole nature to be modelled after numbers, and numbers seemed to be the first things in the whole of nature, they supposed the elements of numbers to be the elements of all things, and the whole heaven to be a musical scale, *i.e.* a number " (*ibid.* 985^{b}23 ff.).

Number then is the early Pythagorean substitute for Milesian matter, and Aristotle anticipates if he means that the separate study of mathematics is present in this theory save in germ. In 989^{b}29 ff. he well expresses the difference : " They employ less obvious principles and elements than the physical philosophers (because they got their principles from non-sensible things, for the objects of mathematics except those of astronomy are of the class of things without movement) ; yet their discussions and investigations are all about nature."

We can guess from Aristotle's further account how this numerical ὕλη divides as it were by fission into a material and a formal cause. " These thinkers also consider that number is the principle not only as matter for things but also as forming their modifications and permanent states,[1] and hold that the elements of number are the even and the odd, and of these the former unlimited and the latter limited ; and the one proceeds from both of them (for it is both even and odd),[2] and number from the one " (*ibid.* 986ª15 ff.). The clue to this is certainly the known Pythagorean classification of numbers in geometrical terms—triangular, square, oblong, etc.—achieved by representing the unit as a point, viz. :

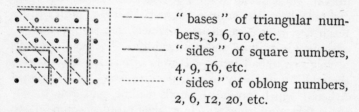

- - - - "bases" of triangular numbers, 3, 6, 10, etc.

———— "sides" of square numbers, 4, 9, 16, etc.

·········· "sides" of oblong numbers, 2, 6, 12, 20, etc.

The explanation of the doctrine is perhaps that it is the successive addition of the odd numbers to the unit which gives squares, whereas, if you start with two, the successive addition of the even numbers from four onwards gives a series of oblongs differing indefinitely in shape.[3] In any case the two original Pythagorean principles seem to have been the Limit and the Unlimited, which unite in the unit to generate the integer series ; and from the integer series as from its real substantial nature—perhaps through geometrical figures of growing complexity—is

[1] *I.e.*, probably, as formal cause. In 987ª19 ff. Aristotle says that regarding the question of the essential nature the Pythagoreans began to make statements and definitions, but treated the matter too simply.

[2] Possibly as the principle of both even and odd numbers. It is not itself a number.

[3] See Ross, *Aristotle, Metaphysics*, Vol. I, pp. 148–9. Yet there are difficulties in this account ; *e.g.* 6 will be both triangular and oblong.

generated " the whole choir of heaven and furniture of
earth," wherein the Limited is good and the Unlimited
is evil. Whatever be the connexion of this bold speculation
with the later stages of Platonism, the linking of goodness
with the definite or determinate is typical of Greek thought,
and foreshadows the whole Platonic and Aristotelian theory
of values.

5

Even this short sketch of the pre-Socratics must give
some account of another type of teacher with philosophic
pretensions, whom Aristotle does not classify.

It was no doubt a growing demand for an education
liberal, yet calculated to assist success in affairs, which
created the fifth-century Sophists.[1] They professed to
teach ἀρετή, or " excellence," which they interpreted as
efficiency in private and political life. The Sophists have
been given a bad name. It was often the discontented
though rich minority in a democratic state—especially at
Athens—which provided pupils willing and able to pay
their fees, and their teaching inevitably accommodated
itself to the demands of men fighting a hostile Demos in
the law-court or the assembly. But the Sophists were
perhaps less to blame than the political situation if the
eloquence and controversial skill which they taught were
sometimes made the tools of revolution.[2] The first great
Sophist, Protagoras of Abdera,[3] was commissioned by
Pericles to frame laws for the colony of Thurii—a sufficient
proof of his credit, and the very respectable humanism of
Isocrates, though antagonistic to fourth-century Sophism,
descends in part from the earlier Sophists.

But Protagoras and his fellows exhibit also a certain
community of philosophic outlook. Though men were

---

[1] What follows is mainly taken from Burnet, *Thales to Plato*, pp. 105 ff.
[2] As Gorgias the Sophist in effect remarks in Plato's *Gorgias* 456d.
[3] Born about 500.

weary of materialism, the times were sceptical. Philosophy —especially after the assaults of Eleatic criticism—seemed only to have estranged itself from the world of sense which it had set out to explain. Moreover the dialectical method created by Parmenides to attack the Milesians depended in fact on a play upon the existential and the predicative significance of the verb " to be," and was a dangerous weapon before Plato's brilliant treatment of the negative judgment in the *Sophist* had shown the true connexion of meaning (see p. 52). Its edge, too, had been sharpened by the famous dilemmas with which his pupil, Zeno, had discomfited Pythagorean mathematics.[1] Hence the Sophists associated themselves with a growing tendency to regard human institutions as conventional and artificial rather than natural, and in the Eleatic dialectic they found a ready instrument for their teaching. That Sophist morality suffered decline and fall is the natural inference from Plato's dialogues. Protagoras, who taught the sub-jective doctrine that the individual is the sole measure of truth and falsehood, is nevertheless pictured by Plato as a firm believer in social convention as the only escape from savage anarchy. Even Gorgias, for all his interest in sheer rhetorical technique, admits that the *dicendi peritus* must be also *vir bonus*. It is only the crude and ruffianly Thrasymachus of the *Republic* who states baldly that right is only might miscalled.

6

There is little doubt that in his earlier dialogues Plato faithfully portrays the life and character of Socrates, moralist and martyr ; and any reader of this book is likely to be familiar with the portrait. The Athenians had failed —ludicrously on the comic stage and tragically in the law

---

[1] " Achilles and the tortoise," " The flying arrow," etc. These all disclose the difficulty which continuity presents to a theory which takes one and not zero as the first term of the number series and proceeds to treat geometrical problems arithmetically.

court[1]—to distinguish the friend of youth from its corrupter ; the man who lived and taught unrecompensed a philosophy for which he was content to die from "the paid huntsman of rich youths," " the peddler of illusory spiritual wares and barren antinomies."[2] And in many dialogues besides the *Apology* Plato consecrated the noblest prose of all time to the duty of ensuring that posterity should reverse their verdict. Yet though in detail the relation of the historical to the Platonic Socrates is matter for controversy beyond our scope, the statements of Aristotle do not justify such a complete identification of the two as some scholars have desired to make.[3] That Plato, save in his very latest dialogues, should speak in the person of Socrates may perhaps signify not falsification of fact but a yet nobler consecration of his own work to the master of whose inspiration it is the ripened fruit—and one that contrasts at least *prima facie* with the confidence of Aristotle's attitude to the past.

[1] Though Aristophanes in the *Clouds* caricatures him no less as a cosmologist than as a Sophist, and though it appears from Plato's *Symposium* that Aristophanes remained the friend of the man he had thought fair game for a skit. No doubt, too, the main charge against Socrates was political. It mattered little to his judges whether his dangerous criticism of existing institutions was idealistic or sceptical.

[2] Phrases from Plato's *Sophist*.

[3] Burnet and Prof. A. E. Taylor. The backbone of their case seems to be that in the dialogues where Socrates is chief speaker, not only the *dramatis personae*, but also the problems discussed belong to the fifth and not to the fourth century. But there is no evidence that the solution of those problems had progressed so far as many of these dialogues suggest, until Plato himself tackled them. The *Phaedo*, which recounts Socrates' last conversation and death, may well be a true historical record (save as regards the theory of Forms—see below, p. 31, note), but I doubt whether it is possible elsewhere to estimate at all exactly the Socratic factor in Plato, or whether we can anywhere profitably divide with a knife. To suggest that from the ages of thirty to sixty (if we may date the *Theaetetus*, 369 B.C.—cp. Taylor, *Plato*, pp. 320, 321—and take it as the beginning of Platonism proper) Plato should have thought nothing worth publication save mere reproductions of his master's philosophy is to deny all power of vital development to the Socratic inspiration. Aristotle's statements, moreover, are as good evidence as we have, and I shall therefore assume that only so much of the Platonic Socrates is historical as they seem to warrant.

In Met. 987ᵇ1 ff. Aristotle says, " Socrates concerned himself with ethical facts . . . and fixed his thought for the first time on definitions." And in Met. 1078ᵇ27 ff., " Two things," he says, " may be fairly ascribed to Socrates—' inductive ' arguments (ἐπακτικοὶ λόγοι), and definition in terms of the universal."

In fact to Aristotle—though he treats him cursorily and as a mere factor in Plato's development—Socrates was the first thinker who more or less consciously sought the formal cause.

We may supplement this from Plato. In the *Phaedo*[1] Socrates recounts how, discontented with the early cosmologists and with the Pythagoreans, he read the book of Anaxagoras with interest because he professed to introduce νοῦς as controller of the universe ; but, when he found that Anaxagoras still relied for all explanation of process on purely mechanical causes, he turned from him in disgust. He was therefore compelled to invent a method of his own for seeking the truth. His account of this method is roughly as follows. Postulate a general statement (λόγος) about the subject in hand, which seems *prima facie* satisfactory. Deduce its consequences. If these conflict with one another or with obvious fact, the postulate (ὑπόθεσις) is overthrown. If they do not, so far so good ; but the postulate itself is not yet proven. If it is attacked, it must be shown as the consequent of a still more ultimate ὑπόθεσις, and so on till a postulate is reached which satisfies all parties to the discussion. But the consequences of the initial postulate must be worked out before its truth is questioned ; and that is what " disputatious people " will not wait to do.[2]

---

[1] I have benefited largely and gratefully by Prof. A. E. Taylor's *Plato* in my analyses of Platonic dialogues in this and the next two chapters.

[2] The reference is to the use made by the Sophists of Eleatic dialectic to reduce an opponent to self-contradiction. It is implied that Socrates argues for the sake of truth, " the disputatious " for the sake of victory.

Now it may seem that this method is in part deductive, whereas Aristotle ascribes "inductive" argument to Socrates. The fact is that a severance of deduction and induction save in the way of emphasis, is a mark of unsound logical theory. Socrates' method is really *dialectic*, and ἐπαγωγή (whence ἐπακτικοί above), though commonly translated "induction," is to Aristotle a *dialectical* procedure. Plato, it is true, ascribes a purely deductive method to current mathematics, and Aristotle makes important use of it under the name of ἀπόδειξις, demonstration ; but both Plato and Aristotle contrast their deduction not with anything like the induction of some modern logicians, but with dialectic. It will be evident, then, that Socrates borrows from the Eleatics something of their method, though there is nothing of their scepticism in his ironical conviction of ignorance.

If we accept Plato's earlier dialogues as essentially Socratic, we find that the Socratic dialectic moves as follows. The definiendum is an ethical fact, one of the ἀρεταί, human excellences or virtues ; courage, for example, or justice. One of the disputants postulates in the form of a general statement a definition which seems to cover a group of particular cases (as when Cephalus in the *Republic* defines justice as telling the truth and paying one's debts). The consequences are examined ; *i.e.* the suggested definition is extended to a fresh set of instances. It is found, when thus extended, not only to be too narrow but actually to provoke its direct opposite (would it be just to tell the truth to a man who had developed homicidal mania, and to return him weapons which he had left in one's keeping ? Similarly Laches, in Plato's dialogue of that name, having defined courage as never turning one's back on the enemy, is forced to admit that it is sometimes a soldier's duty to feign flight). Since the consequences prove contradictory, a fresh ὑπόθεσις must be found to cover the ground divided by the initial contradiction (justice is perhaps to pay, not the amount technically owing, but what is fitting in the circumstances). This reconciling postulate, as its sphere of application is widened, will again provoke its contrary and, together with it, yield to a fresh reconciliation. In the hands of Socrates the definiendum develops from a fragmentary outward sign to an inward disposition of the soul, and—though no claim to finality is ever made—this inward disposition turns out invariably to be a form of knowledge. In the *Laches* courage proves to be a knowledge of good and evil, and in effect the same result is reached in the discussion of temperance in the *Charmides*. The final definition of justice in the *Republic* is reached in the course of an effort to reconcile the four traditional Greek virtues : wisdom, justice, courage, and temperance. It may be that with this we have passed from Socrates to Plato, but, even if that be so, it does not affect the point for which we are contending.

The features, then, of Socratic dialectic are these : (1) it starts with a partial definition ; which (2) on examination contradicts itself ; (3) the fuller definition which reconciles the contradiction, though it negates the initial definition as such, yet contains modified and absorbed within it the grain of truth which that definition held. Hence the initial definition is at once a particular and a confused universal. It is an instance offered as a definition, and therefore contradicts itself in attempting to cover the whole ground. And the succession of definitions offered are still groups of instances ; but they are not merely instances—they are also successively wider and more concrete developments of the universal.

Thus this dialectic is not the induction of an abstract common character from sheerly particular instances. The confused universal, implicit and potential in the instances, is gradually actualised as a concrete whole through ordered stages of differentiation. The movement is in principle self-contained, and not dependent on an unexamined ὑπόθεσις.

That the goal in all thinking is present from the start as a confused universal, dimly foreknown—that thought has direction because its premise is always its conclusion in potential form—is sometimes fancifully symbolised by Socrates (or it may be by Plato) in the doctrine of ἀνάμνησις, " reminiscence."[1] The soul, he suggests, lives before birth in a world of real Being which at birth it forgets. Sense-perception stimulates a gradual recollection, and the soul draws its power to recognise and to appraise the particular objects of the sense world from this remembered reality which they imperfectly embody or reflect.

The same conviction that thought is essentially a learning as well as a knowing is expressed by Plato in the *Theaetetus* (149e ff.), when Socrates describes himself as a barren midwife having no knowledge of his own to impart but capable of bringing to birth the thoughts with which other men are pregnant.

[1] Cp. *Meno*, 80e ff. This doctrine is the first attempt to formulate what has since become known as the *a priori* element in experience. In *Philebus*, 35a ff., anticipation and memory in the ordinary sense of the terms are closely connected.

III

PLATO : THE EARLIER DIALOGUES

THE dialectic of the concrete universal ; the ethical approach to philosophy conceived as a way of life and a learning rather than as a body of doctrine ; the view that virtue is in some sense knowledge : these at least are Plato's inheritance from Socrates.

From Aristotle's curt statements (Met. 987^{a}29 ff. and 1087^{b}9 ff.) we learn that Plato had been brought up a believer in Heraclitus' doctrine of perpetual flux, but, dissatisfied with a theory which by making change the ultimate nature of things renders knowledge of them impossible, was attracted by Socrates' search for a solid and definable reality in the facts of the moral life. Now Heraclitus' metaphysic was purely materialist, and that the object of sense-perception is as such that which is ever changing into its opposite, Plato never ceased to maintain. What he learned from Socrates was to seek what *is* and can be known elsewhere than in the alternating flame and darkness of the world of sense. And to what *is* and can be known Plato gave the name of Forms (εἴδη or ἰδέαι), holding that the things of the world of sense exist by participation in the Forms. The dialogues show clearly what Aristotle's account implies, namely, that the Forms had their source in the moral facts of Socrates, and that in their further development as the real correlate of the whole perceptible world they never lost the trace of their ethical origin.[1]

[1] At any rate until Plato had written the *Republic* and *Phaedrus*, which probably belong to the years just before 369 B.C. ; cp. note 3, p. 26.

Now we might have expected from Aristotle some comment upon Platonism as we know it from the dialogues. But of this he offers rather little. The Platonism on which he concentrates the not always very lucid criticism of Met. I and XIII he regards as in the main a refinement of Pythagoreanism, as a mathematical philosophy which finds in number the ultimate essence of things. The Forms—at least as we know them—play a lesser part, and though Aristotle is clear that they derive from Socrates and not from the Pythagoreans, yet he regards even " participation " as no more than a verbal variant of the term " imitation " by which the Pythagoreans expressed the relation of things to numbers.[1] We are clearly in contact here with a development of Platonism of which the germ only—though certainly that—can be traced in the dialogues. It is true that Socrates and Plato were both influenced by the Pythagorean semi-religious conception of philosophy, and that the Academy was never without a strong interest in mathematics,[2] but it can be safely asserted that this mathematical philosophy belongs to the last twenty years of Plato's life.

On the other hand Aristotle was not in sympathy with this later Platonism. He complains that " mathematics has come to be the whole of philosophy for modern thinkers, though they say it should be studied for the sake of other things " (Met. 992^{a}32 ff.). He is perfectly familiar with the dialogues, and though he attacks the Forms in whatever guise they appear, it is in the earlier Platonism

---

We may agree with Prof. Taylor that up to the end of the *Phaedrus* the influence of Socrates is very strong, but Aristotle never suggests that Socrates taught an actual doctrine of Forms.

[1] Whether Plato ultimately subordinated the Forms to numbers, or equated the two, is not very clear ; see also p. 67.

[2] Plato's first extension of the Forms may well have been from ethical to mathematical facts. In the *Phaedo* the relation of a Form to its particulars is often illustrated as that of a mathematical limit to its approximations—of real equality, *e.g.*, to the rough equality of two perceptible things.

that his own philosophy is rooted.[1] Our immediate need,
then, is a sketch of the theory of Forms as Plato develops
it in the dialogues.

A particular perceptible thing,[2] if we attempt to define
it, quickly shows itself to be, not self-subsistent nor an
isolable object of knowledge, but dependent for its character upon its relations to other things. These relations,
moreover, form a web of more and less significant strands
in the midst of which the object appears as a mass of
confusion. From among them the definer must select,
separating the essential from the irrelevant ; and his task
is the harder that the relations, and with them the thing,
alter with change of spatial position and as time passes.
And not only while it exists is the thing in a perpetual
state of becoming something else, but, as once it *was not*
and then came to be, so when time enough has passed it
will perish and *be* no more. An act of justice or courage—
which may be termed perceptible at least inasmuch as it
first comes to notice embodied in an event occurring in a
particular place and time—may in changed circumstances
prove criminal or cowardly ; and another age or country
may deem it wholly immoral. That which in one
relation we call great or tall or heavy or fast, we shall
call in another little or short or light or slow, and a
thing which is acclaimed beautiful may appear ugly as
soon as its setting is changed. Moreover the multitude
of things which exhibit any given character appears to be
indefinite. Quite apart from their tendency to appear
ugly, the number of particular beautiful things, past,
present, or to come, seems wholly indeterminate, dictated
by no principle.

The ordinary mortal does not look below the shifting

[1] Even some non-mathematical speculations of great importance in
the later dialogues influence him less than might be expected.

[2] The reader may find a comparison of what follows with pp. 9 ff.
some help towards understanding the relation of Plato and Aristotle.
Plato's relatively light emphasis on development should be observed.

surface of things—is hardly aware that it shifts. His delight in his senses has not yet become a craving for knowledge beyond sense. He is none the less opinionated because his opinions seldom remain the same, for he recognises no special significance in the identity that pervades their objects. What remains, then, for one who *has* attempted to define, as he has not ? Shall it content him to unite the philosophy of Heraclitus with the relativist conventionalism of Protagoras ? Not if, by a divine chance, he finds within him some prophetic foreboding of an intelligible reality behind the world of sense. Not if he has known Socrates.

There are two never wholly separate lines of thought which meet in the theory of Forms. Plato is trying to conceive the Form as (1) at once universal and individual, and as (2) the norm by which its particulars are to be judged. (1) Between the objects of opinion there does after all exist some identity ; their changing nature would otherwise have stirred no wonder. And differ as they may—each as its setting changes and all from one another —there are yet groups of particular objects whose identity language itself seals with a common name : every adjective in fact, and every noun if used adjectivally, signifies some community of character. Plato undoubtedly finds difficulty in this when he extends the Forms beyond the Socratic sphere of enquiry, and is compelled to oppose indifferently " the many beautiful things " and the multitude of particular men to " the Beautiful itself " and to Man as the Forms in which these pluralities respectively participate. It was indeed once the fashion to say that a Form was just a common character abstracted from particulars and hypostatised as a real entity ; and because a character taken apart from what it characterises seemed an abstraction due to thought, the Platonic Form was called an " Idea " and regarded as a re-ified concept. But the suggestion that a Form is a thought in the sense of a " subjective " conception, is emphatically denied in the *Parmenides*, and Plato is always clear that a Form, though universal, is a real individual—not a mere character first abstracted and then hypostatised, but an entity whose being and character (existence and essence) are one and the same. Yet this does not altogether avoid the difficulty. The postulate of such a real entity may help us to show that the indefinite multiplicity of particulars is the sign of their unreal or merely apparent nature, but we should not thereby have accounted for a further fact. The particulars of sense-perception are not merely unintelligibly multiple, and not merely liable to exhibit contrary characters : they are also, in virtue of the diversity of relations which each exhibits, meeting-points of different characters that are at least to some extent mutually complementary. Confused as may be the web of characters and relations in which each particular perceptible thing is centred, yet it is only the complexity of the web which makes the thing at its centre intelligible at all. Quite obviously the perceptible world reflects an interrelated reality and not a mere number—not a new indefinite plurality— of separate reals. And if the constituents of this inter-related reality are the various Forms, then each Form, since it is not a mere abstract common character reached by omission of differences, must itself exhibit internal diversity.

To discover the true nature of a Form we must pursue another line of attack. (2) If, as Socrates divined, there are real facts of justice or courage or temperance to be dialectically elicited from the particular moral acts in which they are instanced, it will follow that the instances are not merely linked by a common character, but also embody these facts in different stages or degrees of perfection, which can be shown to present some order of development. *Per contra* the common terms of language signify identities of any and every degree of importance from fundamental to superficial. Hence not in linguistic form but in value lies the clue to the endless relativity of the perceptible world ; and the Form thus turns out to be not only (1) a real entity as well as a universal, but also (2) the norm or standard of the imperfect particular which participates in it. From Socrates comes Plato's conviction that Being and value are ultimately one. The Form is the standard by which we judge both how far real and how far good the particular is. The Form, in short, would contrast with the plurality of its particulars as a real one of many significant and complementary differences with a confused sense-aggregate only real and significant so far as it partakes in the Form.

Aristotle did not consider that Plato had discovered a solution of the problem in either of these two directions. In respect of the first, " The Forms," he says (Met. 990ª4 ff.), " are practically equal to or not fewer than the things in trying to explain which the Platonists proceeded from them to the Forms. For to each nameable set of substances there answers a Form expressed by the same word, and existing separate from the substances ; and so also in the case of the other groups of nameable things which are not substances there is a One predicable of Many, whether the things are in this changeable world or are eternal. . . . According to the argument that there is one attribute common to many things, there will be Forms even of negations ; and according to the argument that there is an object for thought even when the thing has perished, there will be Forms of perishable things." Plato has failed in fact to reconcile universality with individuality within the Form : his universals turn out to be merely a second set of particulars which stand to the first set in no intelligible relation. In many passages Aristotle complains that through emphasising their individuality, and through contrasting their reality and value with the imperfection of their participants, the Platonists " separated " the

Forms from their particulars.[1] In short, Aristotle's objection to the theory is that the Forms (1) reflect all the confused groupings and distinctions of the perceptible world, and (2) in virtue of their self-subsistence and transcendent value constitute a real world of their own totally divorced from the world of sense. The real world of Forms merely reduplicates the sense world, and repeats all its chaotic and shifting cross-divisions.

These are ungentle criticisms : the first part of the *Parmenides* shows Plato familiar with most of them, and they raise difficulties which Aristotle himself never quite successfully solved. It is true that much of Plato's language suggests that the Forms are not the Real immanent in the world of appearance, but wholly transcend it. He calls them patterns of which the particulars are copies, originals of which perceptible things are the endlessly multiplied images, fugitive reflexions which leave the Form unchanged. Nevertheless the dialogues show more than one attempt to solve the two pressing problems : (1) the relation of particulars to Forms, and (2) the inter-relation of the Forms.

When Plato uses myth and simile he signifies that wonder has not yet found full satisfaction in knowledge, and in the famous similes of *Republic* VI and VII— perhaps his first effort to unify his philosophy—he reaches upward tentatively and by analogy from the perceptible to the real world and the Form of the Good.

In the world of the senses vision and visibility form the noblest " linking " of faculty with power in the object of exciting sensation. For the bond that couples them is light—a noble thing—and the other sense functions are conditioned by no such third element. Without light there is no seeing and no colour seen ; and there is not clear

---

[1] He definitely states in Met. 1078b31–32 that this " separation " was a Platonic fault which Socrates had not committed. For a slightly different interpretation of it see p. 187, note 1.

D

vision of colour at its fairest save in the light of the sun. The sun is not vision and the sun is not the eye—though the eye is the likest to the sun of the organs of sense.[1] But from the sun as αἰτία the eye derives its power of seeing both the sun itself and the objects which the sun illumines. The sun again is not γένεσις, " coming-to-be," but it is the αἰτία not only of visibility in the object but also of the whole coming-to-be and development of the object of vision. Analogously in respect of the invisible world of intelligible Being, the Form of the Good is not knowledge in the soul, and it is not the being of what *is*, but it is the αἰτία of knowledge and of the being and ἀλήθεια (truth, or perhaps " knowableness ") of what *is*.

Plato then passes to another simile. Conceive a vertical straight line AE to divide the whole objective world from the corresponding faculties in the apprehending subject. Divide AE into unequal segments at C, and on the one side of AC set opinion, and on the other the visible world. On one side of CE set knowledge, and on the other what *is*. Then divide AC at B, and CE at D, so that AB : BC :: CD : DE :: AC : CE,[2] and the corresponding subdivisions of Being and knowledge will be as follows :—On one side of DE will lie the Forms as constituting a perfect and coherent system of which the crown and αἰτία is the Form of the Good ; on the other, Reason (νόησις). On one side of CD will be the Forms as relatively isolated from one another to constitute the object of mathematics ; on the other the discursive understanding (διάνοια).[3] Finally,

---

[1] Plato holds a theory of vision which descends chiefly from Empedocles' theory that colour is an emanation from the object of vision, symmetrical with, and therefore perceptible by, the organ of vision ; that the eye contains light (" a gentler fire," Plato calls it), which issues to meet a ray of light—*i.e.* the colour-emanation from the object. The union of these two like elements is the physiological aspect of the act of vision. Aristotle's theory of sense-perception should be compared ; see Chap. VI.

[2] *e.g.* in the proportion 3 : 6 :: 6 : 12 :: 3+6 : 6+12.

[3] Understanding and Reason are convenient terms, but they must not be taken to convey more than the germ of the Kantian distinction.

subdivide the visible world and opinion, setting on one side of AB the reflexions and shadows cast by solid objects, and on the other " conjecture " (εἰκασία) ; and on opposite sides of BC set all solid visible objects and, to correspond to them, " confident belief " (πίστις). At the bottom the object side of the line terminates in not-being, the subject side in blank ignorance.

The result will be as follows :

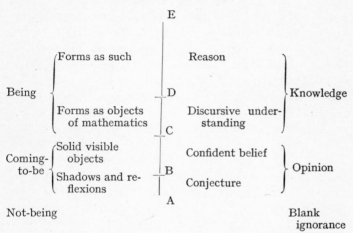

FORM OF THE GOOD

E

Being {
Forms as such — Reason
D
Forms as objects of mathematics — Discursive understanding
C
} Knowledge

Coming-to-be {
Solid visible objects — Confident belief
B
Shadows and reflexions — Conjecture
} Opinion

A

Not-being — Blank ignorance

Plato adds that opinion is to knowledge as a dream to a waking vision, and that the whole object world below the Forms is in different degrees unreal, " between being and not-being."[1]

Of εἰκασία Plato says little. Its meaning is as conjectural as its name. The proportion of the segments suggests that it is an immature state in which images (reflexions and shadows) are confused with solid objects[2]

---

[1] The " divided line " is the germ of Aristotle's classification of the sciences (see Chap. X), and in " between being and not-being " the reader will recognise something like Aristotle's definition of matter.

[2] Plato plays deliberately on the connexion of εἰκασία with εἴκων, "image."

—a state which passes with reflexion into the condition of confident opinion which characterises the ordinary adult.[1]

We learn as the dialogue proceeds that as reflexion becomes aware that perceptible objects exhibit contradictory characters—particularly in respect of their quantitative properties—it resorts to measurement to reduce to order the chaos of quantitative variation. Hence it is the mathematical sciences which fill the subject side of the segment CD. The successive study of arithmetic, plane geometry, stereometry, and finally astronomy, the science of solids in motion, and harmonics, the mathematical investigation of the ratios of the chief musical intervals[2]—this constitutes the first part of the education which Plato destines for the philosophic rulers of his ideal state.[3] Now the mathematician uses visible objects as symbols in his demonstrations ; but his conclusions hold, not of solid numerable objects nor of the triangle or square which he draws as an illustration, but of numbers themselves and of the triangle or square itself. To the pure astronomer the visible heavens are but a symbol of real solids in real motion. In short, the subject-matter of mathematics is Forms. But it is not the full reality of the Forms. The transition from the sense world with its chaos of oscillating characters first to empirical calculation and then to pure mathematics, is achieved by taking the contradictory quantitative characters in separation from one another ; but this separation has its price, for the Forms of the mathematician are isolated groups. The mathematician posits them as

[1] Or Plato may be thinking of the perception of objects too distant to be seen distinctly—a form of conjecture with which any short-sighted man is familiar ; cp. *Philebus* 38 c and d.

[2] Possibly Plato means by astronomy the study of an ideally perfect and therefore intelligible celestial system. If so, the connexion of astronomy with harmonics indicated in the *Timaeus* (see p. 65) becomes clearer.

[3] This is the context in which the simile of the divided line appears in the *Republic*.

ὑποθέσεις which, *qua* mathematician, he does not examine :
he assumes that they exist as he defines them, and argues
from them by demonstration to the conclusions which
constitute the body of his science. If anyone questions
the existence, for example, of the triangle or the square
as the geometer defines them, the geometer is dumb, for
these ὑποθέσεις are the starting-point of his investigation,
and the limit of its sphere.[1]

The philosophic ruler, then, has farther yet to go.
Reason, which apprehends the Forms as such in the light
of the Form of the Good, moves not deductively but
dialectically. The philosopher starts with the ὑποθέσεις of
the mathematician, but from them he climbs, not descends.
He " destroys " them as he ascends through them to a
goal which is not an unexamined assumption—to the
Good, which is directly known and the αἰτία of his
dialectic. Then the Form of the Good becomes his starting-
point, and he descends again through the isolated Forms
of the mathematical realm, now become a coherent whole
of Forms unified by the Form of the Good, from which
they draw their being and their truth.

Plato's meaning in this passage is not altogether clear.
The perceptible world figures almost purely as a *visible*
world, and though Plato speaks of colour, it is the susceptibility of visible shapes to *measurement* which effects
the transition from belief to understanding. Moreover,
under the influence of the analogy, while philosophic

[1] The development of the deductive element in the Socratic dialectic
as illustrating current mathematical method is obvious. Euclid's
procedure is a fair illustration. Aristotle attributes to Plato the doctrine
that between the Forms and sensible objects there are the objects of
mathematics. These " mathematicals," like the Forms, are eternal
and immutable, but, like sensible objects, multiple. This theory is
perhaps constructed to meet the case of theorems which require two
or more identical geometrical figures for their demonstration. There
is evidence both for and against its presence in the *Republic*, but discussion is beyond our scope. In the text I have decided against it, but
without confidence. Aristotle himself appears to hold something like
it ; see Chapter X, § 1 (c).

thinking is described as a dialectical movement, its consummation seems to be an immediate vision of the Form of the Good.

Alternative extremes of interpretation seem possible. (1) We may stress the letter of Plato's words and hold that he exalts mathematics as the group of sciences which interpret the most important character revealed in things by sight, the noblest of the senses. We shall then explain the " destruction " which dialectic performs as the reduction of the current mathematical sciences with their groups of isolated ὑποθέσεις to a single articulated whole of necessary connexions, each stage of which is then transparently deduced in the light of the Form of the Good ; a whole in which no bare fact—no indefinable or indemonstrable—survives. And this single whole will be a single science of numbers, a " sort of teleological algebra," as Burnet calls it.[1] This view we might support by appeal to Aristotle's account of Platonism and his complaint that " philosophy has become mathematics," and also to the *Epinomis*—if the *Epinomis* is a genuine Platonic dialogue. There are also, I think, indications in other later dialogues that Plato's conception of dialectic moves in the direction which this interpretation suggests.

On the other hand (2) we may follow the general trend of the later nineteenth-century interpretation. We may say that Plato gives prominence to mathematics because in his time only the mathematical sciences were at all developed,[2] and we may find in the fact that in the divided

---

[1] *Thales to Plato*, p. 230. It is not esay to see exactly what form the dialectical movement takes on this interpretation, but the doctrine of " mathematicals " (see note, p. 41) suggests that Plato may have found the theory of Forms specially easy to apply in mathematics, because there the particulars are not sensible ; see Burnet, *op. cit.*, p. 257.

[2] The suggestion that Plato would have included other special sciences had they reached an adequately developed condition is perhaps not incompatible with the first interpretation, which might be extended to the hypothesis that Plato intended something like the Cartesian re-

line BC is not related to CD as CD to DE and as AC to CE,
evidence that Plato intends to mark the essentially abstract
character of mathematics. We may point out that the
line is only a simile, and claim the right to extend the
narrow limits which the analogy from sight imposes. We
shall then include in the sphere of opinion ethical and all
other dogmatic judgments limited to particular instances :
and in εἰκασία we shall find a stage of consciousness
prior to judgment proper, in which distinction of subject
from object, and of fancy from fact, are only beginning
to emerge.[1] We shall see in the whole line a continuous
development from potential to actual or real. The Form
of the Good will be the universe as a single teleological
system to which all lesser ends and purposes contribute as
constituents ; in and as which they culminate. We shall
regard the dialectic as the apotheosis of Socratic dialectic,
interpreting its " destructive " phase as the successive
negation of inadequate definitions of what ultimately *is*,
and its upward and downward movements as complementary moments of a single process from abstract to
concrete. We shall urge that Plato can hardly have
forgotten that to level down the series of successively
more concrete mathematical sciences to algebra, and to
look for the ultimate expression of reality in a single
science of numbers, would be to reverse the true order of
dialectic and to mistake the abstract for the concrete, the
potential for the final and actual.

We have seemingly to choose between algebra and

duction of the physical sciences to geometry and a further reduction of
geometry to arithmetic, or rather to an algebraical *Mathesis Universalis.*
There is some evidence that Plato had overcome the Pythagorean
difficulties which arose from beginning the number series with one
instead of zero.

[1] Or we might include in εἰκασία all individual dogmatic judgments
of value, and regard them as shadows of comparatively real originals
in the sphere of πίστις—of the best public opinion as embodied, *e.g.* in the
established legal system. We might, again, even relate εἰκασία to
Plato's theory of art, and discover in it the germ of Croce's view of the
nature of aesthetic experience.

teleology, for the two are scarcely compatible. We might think that in the *Republic* the Socratic impulse towards an ethical and teleological interpretation of the universe is beginning to give way to a purely mathematical philosophy ; but in the later dialogues we do not find this revolution accomplished—there are signs that the conflict still continues—and there is a strong tradition that the contents of Plato's unpublished lecture on the Good seemed to his hearers at a much later date than that of the *Republic* mystifyingly mathematical in character.

Before we carry forward the discussion to the later dialogues, we must touch on a kindred problem arising out of the divided line and vitally affecting the question how the Forms interrelate, and how a Form relates to its particulars. We must ask, in fact, how the two sides of the line relate to one another ; and we must answer with caution. Plato (and the same is true of Aristotle) was neither a realist nor an idealist. Whether this or that modern metaphysic most fully realises the germ and potency of Greek philosophy is legitimate matter for controversy, and there is much to be said for the view which traces a main stream of development from Plato and Aristotle to Hegel ; but to read into Greek philosophy distinctions that are only present in germ is to destroy the whole value of its study. Even to conceive Platonism as no more than the germ of a Kantian or a Hegelian system[1] is to forget once more that men are more as well as less than movements.

To Plato the mind and its objects are linked by an essential kinship which he never questions. A conspicuous feature of the divided line is the even-handed balance which at every stage he maintains between faculty and

[1] Or, for that matter, of the mathematics of a Peano or a Frege. False stress can wrest Greek philosophy into almost any shape, and in Plato's case the danger of distortion is increased by the large speculative liberty in which the use of dialogue form allows him to indulge.

object. He utters a not always heeded warning to
psychologists in the statement that a faculty of apprehension is definable only in terms of the object upon which
its function is directed. But this implies no realist doctrine
of a Being self-subsistent in virtue of its essential independence of mind, for, as we have seen, the Form of the
Good is said by Plato to be the αἰτία not only of being
but of truth in objects. Plato does, moreover, in *Republic*,
526e apply the term εὐδαίμων (" blessed " or " happy ")
to the Form of the Good, and in *Laws*, 903c to the Whole
for the sake of which occur all partial processes of becoming.
We might therefore incline to regard the Form of the
Good as a single self-conscious unity above both finite
being and finite knowledge, a sort of Hegelian Absolute
Spirit. But though there are certainly hints of such a
notion in Plato (see, too, pp. 54 ff.), he was not in full
possession of it. Despite their kinship there seems to be
a certain separation between mind, or soul, and its objects
as Plato treats them, which has led many interpreters
not to regard their ultimate identity as the crown of his
teaching. It may therefore be well to summarise briefly
what Plato actually says of the soul.

In *Republic* IV, the soul of man is analysed provisionally
into an intelligent ruling element, a desiring element, and
between them a spirited (θυμοειδές) element, which is
nobler than the latter, and tends to side with the rational
part against the lusting of the lowest element. We learn
later that the spirited part is less real than the intelligent,
the desiring element than the spirited, and that each finds
its satisfaction in an appropriate pleasure—in truth, in
honour, or in the lusts of the flesh—which possesses the
same degree of reality as itself.[1] The soul is disordered
when either of the baser parts wrests control from the
specifically human rational element. This Plato aptly

[1] Aristotle's doctrine of pleasure is very close to this ; see Chapter
VII, § 6.

symbolises in *Republic* X, likening the whole soul to the figure of a man, within which are concealed lesser figures of a man, a lion, and a many-headed monster. In a myth contained in the *Phaedrus* the charioteer of the soul drives heavenwards a pair of horses : the one white, a generous thoroughbred, well schooled, the other black, a rogue and a runaway. To the elements of the soul thus analysed from a moral point of view, corresponds the graded series from εἰκασία to true knowledge, which results from analysis in purely cognitive terms. In *Laws* X the soul is defined as a self-moving motion, and is regarded as the seat of all intelligence and purposive initiation.[1] On the other hand, in no passage does Plato treat soul as a Form, and Aristotle, to whom soul was essentially form in his own sense of the word, complains as of a defect in Plato's metaphysic that the Forms are neither efficient nor final causes (Met. 988ª9 ff.).

---

[1] In the *Phaedo* Plato argues the immortality of the soul from (*a*) the doctrine of "reminiscence" (p. 30) ; (*b*) its kinship *qua* ruling element with the divine ; (*c*) the fact that life is an essential attribute of soul as heat is of fire ; in *Republic* X by urging that its natural evil, wickedness, does not kill it. In the *Timaeus* (see pp. 64 ff.) and in *Laws* X Plato speaks of a personal God as of a supreme soul. On the strength of such passages Plato has often been credited with a belief in theism and in personal immortality. But the theism of the *Timaeus* is "mythical," and in the *Laws* Plato speaks the language of the practical legislator. And as regards immortality, if we exclude the *Phaedo*, which in its teaching as to the soul is very probably Socratic (perhaps also Pythagorean), and also explicitly "mythical" passages in which Plato never pretends to be expressing literal truth, then there is no passage in the dialogues which can be quite safely interpreted to mean that that which is immortal in man's soul is also as such personal and individual. Aristotle, who certainly did not believe in personal survival of death (cp. p. 175, note 1), expresses no disagreement with Plato on this point, and more probably they both held that men *qua* singular individuals do not differ essentially but in respect only of their perishable bodily natures. On the other hand, Plato does not seem to link the soul *qua* individual with its body so intimately as does Aristotle. Both of them regard the body as the instrument of the soul and as less real than the soul, but Aristotle interprets this to mean that body relates to soul as matter to form ; and that, even if it is the proper logical development of Plato's teaching, represents a new point of view. See for Aristotle's doctrine and for the difficulty he has in maintaining it, Chapters VII and VIII.

The fact seems to be that Plato offers the Forms as an explanation of what ultimately *is* and is object of knowledge, and if the Form of the Good, because it constitutes all that is real, tends inevitably to include subject with object, Plato, though he regards knowledge of the Good as something ineffable and only to be won as a flash of insight after long intercourse with the subject, finds here no precise problem to formulate. Only a lifelong activity in which noble action and a passionate love of beauty are hardly divided from stern intellectual endeavour can turn the eye of the soul to the Form of the Good, and for that reason we can speak of the Good only in terms of simile and myth. But the Form of the Good is " beyond Being," and it is just this faith in a unity of values which transcends, though it sustains, both Being and knowledge,[1] which relieves Plato from examining further the kinship of mind with its object. We might incline to say that, at a level of experience on which an individual soul apprehends an object, the soul, like its object, not only knows but also *is*—that its knowing is a function which does not absorb its whole nature but leaves an inactive residue, to which corresponds an unknown remainder in the object ; and with this experience we might contrast the Form of the Good as an identity without residue of knowledge with its object. But on that account the Form of the Good becomes more than a Form, and, though he speaks more often simply of the Good than of the Form of the Good, if Plato had been fully conscious of this implication he must have seen that the culmination of thought and Being could be equally well approached from the subjective side and called a supreme intelligence. And Plato's doctrine of the soul, despite hints which turned Aristotle's speculation somewhat in this direction,[2]

[1] It is to be remembered that to Plato " truth," ἀλήθεια, is as much a character of the object as is beauty.

[2] Cf., *e.g.*, p. 171.

scarcely allows us to regard absolutism as the explicit intention of his metaphysical teaching.[1]

[1] Plato is never fully conscious of a problem in the opposition of an individual mind which *is*, and can in some sense be an object of knowledge, to mind as the presupposition of objects. Cp. *Sophist*, 248a ff.

PLATO : THE INTERRELATION OF THE FORMS

THE *Republic* leaves the general impression of an effort, not wholly successful, to show the Form of the Good, and correspondingly, the lesser Forms which it comprehends, not only as transcendent but as also immanent ; to conceive what *is* not as two worlds in juxtaposition but as a single coherent system of Forms which the perceptible world of becoming partially reveals as its own real nature. So far as the *Republic* is concerned, Aristotle's criticism of the Forms is justified, inasmuch as Plato has neither clearly traced the manner of their interrelation within the Good nor altogether avoided the appearance, at any rate, of sheer transcendence. Moreover, an evident tendency to seek in the sharpness and clarity of mathematical distinctions an earnest of true knowledge foreshadows, perhaps ominously, that absorption in mathematics which developed Platonism implies to Aristotle.

From the later dialogues we have space only to select a few points. And it is to be remembered that Plato always avails himself of the independence of treatment which the dialogue form allows. We can expect to trace no rigid course of development, though at any rate in the *Theaetetus*, *Parmenides*, and *Sophist*, Plato is mainly concerned with the interrelation of the Forms.

In the *Theaetetus* Plato asks " what is knowledge ? " An attempt is made to identify knowledge with sense perception by combining the relativism of Protagoras with Heraclitus' doctrine of perpetual flux. When this

---

[1] This chapter owes a special debt to Prof. Taylor's *Plato*.

pure sensationalism has broken down in contradiction, it
is pointed out that the bodily organs of sense are not
themselves percipient, but are instruments by means of
which we perceive. Now we cannot perceive sound by
sight nor colour by hearing, but we obviously do have
thoughts of things common to colour and sound. Hence
there must be something other than seeing or hearing, by
means of which we grasp these common characters of the
objects of the special senses. In fact there must be some
one element—the soul perhaps—in which the objects of
the special senses converge in actual perception of a
sensible thing. It is apparently implied that until the
soul relates the simple data of the several special senses
there is no apprehension of any perceptible thing, but it is
these " thoughts of things common " to the objects of more
than one special sense which Plato proceeds to discuss.
As his instances will show, Plato is beginning here to
consider the fact that relations as well as substances and
qualities appear to imply Forms.[1] We have such thoughts
as " colour and sound *are*," " each (*i.e.* colour and sound)
is other than the other and the same as itself," " both
taken together are two, and each is one," " they are like
or unlike one another." We may ask, then, by what power
and through what instrument do we apprehend such
characters as being and not-being, likeness and unlikeness,
sameness, otherness and contrariety, unity and number,
odd and even ; and again predicates implying value such
as beautiful and ugly, good and bad, etc. ? Clearly, by
no specific instrument such as a special sense-organ; rather
the soul acts by itself in their apprehension. Simple sensation of simple qualities begins at birth and is common to all
animals ; the grasp of these common characters involves
comparison and reflexion, and this perhaps is knowledge.[2]

[1] Beginning perhaps to discover that relation and quality are two
sides of the same thing.
[2] Aristotle's doctrine of *Sensus Communis* (see pp. 109 ff.) should be
compared and contrasted.

But this initial definition of knowledge is defective, for it gives no account of error. What then is error ? It cannot, for instance, be the mistaken recognition of a present sensation as identical with an impression retained in the memory like a print on wax ; for there is also purely intellectual error, such as often occurs in the calculation of large numbers. Can we explain this by means of a distinction between actual and potential knowledge ? Can we say that we may *have* knowledge which we are unable to *use*—as we may have a bird secure in an aviary but be unable at the moment actually to put our hand on him ?[1] No, for the content of a false judgment is something actual and not potential (*i.e.* error must be more than mere absence of knowledge), and we should have to maintain, absurdly, that there are positive " ignorances " flying about in our aviary. Moreover, how can we know if our judgment is true or false ? It may even be true, but by sheer accident ; and right opinion is not knowledge.

The final suggestion recalls the first definition. Perhaps there are simple intellectual elements, which, like the data of the special senses, are significant only in determinate combination—just as letters have meaning only within a word.[2] We should perhaps abandon the search for a psychological criterion of truth, and say that knowledge is right opinion combined with a λόγος of the complex, a formula, *i.e.*, which gives the differentia distinguishing the complex from all other things. To this view too there are objections, and the dialogue ends with an apparently negative conclusion.

The *Parmenides* opens with a discussion of the difficulties of relating a Form to its particulars. The admission is made that Forms which obviously imply value are more

---

[1] For Aristotle's development of this distinction cf. pp. 104 and 147.
[2] Aristotle's theory of judgment should be compared ; see Chapter X, § 2 (A).

readily tractable than those which do not, and the first part of the dialogue seems meant to preface a continuation of that attempt to reconstruct the theory of Forms by tackling the problem of their interrelation, which had already begun in the *Theaetetus*. We may say in advance that in this process the Forms lose a good deal of their original character, and in the *Theaetetus*, *Parmenides* and *Sophist* the unambiguous use of the term εἶδος in its original technical sense is rare.

The second part of the *Parmenides* is obscure and variously interpreted. It seems intended to show that if, as the Eleatic dialecticians insist, the common characters of the *Theaetetus* are to be taken as predicable of a subject severally and in total isolation one from another, the result is hopeless contradiction. The argument therefore starts, not from the position of Heraclitus and Protagoras, but from the Parmenidean one. Additions made to the list of common characters are motion and rest, equal and unequal, limited and unlimited.

It is probable that after writing the *Parmenides* Plato was for some time occupied with practical affairs in Sicily, and that the *Sophist* was not composed before 360 B.C.[1] But the thread is not broken. Plato reopens the question of the interrelation of the Forms, and starts again from the Eleatic dialectic.

According to the Eleatics, to judge that A is B is a contradiction, and to judge that A is not B is to judge nothing ; for being alone *is*, and there is no not-being. Plato replies with a brilliant treatment of the negative judgment. He shows that being and not-being have their meaning in λόγοι, judgments. " A is not B," means simply " A is other than B " ; not-B is not a non-entity but a real character excluded from A, and A is significantly characterised by the exclusion. Moreover, since there is no predicate which cannot be thus significantly excluded

[1] See Taylor, *Plato*, p. 371.

from some subject, not-being comprises all that is, and has as many parts as knowledge ; and being is equally multifarious. This enables us to interrelate a few of the greatest Forms. These will not all combine so as to participate in one another, any more than all combinations of letters will make a syllable, or all sets of words a sentence.[1] Some, like vowels amid consonants, will be more pervasive and productive of combination than others. Plato selects five " greatest kinds " ; being, not-being or " otherness," sameness, rest, and movement.[2] Of these, rest and movement will not blend and mutually participate ; but both will participate in being, since both rest and movement *are.* Again, each of the three, rest, movement and being, is other than the other two and the same as itself, although sameness and otherness are neither rest, movement, nor being. This systematic division of being into its subordinate kinds—the blending and severing of the forms so that they give rise to λόγος—is said by Plato to be the true dialectic which is philosophy.

So Plato becomes the founder of logic ; yet of a logic not formal but philosophical and concrete. He does not answer the Eleatics by treating the " is " of predication as a mere copula without existential significance. The blendings and severances of the Forms are not mere *distinctiones rationis* : they are *distinctiones in re,* the real ground of significant judgment ; and later in the dialogue Plato treats judgment (λόγος), in which the Forms systematically blend with or repel one another, as itself a Form. Thus it is his clear purpose again to emphasise that kinship of mind and object which makes it impossible to interrelate the Forms unless they are treated in union

---

[1] Cp. p. 51.

[2] Κίνησις here translated " movement," covers all forms of change and activity, though Plato tends to think of locomotion as the primary form of change—a doctrine which Aristotle definitely holds, though he greatly restricts the meaning of κίνησις ; cp. pp. 77 ff., esp. p. 78, note 3, and p. 80.

E

with the thought that thinks them ; but how precisely this kinship is to be understood is not so clear. He introduces his account of negation by criticising a doctrine of static and immutable Forms. The mind in knowing, he argues, is active, and the object known is passive : therefore neither is static nor immutable. There must correspond movement and variety in the object to the activity in the soul ; purely static Forms would be as unknowable as the flux of Heraclitus. Certainly what is fully real and knowable must as such be stable and self-identical, but it must also possess life and thought and, therefore, soul.[1] Hence we must say that Reality as a whole both rests and moves. Now if judgment is itself a Form, and if whatever is fully real and intelligible must possess soul, one might be tempted to infer that soul too is a Form. Plato might seem to be approaching the view that philosophic inquiry should not assume the distinction of subject and object, but exhibit its emergence in experience—that, in fact, the kinship of mind and object implies their ultimate identity. But the doctrine of soul which Plato develops in later dialogues precludes this interpretation. Soul is never a Form to Plato, and its kinship with the Forms is never made fully explicit.[2]

The *Sophist* suggests that the problem of how particulars participate in a Form and of how Forms are to be ranked, would be solved by a reconstruction in which many of the early Forms, posited to correspond with the groups and characters of linguistic usage or common sense, would, as such, disappear.[3] They would be absorbed within a system of all-pervasive characters—universal, though variously partial and abstract, definitions—of Reality. The dialogue however, offers little more than hints of such a system, hints dropped in the course of special arguments. Of the

[1] Heraclitus in fact regarded soul as that which knows moving objects because it is itself in ceaseless flux ; cp. Aristotle, An. 405^{b}25 ff.
[2] See also pp. 44 ff.
[3] Rejected as something like what Croce calls "pseudo-concepts."

greatest kinds, being, sameness, and otherness are all-pervasive : they participate in and are predicable of one another, and all other Forms participate in each of them. Rest and movement, on the other hand, are said to be mutually exclusive contraries, and on what we take this statement to mean our view of the system will chiefly depend.[1] Alternative interpretations seem possible, and neither reconciles all the evidence.[2]

(A) The logical conclusion to be drawn from Plato's account of significant negation would seem to be that, though the negative judgment, to have meaning, must exclude a more or less determinate predicate from the subject, yet the subject is not thereby precisely characterised unless the excluded predicate and the resulting positive qualification of the subject are precise contraries. For example, " A is not greater than B " leaves it doubtful whether A is equal to or less than B,[3] but " Prime numbers are not even " implies that they are necessarily odd. Thus negation points the way to the disjunctive judgment, within which it is precisely related to affirmation ; e.g. in " Number is either odd or even," or " Quantity is either discrete or continuous," the subject is characterised by a pair of contraries such that either is precisely defined by the denial of the other. The difference, in fact, between the negative and disjunctive judgments—between otherness and contrariety—measures nothing but the degree of our ignorance. In a fully real and intelligible system ignorance is irrelevant, and negation would only appear as disjunction. Moreover, in a judgment such as " Quantity is either discrete or continuous," the subject is not only characterised by each of the contraries, but by the two together as a disjunctive correlation : quantity as such is *both* discrete

---

[1] Plato does not here discuss contrariety, though it is one of the common characters of the *Theaetetus*.

[2] The analysis which follows is based on some unpublished work of Prof. Joachim, which I have been privileged to read.

[3] Cp. 257b, where Plato recognises this.

and continuous. Only in empirical judgments expressing partial ignorance is this not true. Hence when Plato tells us that Reality as a whole both rests and moves, we might infer that (*a*) rest and movement are each all-pervasive characters of Reality, and (*b*) both together as a disjunctive correlation characterise the real as such—*i.e.* that (*a*) " Reality as such rests (abides)," and " Reality as such moves," are each true, though partial, definitions of the real, and that (*b*) in " Reality is stable in change " (*i.e.* " is characterised by rest-and-movement ") the real is yet further and more fully defined. In such a system this disjunctive correlation, or synthesis of contrary characters, would in its turn be found partial, in the sense of still abstract, and point the way to a further definition, which would be *its* contrary. In this process from abstract to concrete, in which analysis and synthesis would alternate, every determination of the real would stand to one other determination of the real in a special relation of contrariety ; every successive disjunction would be realisation at a more concrete level of an initial opposition of contrary characters ; every successive synthesis would further develop an initial correlation. Reality as a whole, present from the beginning as the definiendum, would exhibit itself more and more concretely through these stages. One of them would be λόγος, the real as self-expressive in judgment—and the final stage perhaps the Form of the Good. In fact, the process would present the essence of the Socratic dialectic as the true method by which philosophy defines not one of the virtues but Reality.

But much that Plato says runs counter to this interpretation. We might take being—in the sense of the minimal characterisation of Reality—and not-being, in the sense of otherness, as the initial pair of contraries, and rest and movement as the second pair. As the intervening synthesis we might perhaps suggest γένεσις, coming-to-be, in the sense in which in the *Republic* Plato applies it to that

which both *is* and *is not*. But Plato does not introduce
γένεσις as a Form in the *Sophist*. Moreover, the interpretation which we have offered compels us to identify sameness
with being. This, however, Plato explicitly forbids us to
do. Though he does identify otherness with not-being, he
then introduces a distinction between self-subsistent and
dependent (relative, adjectival) being, and identifies otherness with dependent being—a proceeding dubious enough
in itself, and one which increases a certain confusion present
throughout the discussion between being in the sense of
the abstract, minimal, characterisation of all that is, and
being in the sense of Reality as a complete whole. And
there is further evidence for a different interpretation.

(B) When Plato defines rest and movement as mutually
exclusive contraries, he states that they are embraced
ab extra by being ; *i.e.*, it would seem, they are not first,
each separately, and then as a correlated pair, all-pervasive
characters of Reality—further and fuller determinations
of being and not-being—but divide the universe between
them into that which rests and that which moves. If
we follow this line of thought, the system seems likely to
develop as follows. Rest and movement will each divide
into a pair of contraries and embrace them purely *ab extra*.
These fresh contraries will each again divide, and the
process will be throughout one of analysis unpunctuated
by synthesis. The final result will be, not Reality as a
single organic system, but a number of more or less
remotely related infimae species. We approach the conception of a genus of species embodied in Porphyry's Tree
—the notion of genus as abstract common character, and
of species as formed by the addition *ab extra* of differentiae
to the generic character. And hints of such a degradation
of dialectic towards mere classification are traceable in
Plato's dialogues. Already in the *Phaedrus* Plato had
split the Socratic method into two processes : (*a*) definition
by means of " composition " (συναγωγή)—a collecting of

the definiendum by eliciting it from its scattered and fragmentary instances ; (b) successive " division " of the Form thus reached, by exhaustive couples of alternative differentiae which articulate it into its species. Now the Socratic dialectic was a single self-contained movement ; its starting point was at once a particular and a confused universal, its conclusion a universal individualised in concrete difference. But if "composition" and "division" are to be distinguished as two processes, it would seem that composition must start from sheer particulars, and division from a sheerly abstract universal. In the *Republic* the relation of upward and downward processes was not very clear, and in the *Philebus* we do not find the conception of dialectic as a single self-contained movement.

In practice Plato uses division as a method of defining a species. To define X, take a genus A, of which X is well known to be a species. Divide A into two mutually exclusive subgenera, B and C, which exhaust A and are distinguished by the fact that B is, while C is not, characterised by a differentia well known to belong to X. Neglect C and again divide B, so proceeding until X itself is reached. The definition of X will then be X as successively specified in the series of differentiae which terminates in X ; *e.g.* if A is animal and X is man, " animal—terrestrial—biped—rational—man." If the neglected divisions can now be completed, we get just such a system as I have outlined in (B).

Thus Plato in the *Sophist* seems to halt at a parting of the ways. If he ever pursued further the method of this dialogue he may perhaps have decided to arrest the disintegrating process of division at a comparatively abstract stage, and have taken number to be the ultimate essence of things—certainly he did not incline, as Aristotle did, to regard the infima species as the ultimately real.[1] Yet his

[1] For the relation of Aristotle's doctrine to Plato's problem in the *Sophist* see pp. 180 ff.

very different method of approaching the problem in the
Philebus and *Timaeus* should warn us against pressing too
far the implications of the *Sophist*. We will close our
sketch of Platonism with a brief account of these two
dialogues, dismissing for the present the *Politicus*, an essay
on government linked externally to the *Sophist*, but paving
the way for the *Laws*.

The *Philebus* not only throws light upon Plato's metaphysical development, but its psychology provides much
of the material for Aristotle's ethical teaching.[1]

Primarily it discusses what is the good life for man ;
but man is treated as a microcosm, and the question, as
Taylor puts it, is " what is really meant by the Platonic
Form of the Good." The good for man is a state of soul
which makes him happy ($\epsilon\dot{v}\delta a\dot{\iota}\mu\omega\nu$). Philebus suggests
that this is pleasure, Socrates that it is thinking. Socrates
points out that pleasure, like colour, is a genus comprehending different and contrasted species. We must divide
this genus dialectically, and we must go farther than the
Pythagoreans, who distinguish in all things a one and an
indefinite plurality ; we must discover just how many
are the different species, and be content to leave an
indefinite plurality of singulars as logically indiscriminate
only when infimae species are reached. And in any case
no man would choose either a life of sheer pleasant feeling
without power of conscious reflexion on past, present, or
future feeling, or a life of sheer thought, neutral in respect
of feeling : either would be something unfinished and
imperfect, and therefore not the good for man. All things
that are, continues Socrates, fall into one of four classes :—
(*a*) The unlimited (indefinite).[2] In this class falls everything
that is " a great and small," or " a more and less " ;
i.e. all things that admit of degree, such as temperature.
(*b*) Limit ; *i.e.* the exact mathematical number, ratio, or

---

[1] See esp. Chapter VII, § 6.
[2] The term is at present used without prejudice.

measure, which limits a continuum of degree.[1] (c) The
" mixed " ; i.e. anything which is a " mixture " of limit
with the unlimited. Thus the continuum of temperature
variation is an unlimited, 60° is a limit, and a temperature
of 60° F. is a mixture. The introduction of limit is a
" γένεσις into being," a process of coming to be. Mixed
products so formed are good climate, sound articulate in
definite differences of musical rhythm and pitch, the health
of the body and the excellence of the soul. All these are
brought into being by the introduction of exact ratio to limit
intensive continua, and their goodness depends on their
being neither a too much nor a too little. (d) The cause—
that which makes—the mixture. Now the whole universe
submits to this analysis, but within it man relates to the
cosmos as microcosm to macrocosm. At least as a
" mixture " he draws from the mightier and purer masses
of the cosmos the earth, air, fire and water that constitute
his body ; and since in him the intelligence residing in his
soul is the cause of order in his body (e.g. it is the medical
art which restores the disordered body), we may complete
the analogy and place in (d) an intelligent soul as cause
of the proportioned structure of the universe.

We can now review the proposed constituents of the
good life. Pleasure and pain as such clearly belong to the
class of the unlimited, for of pleasure and pain as such there
is no maximum or minimum (cf. p. 150). They occur in
the living creature, who is a mixed product, and one kind
of pleasure accompanies the restoration of organic equilibrium which has been disturbed ; i.e. it accompanies the
re-introduction of limit, the " γένεσις into being " in which
this restoration consists. Dissolution of the normal state
is correspondingly painful. Permanent equilibrium would
be neutral in respect of feeling, and though such a state

[1] Plato's conception of limit is in principle the same as Aristotle's
(see note 2, p. 83), and the germ is here of Aristotle's theory of matter
and form.

may be that in which God lives,[1] yet human life inevitably
fluctuates in alternate pain and pleasure. When this
disturbance and restoration is merely remembered or
anticipated, another kind of pleasure and pain occurs in
the soul alone without organic accompaniment. To
explain this some definitions are required. Sensation is a
process beginning in the body, penetrating to the soul,
and affecting both together. Memory is the retention of
this sensation, and recollection is the purely psychical
recovery of a memory. Desire occurs in its simplest form
when the body lacks something of its normal condition,
but desire is a *psychical* tension—a state of the soul in
some sense apprehending the contrast of actual bodily
depletion and anticipated restoration. Hence arises a
problem ; for the pains and pleasures of this second kind
are often simultaneously experienced, and often—in the
case of the so-called bodily pleasure commonly—become
intensified by contrast. And the present pleasure of
anticipation may not only contrast with the pain of a
present situation, but may rest on a false judgment as to
the future. Hence pleasure itself may be false—though
this does not mean that a false pleasure is not a
pleasure at all, any more than a false judgment is not a
judgment.[2]

Now both the types of pleasure which we have discussed depend upon a process of satisfying a felt

---

[1] Aristotle disagrees ; cf. p. 151.

[2] 37c. Plato's point, I think, is that a man is certain *that* he feels,
just as he is certain *that* he judges ; but *what* he feels—even, in the case
of mixed states, whether it is pain or pleasure—is just as much open
to doubt as *what* he judges. Feeling is inseparably connected with
apprehension of an objective situation—hedonism in fact can only be
made plausible by covertly ascribing to pleasure a character undeter-
mined by the features of this situation—and Plato, to whom being,
intelligibility, and value are not ultimately divisible, could hardly hold
any other view. It is because feeling isolated from the apprehended
situation has a merely formal existence that Plato assigns it to the
class of the unlimited. In An. 403ᵇ5 Aristotle says that emotions are
" intelligible contents (λόγοι) embodied in matter." For Aristotle's
view of states in which pleasure and pain are mingled see p. 150, note 3.

want.[1] Hence they both involve mixture of pleasure and
pain and are deceptive and unreal.   Moreover—to express
the same thing from a different point of view—coming-to-
be is for the sake of being,[2] a process exists for the sake
of the end which it subserves : only the end, and not the
means to it, can be intrinsically good.   Hence pleasure
such as intrinsically belongs to a process cannot be intrinsically good.   But there are pleasures preceded by no
felt want and accompanied by no conscious process of
restoration or repletion.   The pleasures of perceiving
geometrical figures, colours, sounds, and some odours,
and again the pleasure of acquiring knowledge—these are
true and real pleasures, pure of any pain.

Plato implies here, and in *Timaeus*, 64a ff. definitely
states that a depletion *is* in process of repletion when the
pure pleasures of sense are experienced, but this does not
falsify the pleasure, because it is not a conscious want.[3]
He would thus appear to retain the view that the perfect
spiritual equilibrium of God would not involve pleasure ;
and it would seem to follow that even the highest pleasures
are only relatively real.   But here the discussion of pleasure
ends—though with a remark which reveals the essence of
Greek ethical thinking, namely that the judgment predicating moral goodness of a man relates to any other
judgment asserting excellence of him, as the whole to the
part which it includes (cf. p. 127).   It would be absurd,
says Socrates, to deny goodness to beauty in the body
and to courage, self-control, and intelligence in the soul,
and to maintain that a man is good merely in proportion
to the amount of pleasure which he is feeling.

We need now a corresponding analysis of knowledge.

---

[1] The only difference between them seems to lie in the degree to
which the felt want becomes desire of a consciously formulated end.
Aristotle's view is different ; see p. 150.

[2] Cp. the quotation from Aristotle with which Chapter I, § 2 begins.

[3] That unconscious depletion precedes intellectual pleasures Plato
seems to imply in *Republic*, 583b ff.

In the operative arts, or crafts, there is precisely as much knowledge as there is mathematics ; the rest is empirical conjecture. Building typifies the purer kind, music the less pure. Pure mathematics is a yet truer form of knowledge than applied mathematics ; and, despite Gorgias' plea for rhetoric as the most practically useful of arts, the highest place belongs to the truest form of knowledge, namely dialectic, which studies not the shifting realm of opinion and coming-to-be to which the crafts belong, but the ultimately and eternally real.

Hence the good life will include knowledge—even of the less exact kind, since it is human life that we discuss—and all pure and harmless pleasures. But we must add a third ingredient, ἀλήθεια, " truth " or " reality," without which the mixture cannot come to be ; and this brings us to the threshold of the good, that element of intrinsic value in the mixed life which we wish to seize. Now the goodness of any mixture lies in measure and proportion ; but these, everywhere and in all things, are—beauty. It is then this triple unity of values, beauty, measure and truth which causes the mixture—causes it to be good,[1] and we can now set the ingredients of the good life in an order of value : (i) measure ; (ii) proportion, beauty, completeness ; (iii) intelligence and wisdom (since mind is either identical with or likest of all things to ἀλήθεια) ; (iv) the intelligent crafts and true opinion ; (v) the unmixed pleasures.

The *Philebus* is primarily an attack on hedonism, and its metaphysical background—*e.g.* the position, if any, occupied by the Forms—is elusive. We may hazard a few suggestions. (1) Despite the hinted identity of mind with ἀλήθεια the point of view is not that of the *Sophist*.

---

[1] Though Plato characteristically emphasises unity rather than difference, the single Form of the Good of the *Republic* here first begins to exhibit internal diversity. Plato had, however, already in the *Symposium* and *Phaedrus* treated the Form of the beautiful as an ultimate value and the object of a passionate spiritual love. Aristotle would have called the triple unity both formal and final cause.

Plato seems to envisage the universe as a correlation of intelligent soul with its object in the macrocosm and, analogously, in the microcosm.[1] The constituents of the good life would perhaps thus correspond with the initial fourfold classification of the universe : (i) and (ii) with (B) ; (iii) and (iv) as inherent in the human soul, with (D) ; (v) with (A) ; the good life, as a mixture, with (C). (2) The mathematical implications of measure are clearly prominent in Plato's mind, and in the concept of the unlimited we have perhaps a foretaste of " the dyad of the great and small "[2] from which, together with the One, Plato is said by Aristotle to have derived the Form-Numbers.[3] We learn from Aristotle (Met. 987ᵇ25 ff.) that whereas the Pythagoreans treated the indefinite as one and identified mathematical numbers directly with things, Plato introduced Form-Numbers and Forms,[4] separating them from things. (3) The four classes with which the dialogue opens are certainly not Forms, and we might perhaps infer that the Forms—become Form-Numbers—are to be identified with (A) and (B) taken together ; but it is hard to be sure that the Forms have any place at all in the Philebus.[5]

The Timaeus is suspect as a source of Platonic doctrine. Its teaching is markedly Pythagorean, and though we may assume Plato's sympathy with the theory which it expounds, it is in any case a study in what is to Plato the merely probable and therefore only mythically expressible science of cosmology.[6] We have space only for an outline

[1] This, as we shall see, is the teaching of the probably contemporary Timaeus. [2] I.e. mathematical continuity.

[3] The integers, two, three, etc., not the mathematical numbers with which the mathematician operates. The latter are the particular pairs, triplets, etc., which participate in the former ; see note 1, p. 41.

[4] See note 1, p. 32, and p. 67.

[5] See Taylor, Plato, p. 417. Even the categories of the Sophist have developed so far from their origin in the early Platonic doctrine of Forms that the question of terminology becomes difficult.

[6] Yet the Timaeus is the background to Aristotle's cosmology (see Chapter V, §§ 4 and 5), and its influence on medieval thought is great ; see pp. 238, 239.

of the dialogue and a brief selection from the mass of nascent special science embedded in it.

The world of real and timeless being is twofold. It contains the Forms, and it contains God. God out of chaos created the cosmos as a live creature, fashioning it after the pattern of the Form of living being. Himself a soul, to make the soul of the world he blended, according to the intervals of a musical scale, Being that is self-same and indivisible with Being that is other and divisible. Out of this mixture he formed an outermost governing circle of " the same " (the sidereal equator), and, obliquely inclined to it, an inner circle of " the other " (the ecliptic),[1] and he subdivided the latter into six concentric circles (the orbits of the planets). These two soul-circles revolve in opposite directions unceasingly ; for time, " a moving image of eternity," was created with the cosmos as its mode of being, and is measured by the revolutions of the planets. This world-soul is (a) a knowing of the eternal and a true opining of the temporal, and (b) the source of movement, the efficient cause, of the cosmos.

Looking to the organisms of which the single Form of living being is constituted, God made " the gods "—the fixed stars—and set them in the circle of " the same." Each is an individual and each has a body of fire. These and certain other gods—created, but by their creator's will not destined to perish—fashioned man. Man's soul was made from a weaker brew of the same constituents, and it is so far analogous to the world-soul both as knower and as initiator of movement ; but with its body, which is compacted of the four elements, it acquired two inferior parts, a spirited part and a desiring part. These were placed respectively in the thorax and below the diaphragm, whereas the intelligent element resides in the brain. The disquisition on anatomy, physiology, medicine and hygiene, which follow this statement, have a fantastic air, but the

[1] Cp. p. 89.

guiding principle is the construction of the body to serve
the soul as its instrument.[1]

An essay in geometrical physics provides a further
analysis of the elements, by resolving them into two
species of triangle as their ultimate constituents. It serves,
as Professor Taylor remarks, " to connect the two main
currents of scientific thought, the biological and the
mathematical, by providing a geometrical construction
for the corpuscles of the four elements which the biologist
Empedocles had treated as the ' simples ' of his system."

The permanent substratum of the world is not the four
elements, for these are impermanent and constantly change
into one another by processes of rarefaction and condensation. Nor is it the simple triangles. It is simple
space, or extension. It is a " not-being apprehended by
a kind of bastard thinking," *i.e.* by the negation of any
positive character ; for it is a mere indeterminate matrix,
the bare omnirecipient medium of the percepta which
come to be in it, the mirror—" hardly matter of belief,
beheld as in a dream "— which sustains those reflections
of the Forms in which the things of sense consist.[2] The
constituents of these sensible bodies, if you analyse below
their appearance as earth, air, fire and water, are the
simplest and most beautiful triangles—those which combine to form the regular solids. This geometrical structure[3]
is the basis of all more concrete physical differentiation.
Since " Necessity " is a part cause with mind of this
physical creation, no more than a probable and inadequate
account can be given either of this or of the physiological
side of man's psychical life.[4]

[1] Cp. pp. 96 ff. for Aristotle's elaboration of this view.
[2] For Aristotle's debt to Plato's omnirecipient substratum see p. 72,
note 3.
[3] In the last resort presumably the Number-Forms.
[4] This " necessity " is not that of rational order, but " an erratic
cause," recalcitrant to (though ultimately plastic to and persuadeable
by) intelligence. It seems to contrast with intelligent purpose as (*a*) an
element in things of never fully intelligible brute fact, perhaps actual

Thus, if we omit the " mythical " element, the attitude of the dialogue, like that of the *Philebus*, is on the whole scientific in the sense that the universe is assumed as an object of investigation without question of how knowledge of it is possible. The hints of the *Republic* and the *Sophist* are not pursued. The Forms are once more objects of knowledge, not categories ; mind is not a Form but the functioning of a soul. It seems probable that, as Aristotle so often says, the Forms—reality *qua* object of mind —became in the end the Form-Numbers, and the later stages of Platonism remain unintelligible unless we remember that mathematical truth has in all ages tended to dazzle the mind of man ; that in Plato's day its higher branches were a new-discovered continent of intellectual adventure, and that in his old age the success of astronomers like Eudoxus in calculating planetary movement had seemed to reveal at once a supreme vision of divine order and an infinite promise of reconciling theory with observed fact. Yet to Plato number was never the whole of reality. We do not know whether, like Speusippus, he ever came to identify the Good with the One, but it was left to Xenocrates, the third head of the Academy, to force all reality within the compass of the Form-Numbers, and to call the soul " a self-moving number."

To leave Plato's dialogues for the treatises of Aristotle is to exchange a gallery of bright landscape paintings for a map, and a map that Aristotle sometimes seems to be constructing with special intent to convict his master of errors in perspective. But it is still Plato's country that he charts. The reader who has followed our account of the dialogues with the fourfold causal analysis in mind has already seen that for Aristotle to philosophise means

indeterminacy ; (*b*) something like the mechanical necessity governing Kant's world of phenomena. It is the necessity of which the complementary moment is contingency, the conditioned which is *eo ipso* conditional. For Aristotle's use of the notion see p. 92, note 1.

to Platonise,[1] and in the chapters now to come he will readily observe how closely Plato dictates the main lines of Aristotle's efforts to discover and define the substantially real.

[1] Cp. Jaeger, *Aristoteles*, p. 1.

PART II
THE PHILOSOPHY OF ARISTOTLE

V

SUBLUNARY DEVELOPMENT : ITS FIRST STAGES AND ITS SOURCE

1. ELEMENTAL TRANSFORMATION

ARISTOTLE's search for substance begins in the perceptible universe where all things change, and all are composite of form and matter—the world of nature. For " nature " in its strict and primary sense is to Aristotle the essence of things which have in themselves as such a source or impulse of change and cessation from change ; and the " nature," in the strict sense, of these natural things is the form which their changing actualises.[1] Within this universe Aristotle distinguishes the lower or sublunary cosmos as more especially characterised by change. And the negative moment of it—or, if we view it dynamically, the *terminus a quo* of its total change—is what he calls " primary matter " ; a matter, that is, bare of all form ; a potentiality quite inactive and unactual, which has for its complementary moment a privation that is sheer negation, not a shadow that darkens but darkness absolute.

But primary matter is not by itself the substratum of any actual change. It is neither a separately existing physical body, nor a chaos which precedes the evolution of the sublunary world ; it is a purely logical *terminus a quo* of process, a moment distinguishable but not separable in any concrete of matter and form. For the simplest *bodies* of the lower cosmos are the four elements, fire, air, water and earth. Logical analysis in fact reveals also a

---

[1] See Met. 1015ª13, Ph. II, 1. Also pp. 10 ff.

stage of actualisation *between* primary matter and the elements. The latter are being incessantly transformed into one another, and the termini of transformation—the simplest form of substantial change in which that comes to be which was not, and vice versa[1]—are always specifically contrary states of a generically identical substratum, which are further related as agent and patient.[2] Hence transformation implies a matter more than primary ; it implies a matter potentially capable of alternative actual qualification as either the one or the other member of certain pairs of contrary qualities which are such as to act upon one another. These pairs of contraries—which *exist* only as qualifying bodies—are thus a second merely logical implicate of transformation. They are in fact such of the tactual qualities of bodies as are fundamental, viz., hot and cold, and fluid and dry.[3]

---

[1] See p. 10.

[2] Cp. GC 331ᵃ14 and below, p. 73 ff. Moreover, of any pair of contraries, though each may be regarded either as positive or as the privation of the other, yet one is always more strictly a positive qualification and the other a privation—as, *e.g.*, in good and bad, hot and cold. Strictly speaking, contraries are the two most sharply opposed species of a genus—*e.g.* black and white—though an intermediate serves as contrary to any other intermediate or to either extreme. Elsewhere Aristotle treats the termini of substantial change as *contradictories*, thus contrasting it with the derivative forms of change (Ph. 225ᵃ12 ff.). His point is that though its termini are *logically* contradictories, yet all *actual* substantial change is transformation : nothing comes to be or perishes absolutely. Yet he does not wholly avoid confusion of physical with logical analysis.

[3] For this doctrine of the three postulates of substantial change see GC 329ᵃ24 ff. : " Although there is a matter of the perceptible bodies, a matter out of which the so-called " elements " come to be, it has no separate existence, but is always bound up with a contrariety. . . . We must reckon as an " originative source " and as primary the matter which underlies, though it is inseparable from, the contrary qualities ; for the hot is not matter for the cold, nor the cold for the hot, but the substratum is matter for them both. We therefore have to reckon three " originative sources " : (i) that which is potentially perceptible body ; (ii) the contrarieties (I mean, *e.g.*, hot and cold) ; (iii) fire, water, and the like." Cp. also Ph. I, 4–7.
In GC 329ᵃ13 ff. Aristotle develops the notion of primary matter by criticising Timaeus' omnirecipient substratum as ambiguous : has it, or has it not, separate existence ? In Ph. I, 9 he criticises Plato for failing to differentiate the two moments of matter, privation and positive sub-

Aristotle's explanation of how he arrives at these four
qualities, and of how they combine to constitute the four
elements, is as follows: " Contrarieties correlative to touch
are hot-cold, dry-fluid, heavy-light, hard-soft, viscous-
brittle, rough-smooth, coarse-fine. Of these heavy and
light are neither active nor susceptible. On the other
hand hot and cold, and dry and fluid, are terms of which
the first pair implies power to act and the second pair
susceptibility. " Hot " is that which associates things of
the same kind . . while cold . . . associates homogeneous
and heterogeneous things alike. Fluid is that which, being
readily adaptable in shape, is not determinable by any
limit of its own ; while " dry "[1] is that which is readily
determinable by its own limit, but not readily adaptable
in shape " (GC 329^{b}18-32). He dismisses the remaining
tactual qualities as derivative, and links these four to
form the elements : " The elementary qualities are four,
and any four terms can be combined in six couples.
Contraries, however, refuse to be coupled : for it is impossible for the same thing to be hot and cold, or fluid and

stratum ; but by complaining that Plato's matrix metaphor contradicts
Plato's own assumption that the non-formal element in things which
come to be is sheer not-being, Aristotle confesses the source of his
own doctrine of matter. (From Plato's omnirecipient Aristotle largely
derives also his doctrine of " place " : see p. 82 and Ph. 209^{b}12 ff.).
The contrarieties replace Plato's intermediate stage of geometrical
figures (see p. 66. Aristotle vigorously attacks all theories—Pythagorean, Platonist, and atomistic alike—which he regards as resolving
the physical elements into mathematical constituents, on the ground
that they all ultimately involve the erroneous view that points are
constituents of lines and not—as in fact they are—their limits.
It is tempting to take primary matter as the ideal limit of matter
qua privation, and the contrarieties as the lowest limit at which matter
qua substratum can be detected. For hot, cold, fluid, and dry are in
fact rather *qualia* than qualities, as the hardly translatable Greek use
of the neuter adjective by itself implies. Though Aristotle deduces
them from the fundamental tactual qualities of bodies, they are not
adjectives divorced from substances. Nor are they qualified substances,
but something more rudimentary—essences one with their existence
below the level of physical existence. But Aristotle in treating prime
matter as substratum does, as has been said, confuse physical with
logical analysis.
[1] " Solid " might better translate the term ξηρόν, but fire is hot—ξηρόν.

dry. Hence the couplings of the elementary qualities will obviously be four : hot with dry and fluid with hot, and again cold with dry and cold with fluid. . . . Fire is hot and dry, whereas air is hot and fluid (air being a sort of aqueous vapour) : and water is cold and fluid, while earth is cold and dry. Thus the differences are reasonably distributed among the primary bodies, and the number of the latter is consonant with theory."[1] Thus fire, air, water, earth, form a cycle of pairs, each of which shares one quality with its predecessor and the other with its successor ; though in each pair one contrary predominates, fire being primarily hot, air fluid, water cold, and earth dry. All four elements pass into one another in cycle, and always the coming-to-be of one is the passing-away of another. Neighbouring pairs readily change a single quality and transform into one another, but transformation occurs also (a) by dual change between non-consecutive elements, and (b) when two elements taken together each lose a quality and become alternatively one or other of the remaining elements.[2]

2. CHEMICAL COMPOUNDS

We may now momentarily abandon elemental transformation and consider the next stage of actualisation in the sublunary world. This is the formation from the elements by μῖξις, " chemical combination," of ὁμοιομερῆ, " compounds of homogeneous parts " ; namely, the various minerals, and also the tissues of plants and animals taken in abstraction from the living organism.

This formation—in which all four elements are always concerned—may be described in terms of its material cause as follows : (a) within the whole cycle of transforma-

---

[1] *I.e.* with the views of Aristotle's predecessors. GC 330ª33–ᵇ7.
[2] They must be non-consecutive ; otherwise two identical or two contrary qualities would result.

tions each contrary now overcomes and is now overcome, and here the action and passion of contraries is clearly reciprocal; but (*b*) in any given case of transformation each contrary is either completely established or completely cancelled. A ὁμοιομερές, on the other hand, occurs when the conflict of contraries is indecisive. In μῖξις, therefore, the action and passion of contraries is reciprocal; each acts upon the other, assimilating it to —converting it into—itself, but each also reacts. Hence both contraries survive in varying degrees of relative intensity—*i.e.* the compound is essentially characterised by an intermediate, derivative, quality determined proximately by the precise ratio (λόγος) in the compound of the elements, ultimately by the ratio in it of the four elementary contrary qualities. The product of μῖξις is thus not an aggregate, but — as the term ὁμοιομερές implies—a chemical compound, the least particle of which will exhibit this characterising ratio.

The formal cause of a ὁμοιομερές is of course this ratio : its form is given in the formula of its chemical constituents. But Aristotle further specifies the activity of the form. The hot and the cold are, as we saw, *par excellence* active qualities ; and the dry and the fluid are a matter passive to their formative control. The function of the hot, and in a secondary sense of the cold,[1] is, when they are present in a given ratio to each other and to the dry and the fluid, to induce a substantial change—the generation of a given ὁμοιομερές (cf. Meteor. 378ᵇ31 ff.). Thus : the conflict of hot and cold—their reciprocal action and passion—produces a tempered heat ; and this governs and completes a tempering of dry by fluid which their own interaction as contraries has initiated.[2] The im-

---

[1] Because cold is the privation of hot (as fluid is of dry). Cp. note 2, p. 72.

[2] This formative control may be contrasted as " immanent " with the " transient " activity of contrary on contrary ; see Joachim, " Aristotle's conception of chemical combination," *J. of Philology*, Vol. XIX, p. 72. I owe much to this article and to Professor Joachim's edition of GC.

manent, formative, action upon a body of its own natural heat is described in Meteor. IV, 2 and 3, chiefly—though not wholly—with reference to the more complex stage of development in organised tissue. Aristotle, who regards art as Nature's closest analogue, treats of it in terms of a sort of natural cookery.

The species of ὁμοιομερῆ are classified according to their temperature and the ratio in them of earth to water—*i.e.* ultimately by the specific ratios of the contraries which they severally embody. Aristotle groups their properties according to (*a*) their power of acting upon the special senses, and (*b*) their passive response or resistance to different types of pressure.[1]

If the control of the tempered hot remains incomplete, the product is crude and immature. When it fails altogether, the inevitable converse process sets in. Under the influence of external heat the compound rots and dissolves : its fluidity evaporates with the passing of its natural heat, and nothing is left but dry dust. " Putrescence is the end of all natural objects, except such as are destroyed by violence. . . . Everything except fire is liable to putrefy ; for earth, water, and air putrefy, being all of them matter relatively to fire " (Meteor. 379ª5-16).

The formal cause of a ὁμοιομερές is the ratio of its constituent elements, and the tempered heat of the fire in it plays a specially formative rôle. Its final cause we must at present take on faith, assuming it to be constituted such as it is best for it to be. When we come to pursue sublunary actualisation into the realm of organic structure, there will be life as well as warmth ; the meagre chemical formula of the ὁμοιομερές will give place to definition in terms of purposive function ; form and end will more nearly reveal their real identity. But at the level on which we are now investigating we have to do with what is

[1] Soluble or insoluble ; malleable or non-malleable, etc. *Ibid.* IV, 8 and 9.

largely potential and unreal, and we cannot expect here precise differentiation and intelligible coalescence of the non-material causes. Aristotle himself warns us : " The end is least obvious where matter most predominates. If you take the extremes, matter is pure matter and substance is pure definition ($\lambda\acute{o}\gamma os$)[1] ; but the things between these two are matter or definition in proportion as they are near to either (*ibid.* 390ᵃ3 ff).

Because it offers no account of efficient causation, Aristotle rejects the Platonic explanation of substantial change in terms of Forms and their participants (GC 335ᵇ7 ff.). But though heat is a partial efficient as well as a final cause at this level, it functions mainly as the instrument of an efficient cause which is altogether beyond the sublunary world. Before, however, we approach the upper cosmos something must be said of the three secondary forms of change which Aristotle distinguishes from change of substance.

3. SECONDARY CHANGE

The termini of all change must, we saw, be contrary states of an identical substratum, of which the one will be the more strictly positive, the other the more strictly privative. In substantial change—coming to be and passing away—the substratum, considered either as primary matter or as the primary contrarieties, is a mere logical postulate ; the termini are, properly speaking, contradictories (see p. 72, note 2). But throughout the process of each secondary form of change a *perceptible* substratum persists. Alike in (i) increase ($a\check{v}\xi\eta\sigma\iota s$) and diminution, (ii) qualitative alteration ($\dot{a}\lambda\lambda o\acute{\iota}\omega\sigma\iota s$), and (iii) locomotion ($\phi o\rho\acute{a}$), a single physical body retains its substantial nature ; the form which defines it does not change ; we call it by the same name before and after,

---

[1] $\lambda\acute{o}\gamma os$ here might equally well be translated " form " ; see p. 14, note 1.

whether it alter in bulk, or in some perceptible affection, or in spatial position.

This is enough to show that the matter which actualises[1] in the course of these three processes is not in each case physically distinct. Moreover, it is true that each process in its operation involves the others, and in its anabolic moment contributes specially to the total development of the physical body.[2] Nevertheless Aristotle often makes a sharp—perhaps questionable—distinction between (a) the substantial characters in virtue of which a thing possesses its definable form—its genus and differentia— and (b) properties which, though they *must* inhere in some degree, yet fluctuate between contrary poles and therefore do not affect the unchanging substantial character of the thing ; *i.e.* are not a part of its τί ἦν εἶναι, or essence. More reasonably, perhaps, he discriminates as logically separable the three matters, the three potentialities, of contrary actualisation, which the three forms of alteration[3] imply.

Ἀλλοίωσις and αὔξησις[4] become important at a higher level of sublunary actualisation. At the level which now concerns us by far the most vital part is played by locomotion.

It will be remembered that one pair of fundamental qualities were not directly involved in elemental transformation—" Light and heavy are neither active nor susceptible." Aristotle's conception of gravity (see Cael. IV, 3–5) assumes that the four elements have each a natural place in the universe. If there were no disturbing influence, earth would rest, an undiluted spherical mass, about

---

[1] I have found it convenient to use this verb intransitively. The reader will, I hope, forgive the solecism.

[2] Every sublunary body is in fact subject to all four forms of change.

[3] " Alteration " serves to translate the term κίνησις which Aristotle, when speaking strictly, uses to distinguish within the genus μεταβολή these three processes from substantial change. ἀλλοίωσις and φορά are distinguished as species of κίνησις by Plato in *Theaetetus*, 181c. Αὔξησις occurs in *Phaedo*, 171d, in the course of an argument that the termini of all change are opposites.

[4] In its full sense of growth.

the centre ; water, air, and fire would surround it as
successive enveloping shells. And when any portion of
an element is forcibly displaced, it tends to return in a
straight line to its station. This tendency is its " nature,"
its essential source of change, its impulse to actualise ;
and this tendency determines its weight. " Whenever
air comes into being out of water, light out of heavy, it
goes to the upper[1] place. It is forthwith light : becoming
is at an end, and in that place it has being. Obviously,
then, it is a potentiality which in passing into actuality
comes into that place and quantity and quality which
belong to its actuality."[2] For, as Aristotle explains later,
" Alike in the domains of quality and quantity,[3] there is
that which corresponds rather to form, and that which
corresponds to matter. Analogously among spatial distinctions, the above belongs to the determinate,[4] the below
to matter " (*ibid*. 312ᵃ14 ff.). Thus light and heavy are
qualities determined in an element by relation to its
natural station, in a ὁμοιομερές, or any more complex
body, by the proportion of the elements that constitute it.
Hence absolute lightness belongs only to fire, the outermost—" uppermost "—shell, absolute heaviness only to
the central core, earth. The intermediates, air and water,
are only relatively light and heavy respectively ; for
though air liberated in earth or water will *rise* to its own
station, yet it will *sink* to that station if released in the
fiery region. And correspondingly water sinks in fire and
air rises in earth. Fire alone rises from any alien region,
and earth goes downward always to its own place.[5] Light

---

[1] *I.e.* outer.

[2] *Ibid*. 311ᵃ1 ff. Apparently ἀλλοίωσις and αὔξησις are in some degree
present at this level ; cp. also *ibid*. 270ᵃ30 ff.

[3] *I.e.* in ἀλλοίωσις and αὔξησις.   [4] *I.e.* informed, actualised.

[5] Cp. *ibid*. 312ᵃ25–30. But Aristotle is then forced by obvious facts
to contradict this and allow the intermediate elements weight *in their
own stations* : *i.e.* air would sink if the water below it were removed,
water if earth were removed. The attraction to which he attributes
this is similarity of matter—a fresh principle which confuses his doctrine.
Cp. 312ᵇ2–19.

and heavy are thus contraries ; light the more formal
and positive, heavy the more privative and material. And
this accords with Aristotle's ranking of the elements :
" The relation of each outer body to that which is next
within it is that of form to matter " (*ibid.* 310ᵇ15).

It follows that what we call earth, air, fire, and water
are not, strictly speaking, those elements. For (i) the
elements cannot exist pure—true to form, so to speak—
save in their own regions, and (ii) what we see and call
elements are in fact bodies in the double process of
elemental transformation and local transition, characterised by the varying preponderance in them of the real
elements.

4. THE UPPER COSMOS

Compared with the other sorts of alteration, locomotion
implies a matter which is (i) *qua* privation a minimum,
(ii) *qua* substratum persisting throughout the change, a
maximum : *i.e.* a body is less altered by φορά than by
ἀλλοίωσις or αὔξησις. Hence Aristotle maintains that
the matter (substratum) of φορά is " nearest to substance "
(Cael. 310ᵇ32)—a body subject only to change of place
would approximate closely to perfect substance. From
this and from his observation that all other change presupposes it, he concludes that locomotion is the most
fundamental form of change.[1] For he does in fact on
other grounds hold that there *is* a body subject only to
φορά, namely aether, the diaphanous fifth element, of
which the upper cosmos is composed.

But the φορά of the upper cosmos is not the rectilinear
movement of the four sublunary elements : it takes the
more fundamental form of revolution. Plato had held all
natural motion to be rectilinear, and the revolution of the

---

[1] Cp. Cael. 310ᵇ33 ff. : " Locomotion belongs to bodies only when
separated from other bodies, and is generated last of the several kinds
of alteration : in order of being, then, it will be first."

heavens to require a soul both to inaugurate and to maintain it eternally ; but Aristotle argues thus : All locomotion is either straight or circular, or a combination of these two, which are the only simple movements. This is because the straight and the circular line are the only simple magnitudes. Now revolution about the centre is circular motion, while the upward and downward movements are rectilinear, " upward " meaning motion from, " downward " motion towards, the centre (*ibid.* 268^{b}17–24). " Circular motion must be primary. For the perfect is naturally prior to the imperfect, and the circle is a perfect thing. This cannot be said of any straight line— not of an infinite line ; for if perfect it would have a limit and an end ; nor of any finite line ; for there is always something beyond it, since any finite line can be extended " (*ibid.* 269^{a}19–23). Aristotle then assumes that simple movement is a movement natural to a simple body, and since rectilinear motion is natural to the four elements, he deduces aether as the fifth element to which revolution is natural. And its revolution is both uniform and eternal as well as natural ; for the circle has no beginning nor end, and aether is consequently not moving between contrary termini—*i.e.* not to or from a natural goal. For the same reason aether is neither light nor heavy. Moreover, since there is no motion in contrary opposition to circular motion,[1] there is no body contrary to aether :[2] hence aether is ungenerated and indestructible, for substantial change takes place between contraries.[3] And it is exempt

[1] Not rectilinear motion, for upward and downward motion are already the contrary species of this.

[2] The only opposite of motion in a circle is rest at a centre : " and to mere central position we should give the last place rather than the first. For the middle is what is defined, and what defines it is the limit, and that which contains—the limit—is more precious than that which it limits ; for the latter is the matter and the former the essence of the system " (Cael. 293^{b}11–15, and cp. note 2, p. 83). Hence the only opposite of aether is earth ; but earth finds its contrary in fire.

[3] See however note 2, p. 72.

from ἀλλοίωσις and αὔξησις, which belong only to a body subject to substantial change. Its position has been already determined; the upper cosmos envelops the sublunary world as an inner core about which it revolves, " unaffected by any mortal discomfort and without effort, needing no constraining necessity to keep it to its path " (*ibid.* 284ᵃ14–15).

Certain attributes of the whole heaven, which the two cosmoi together constitute, follow from Aristotle's doctrine of " place " and from the denial of void which this entails. Place is not the form of a body, for the form of a body (*qua* magnitude) is its own bounding surface, whereas its place may be occupied by another body. And for the same reason its place is not its matter.[1] The place of a body is only definable as the inner boundary of the body which contains it (the first body), so far as that is at rest.[2] This definition accords with the real basis of Aristotle's doctrine—itself a corollary of his theory of natural φορά— viz., that not only has every body its natural place, but all place is the natural place of some body. Hence, although different bodies may succeed one another in occupation of one place, yet place does not exist separate from body. But the notion of void, wrongly postulated by some to explain locomotion, is precisely that of separately existing place—" that in which the presence of body, though not actual, is possible."[3] It follows that the shape of the whole heaven is spherical; for not only

---

[1] See however note 3, para. 2, p. 72. For the reason why place and matter are sometimes confused, see Ph. 211ᵇ29 ff.

[2] *I.e.* the place of an object drifting submerged in a stream is the surface of water in contact with it at a given moment, not that of the water *qua moving* in contact with it.

[3] Cael. 279ᵃ13. For the whole doctrine see Ph. IV, 1–9. Aristotle uses also other arguments against void, such as that the velocity of a moving body is in inverse proportion to the resistance which it meets : therefore its passage through void must be infinitely fast. His own view that body occupies place in varying degrees of intensity accords with his theories of transformation and μῖξις. The atomists whom he is attacking tended to treat all combination as mere aggregation.

(i) " The circle is primary among figures, and the sphere holds the same position among solids " (*ibid.* 286ᵇ23), but (ii) any solid in revolution except the sphere occupies different places as it moves[1]—*i.e.* there is place outside it, and if it were not spherical there would be void outside the heaven. The whole heaven is finite ; for the infinite is (i) essentially imperfect,[2] and (ii) cannot pass a given point in a finite time, " but our eyes tell us that the heavens revolve in a circle " (*ibid.* 272ᵃ5).

This finite sphere, we are told, " is turned with a finish which no manufactured thing nor anything else within the range of our observation can even approach. For the matter of which these are composed does not admit of anything like the same regularity and finish as the substance of the enveloping body ; since with each step away from earth the matter manifestly becomes finer in the same proportion as water is finer than earth " (*ibid.* 287ᵇ15 ff.).

Nevertheless the attributes of the aetherial body remain highly ambiguous. For example, although it moves, the

---

[1] This is, of course, not true of a cone, *e.g.*, or a cylinder, if they revolve only on one axis.

[2] Cp. quotation in note 2, p. 81. Aristotle discusses the infinite in Ph. III, 5–8. It is to him the unlimited and indeterminate—" that outside which there is always something " (207ᵃ1) ; the part rather than the whole ; " the matter of the completeness of the magnitude, the whole as potential and not actual " (207ᵃ21–22). Hence an *actual* infinite is to him a contradiction in terms. Space is *potentially* divisible *ad infinitum*, and the fact that magnitude is infinitely divisible implies that number is potentially infinite in respect of addition : cannot, *i.e.*, be exhausted by adding part to part. Time, the measure or numerable character of change, is potentially infinite in both senses, for change is both continuous and eternal. A limit, on the other hand, is an end or perfection, and the finite, or limited, means to Aristotle (as it had meant to Plato ; see p. 60, note 1) not so much what falls within, or short of, a limit dividing it from a beyond, as a perfect whole which has nothing outside it upon which it depends for its being—something in fact nearer to Hegel's " philosophical infinite " than to " finite " in the ordinary sense of the word. For the difficulty Aristotle has in maintaining this distinction, see pp. 151-2. Ambiguity is already apparent in his inference that the whole heaven is finite from the finite period of its revolution.

whole heaven is not in place, for nothing contains it. Yet Aristotle's apparent explanation[1] to the effect that it can be said to move only in reference to its parts, and that its circumference viewed from within is the ultimate place of its parts, is more subtle than satisfying. And when Aristotle says that it " embraces within itself the infinity of time " (*ibid.* 283^{b}29), one may suppose that it is no more in time than in place. But though the aetherial body presents no other change for time to measure, yet it revolves ; and it is because we can measure this revolution that we can use it as the measure of all sublunary change (Ph. IV, 12).

So far we have spoken as if the aetherial body were a single hollow ball in revolution. It is in fact, Aristotle suggests, a nest of fifty-five contiguous shells, concentric but rotating on different axes and at different though uniform speeds. The outermost shell, or " first heaven," exhibits the most rapid and perfect movement from east to west, and it carries inset in it the fixed stars,[2] which are intensifications of the aetherial body, spherical in shape.[3] The other fifty-four spheres are postulated to explain the apparent movements of the planets (see Met. XII, 8). The principle is this :—Suppose the poles of one sphere so fixed in the inner surface of a second which contains it, that though the two are concentric, yet their axes do not coincide. Then, if both spheres revolve uniformly, the apparent motion of a body on the equator of the inner sphere will be a composite of the two revolutions. On this principle Aristotle's friend Callippus, improving on the

[1] See Ph. 212^{b}7–22, and 212^{a}20 ff. Yet in the latter passage only the inner surface of the aetherial body seems indicated as the ultimate place of sublunary bodies.   [2] Cp. Plato's " circle of the same," p. 65.

[3] We do not see the stars and planets themselves. Their apparent light and heat are due to patches of flame between us and the real stars, caused at the edge of the sublunary sphere by " friction " between it and the aether (cp. Cael. II, 7, and Meteor. II, 3 and 4). How this is possible save, perhaps, in the case of the nearest planet, the moon, Aristotle does not explain.

work of Eudoxus, had ingeniously decomposed the observed path of each planet into several uniform rotations. Callippus' hypothesis, calculated separately for each planet, was purely mathematical. But no Greek astronomer had assigned a free motion to the stars ; Plato and many other cosmologists had conceived them somewhat as jewels of fire set in a revolving ring. Hence Aristotle in natural accordance with his own fundamental assumptions accepted his friend's hypothesis as a literal account of the celestial mechanism. But he found it to require correction in one respect. The aetherial shells form a continuum ; given no interference, the first heaven will impart its motion unmodified to all the inner spheres. Hence, to neutralise the effect of the first heaven and preserve Callippus' calculations, Aristotle interpolates between each group of planetary shells spheres which move in an opposite direction.[1]

The Pythagorean doctrine of the " harmony of the spheres," to which Plato had shown some favour,[2] is rejected by Aristotle as absurd despite its grace and originality. The spheres move without friction, and therefore in silence.

5. THE PRIME MOVER

The motion of the first heaven, which it imparts with decreasing strength to the succession of inner spheres, is natural and not, as Plato thought, a constraint continuously imposed by a world-soul (Cael. 284ª27). But the first heaven is not fully self-moving : it presupposes a mover which moves, itself unmoved.

To make Aristotle's doctrine clear we must return to his

---

[1] Aristotle propounds his astronomical calculations only tentatively. For the details see Heath, *Aristarchus of Samos*, Chap. 16.

[2] It appears in the Myth of Er, *Republic*, 617b, and is suggested by the harmonic ratios used for the blending of the world-soul, etc., *Timaeus*, 35b.

theory of change.[1] Change is an actualisation, but an imperfect one ; for it is an ἐνέργεια of what is imperfect and potential as such—in fact something between a δύναμις and an ἐνέργεια. That is to say that whatever is being changed is (a) actualising a potency of change, and (b) developing towards a fresh ἐνέργεια. But (a) change, as a process qualifying the changing thing qua imperfect, is sharply—if questionably—distinguished by Aristotle from (b) the fresh actuality which the changed thing will exhibit when the process is over and done with. The former is a mere process towards an end ; the latter is pure form viewed dynamically, an activity complete at any and every moment of itself, containing its end fully immanent within it throughout its course—if we can speak of the " course " of an activity which, because it is not change, can have no temporal character.[2] Now a postulate of all natural change is a pair of contraries one of which relates to the other as form to matter, and we might infer at once that, since the first heaven is in a measure material and potential, the cause of its motion must be pure form, pure activity not itself a process of motion. But Aristotle elaborates further. Sublunary locomotion implies (i) an agent possessing a source or potency of moving, and (ii) a patient possessing a source or potency of being moved.[3] The passive body, since it is to undergo a continuous process, must be itself continuous and infinitely divisible, and the active body acts upon it through their un- intermittent[4] mutual contact—i.e. the two bodies must have and retain a common limit, a partial coincidence of surface. And their relation in the change is partially

---

[1] What follows is drawn mainly from Ph. III, 2 and 3, and VIII, 2, 4 and 5. Cp. also An. 431ᵃ6 ff.

[2] Of course the bulk of sublunary things never are completely ἐνεργείᾳ, but Aristotle's use of this conception of timeless activity presents great difficulties. Cp. e.g., pp. 139, 150.

[3] The conditions of locomotion apply mutatis mutandis to all the kinds of alteration.

[4] Aristotle feels the want of a law of inertia.

reciprocal, for the agent suffers some obstruction, and the patient becomes in its turn capable of imparting motion. Thus the whole fact of local change involves an assimilation of agent and patient, and is the single actualisation in the patient of (i) the agent's potency of moving, and (ii) the patient's potency of being moved—a single actualisation in the patient,[1] though definable alternatively as the actualisation of either agent or patient, " just as the same road is both the road from Thebes to Athens and the road from Athens to Thebes " (Ph. 202^{b}13). If we next look beyond what we called " the whole fact " of the change, we see that its two factors are terms in a series any member of which is, in different relations, (a) an agent, (b) a patient, and (c) an instrument through which the term before it imparts motion to the term after it ; e.g. " The rod moves the stone and is moved by the hand, which is itself set in motion by the man " (ibid. 256^{a}6–7). Thus, though the degree of genuine initiation tends to vary with every term of the series,[2] the agent remains always an external efficient cause, discrete from the patient : nothing can be completely self-moving, agent and patient in the same relation.[3] Even a sublunary element has at least an incidental efficient cause of its motion in that which removes an obstacle from its natural path ; man himself is only self-moved so far as one element within him moves another, and even this motion does not occur without reaction to stimulus.

Yet the series of efficient causes cannot be an indefinite regress, and Aristotle finally concludes that the first term

---

[1] This point is vital to Aristotle's proof of the possibility of a mover which moves, itself unmoved.

[2] The four elements appear to move spontaneously because their matter is nearest to substance (Cael. 310^{b}31 ff.), but their nature is really rather a source of being moved.

[3] Aristotle illustrates this by pointing out that otherwise we should have to say that, because teaching and learning have a single identical actualisation, the teacher is all the time learning what he is teaching ; see Ph. III, 3.

which it presupposes is an unmoved mover whose immobility is not rest but a timeless activity which is not a process of change. And this unmoved mover is God.

The prime mover initiates the first heaven's rotation at its circumference so that it spins as with a forward motion from the right imparted by a man's right hand. Yet the prime mover, being not in space or time, clearly does not operate by contact. Aristotle answers that God moves as the object of love and desire, and we are perhaps entitled to postpone discussion of this coalescence of efficient with final cause on the ground that it is metaphysical, and that we are at present only at the level of natural science, for which a prime mover is no more than a postulate necessitated by Aristotle's theory of movement. Yet the precise senses in which the heavens are at once the subject matter of natural science, of mathematics, and of metaphysics, are hard to distinguish. Aristotle's cosmology is strangely ambiguous, and its ambiguity is well illustrated by the hesitant manner in which he describes the transmission of the first heaven's motion, particularly the detail of its action upon the inner spheres.

We may say generally : (1) No two aetherial spheres are in physical contact, for they have no weight ; neither, strictly speaking, touches the other, and there is no mutual assimilation or reaction. (ii) Touched by the aetherial body, the sublunary sphere reacts—*e.g.* by exhibiting the " friction " which creates the phenomena we call the stars ; it does not, however, touch the aetherial body, and this does not react. And to the question we have long carried with us unanswered[1] we find some reply in Aristotle's account of the part played by the celestial revolution as efficient cause of substantial change : " In all things nature strives after the better, and being is better than not-being : but not all things can possess being, since they are too far removed from the originative source. God

[1] See p. 77.

therefore adopted the remaining alternative, and fulfilled the perfection of the universe by making coming-to-be uninterrupted : for the greatest possible coherence would thus be secured to existence, because 'that coming-to-be should itself come to be perpetually' is the closest approximation to eternal being. The cause of this perpetuity of coming-to-be is . . . circular motion : for that is the only continuous motion. That too is the reason why all the other things—the things which are reciprocally transformed in virtue of their 'passions' and potencies of action, *e.g.* the simple bodies—imitate circular motion. For when water is transformed into air, air into fire, and the fire back into water, we say that the coming-to-be has 'come full circle,' because it reverts again to the beginning. Hence it is by imitating circular motion that rectilinear motion too is continuous."[1] But coming - to - be and passing-away are contrary processes, and require contrary causes. Hence " It is not the primary motion that causes them, but the motion along the inclined circle ;[2] for this motion not only possesses the continuity necessary in order that substantial change may not fail, but includes a duality of movements as well. . . . The continuity is caused by the motion of the whole : but the approaching and retreating of the moving body are caused by the inclination."[3] The sun's heat is, in fact, efficient cause of (i) continuous substantial change (and derivatively of all secondary change), by virtue of the sun's diurnal rotation ; of (ii) the regular alternation of coming-to-be and passing-away, by virtue of its seasonal revolution in the zodiac.

But the transmission of movement through the aetherial spheres severely tasks Aristotle's speculative powers. It does not proceed in an obviously ordered series : " The

---

[1] GC 336ᵇ27–337ᵃ4. Aristotle regards all terrestrial process as consequently cyclical.

[2] *I.e.* not the rotation of the first heaven, but the sun's annual revolution in the ecliptic.

[3] Of ecliptic to equator. *Ibid.* 336ᵃ31–ᵇ4 abbreviated.

movements of the sun and moon are fewer than those of some of the planets, yet the former are nearer to the centre, as even observation has shown. . . . We do well in trying to increase our knowledge of these things, though we have little to go upon and are so far away from the scene of these happenings. Nevertheless the problem is not insoluble if we look at it in this way. We must cease to think of the stars as mere bodies—units with a serial order indeed, but entirely inanimate—and rather conceive them as enjoying life and action. . . . We must think of the action of the lower stars as similar to that of animals and plants. For on our earth it is man that has the greatest variety of actions—for there are many goods that man can secure[1] . . . while the perfectly conditioned has no need of action, since it is itself the end, and action always requires two terms, end and means. The lower animals have less variety of action than man ; and plants perhaps have little action, and of one kind only. . . . Thus one thing has and enjoys the highest good ; other things attain to it, one immediately by few steps, another by many ; yet another does not attempt to secure it, but is satisfied to reach a point not far removed from that consummation. Take, for example, health as the end : there will be one thing that always possesses health ; others that attain it, one by reducing flesh, another by running and thus reducing flesh, another by taking steps to enable himself to run, thus further increasing the number of movements ; while another cannot attain health itself but only running or reduction of flesh, so that one or other of these is for such a being the end. . . . That is why the earth moves not at all, and the bodies near to it with few movements. For they do not attain to the final end, but only come as near to it as their share in the divine originating principle

---

[1] He means not a variety of unconnected ends, but a single complex end, requiring a diversity of means (always to Aristotle themselves relative ends) for its attainment.

permits. But the first heaven finds it immediately with a single movement, and the bodies intermediate between the first and last heavens attain it indeed, but at the cost of a multiplicity of movement."[1] In the *Metaphysics* we learn that this active astral life implies for each planetary sphere a mover analogous to the prime mover of the universe : " Since we see that besides the simple spatial movement of the universe, which we say the first and movable substance produces, there are other spatial movements—those of the planets . . . each of these movements must be caused by a substance unmovable in itself and eternal. . . . Evidently then there must be substances which are of the same number as the movements of the stars. . . . In the number of the substances we reach a problem which must be treated from the standpoint of that one of the mathematical sciences which is most akin to philosophy—viz., of astronomy."[2]

The status of these astral intelligences is most obscure.[3] Aristotle teaches that the life, or soul, of any animate *terrestrial* being relates to its body as form to matter. Are we, then, to regard the aetherial spheres as each analogously informed by an astral soul—something like Plato's fixed stars with their bodies of pure fire ? But, if so, the aether should be itself an actualisation of matter. Or are we, on the other hand, to press the analogy of the astral spirits to God,[4] and accept the usual medieval view of them as *formae assistentes*, not *formae informantes* ?

Even a tentative answer to these problems is best postponed until we discuss in its proper place the relation of God to the world (cp. Ch. VIII, § 4). Till then, admire as we may the ingenuity with which Aristotle seeks a primary term in the series of conditions, and exhibits

[1] Cael. 291ᵇ28–292ᵇ25 condensed.
[2] 1073ª28–ᵇ5. The account of Callippus' hypothesis follows.
[3] See GC, ed. Joachim, Introd., p. xxiii.
[4] Aristotle calls them divine, and treats them (Cael. 279ª18 ff.) as no more in space or time than is God.

the aetherial realm as the least possible diminution of God's fully real activity, it is bound to seem to us that he has not winnowed the grain from the chaff of mythology with all the success that he sometimes supposes : " Our forefathers in the most remote ages have handed down to us, their posterity, a tradition, in the form of a myth, that these substances are gods and that the divine encloses the whole of nature. The rest of the tradition has been added later in mythical form with a view to the persuasion of the multitude and to its legal and utilitarian expediency ; they say among other things that these gods are in the form of men or like some of the other animals. . . . But if we were to separate the first point from these additions and take it alone—that they thought the first substances to be gods, we must regard this as an inspired utterance, and reflect that, while probably each art and science has been developed as far as possible and has again perished, these opinions have been preserved until the present, like relics of the ancient treasure. Only thus far, then, is the opinion of our ancestors and our earliest predecessors clear to us."[1]

And yet, even if Aristotle's cosmos is geocentric while

---

[1] Met. 1074[b]1–14. Aristotle's philosophy of history, had he written it, would have been a theory of successive cycles, but not of precise repetitions : " The times—*i.e.* the lives—of the several kinds of living things have a number by which they are distinguished : for there is an order controlling all things, and every time (*i.e.* every life) is measured by a period. . . . The durations of the natural processes of coming-to-be and passing-away are equal. Nevertheless it often happens that things pass away in too short a time. This is due to the " intermingling " by which the things that come-to-be and pass-away are implicated with one another. For their matter is irregular, *i.e.* is not everywhere the same : hence the processes by which they come-to-be must be irregular too, *i.e.* some too quick and others too slow " (GC. 336[b]10–23). This casual " intermingling " due to the material element in perceptible things takes shape in Ph. II, 6 as a doctrine of the fortuitous—or rather the " automatic," that which happens " of itself " by a kind of irrational spontaneity resembling the " necessity " of the *Timaeus* (see p. 66, note 4), and sometimes actually called by Aristotle " necessity " (cp. Ph. 198[b]17 ff.). The term there covers three modes of occurrence : (1) Events which happen to beings capable of deliberate action, and look as if they were the natural result of purpose, but in fact are not. These happy coincidences are attributed to " luck." (2) Events con-

Plato seems to have attributed some movement to the earth (see *Timaeus*, 40b), the physical writings of Aristotle are much closer than the *Timaeus* to the spirit of modern science at its best.[1]

So, by tracing the process of terrestrial change to a divine origin beyond the stars, Aristotle begins a resolute attempt to apply everywhere his fourfold analysis, to leave a minimum of dead matter unactualised and opaque to knowledge. Yet he has succeeded in his first step only by allowing the line of causal explanation to bifurcate. We have next to pursue the further course of sublunary development, and it is not clear how the divergent paths are to meet again ; how the form and substance that we seek are to coalesce with the efficient cause that we have already found.

comitant of the behaviour of beings incapable of choice—brutes and inanimate objects—such as the unreasoned bolting of a horse which saves it from ill-treatment, or the fall of a tripod which kills a man. (3) Nature's failures, her sports and monstrous births. These are unlike (1) and (2), which are due to causes external and incidental, for they come to be " by nature " ; yet they are " contrary to nature." In fact luck is to purposive thought as the merely " automatic " is to the unconscious purposiveness of nature (see Mr. Ross on Met. 1065^{b}2–4). But though Aristotle seems sometimes to hold that the possibility of purpose implies some real indeterminateness in things (see p. 130), he states in Ph. 198^{a}5 ff. that there is no *vera causa* besides intelligence and nature ; which implies rather that the notion of chance is but a cloak for ignorance of the true cause : " The ' automatic ' and luck are causes of effects which, though they might result from intelligence or nature, have in fact been caused by something incidentally. Now since nothing which is incidental is prior to what is *per se*, it is clear that no incidental cause can be prior to a cause *per se*. The ' automatic ' and luck, therefore, are posterior to intelligence and nature. Hence, however true it may be that the heavens are due to the automatic, it will still be true that intelligence and nature will be prior causes of this All and of many things in it besides." The last sentence perhaps indicates that Aristotle wavers.

Aristotle maintains that ultimately the actual is prior to the potential temporally as well as really—this must be so if the efficient cause is always form operant *a tergo*—and this seems to make the theory of historical cycles inevitable as the presupposition of the cyclic character of particular processes (for the latter cp. especially p. 100).

[1] It is too easy to forget (1) how much modern astronomy owes to the telescope, and (2) that its rejection of final causes, however necessary, leaves an unsolved problem.

VI

VEGETABLE AND ANIMAL LIFE

1. LIFE AND SOUL

IN the animate world the identity of form and end appears undisguised ; for the works of men's hands express design no more evidently than do the living works of nature. The early thinker who states the cause of animal form in terms of physical elements—suggesting, for example, that the breath by its passage breaks open the outlets of the nostrils—seems to Aristotle to miss the mark even more widely than the craftsman who tells one that the axe and the auger are the cause of the carven figure. " In fact," he says, " it is not enough for the artificer to say that by the stroke of his tool this part was made concave and that part flat ; he must state why he struck his blow so as to effect this, and what his final object was ; namely that the block of wood should eventually develop into this or that shape."[1] And, analogously, the biologist is concerned with form primarily, with matter only for the sake of form : he must establish the functions definitive of the living thing and of its several organs, and treat its structural constituents not as determining it, but as determined by it.

Since form and function are the clue to the intricate

[1] PA I, 1, 641ª10–14. Aristotle objects further to this type of explanation that it subjects natural development to chance, and that it forgets that, since process is cyclic and the parent must precede the offspring, form is temporally as well as logically prior to matter : cp. PA 640ª19 ff., where he criticises Empedocles' view that the backbone is divided into vertebrae because it happened to be broken owing to the contorted position of the foetus in the womb.

hierarchy of Aristotle's animate world, a general sketch of its stages must preface any detailed description. That some ὁμοιομερῆ are designed by nature for a higher purpose than to be merely compounds of the four simple bodies, we have already noticed (p. 74). The four elements combine also to form the tissues of plants, such as wood and bark, and animal tissues—blood, fat, marrow, brain, flesh, bone, sinews, veins, skin, etc. These are a matter which exists for the sake of the various organs of the living body, and in the ebb and flow of their actualisation they appear successively as nutriment, actual constituents of the organ, and excreta.[1] The organ in contrast to its constituents is an ἀνομοιομερές ; i.e. it consists of heterogeneous parts, and its unity is not that of a chemical compound, but, as the name " organ " implies, that of an instrument with a single function. But the meaning of this developing series still lies ahead. The body is a new, more complex, unity which these organic, or instrumental, functions subserve as an ordered hierarchy ; and it is itself an instrument : " As every instrument and every bodily member exists for some partial end, i.e. some special action, so the whole body must be destined to minister to some complete and comprehensive action" (PA 645ᵇ14 ff.). In fact the dead body is not a body, and the amputated limb is not a limb, for the nature of the body and its organs lies beyond their physical limits. And the form and nature to which a living body is at once matter and instrument, is soul.[2]

[1] The third stage is not present in plants.

[2] Aristotle never abandons the strict sense of the term " nature " (see p. 71) : soul too is an originative source of change. When, as frequently he does, he depicts nature as the great artificer in phrases such as " Nature makes nothing in vain," he does not seem to imply conscious purpose, and Mr. Ross in saying (Aristotle, p. 66) : " Nature is here to be thought of not as a transcendental principle but as a collective term for the natures of all ' natural bodies ' working harmoniously together," perhaps expresses the general trend of Aristotle's thought when his mind is engrossed in biological detail. But Aristotle sometimes thinks otherwise. The phrases "God and nature make nothing

The term " soul," which conveniently renders the Greek ψυχή, covers a wide range ; for the emergence of soul marks the beginning of animate existence, and its culmination sets a limit to that natural developing series of which the four elements were the first term. Plant, animal, and man are each constituted what they are by a specific activity, and that is to say that they embody in an ascending order as their form and purpose three grades of soul. Broadly characterised these are (i) the nutritive and reproductive soul, (ii) the sentient soul, (iii) the rational soul ; and each succeeding stage presupposes, but also modifies and transcends, its predecessor. There may be plants without animals, and animals without men, yet the animal soul of which sensation is the differentia must absorb within itself, and develop to subserve its own sentient function, that capacity for assimilating food and propagating its own kind which distinguishes the plant ; and in man the whole sensating soul with its already absorbed nutritive basis becomes the matter necessary to the fresh form of man's distinctively rational nature.

2. VEGETABLE SOUL

But each soul-form is itself a unity of graded functions. The form and purpose in which consists the minimal nutritive soul is to participate in the divine—its *ultimate* final cause—so far as an organism can, *i.e.* to reproduce its kind (An. 415^{a}26 ff.). But this end necessitates two subordinate functions : growth and, as a precondition of growth, the assimilation of food. In order to preserve

at random " (Cael. 271^{a}33) and " Nature is the cause of order in all things " (Ph. 252^{a}12 ; cp. also An. 415^{a}26 ff.), represent rather the metaphysical notion of a divinely ordered natural world than " a concession to ordinary ways of thinking " (*ibid.* p. 126). There is in fact a certain appearance of contradiction in the suggestion of a *collection* working harmoniously together. It is to be remembered that on the whole Aristotle sets the working of nature above human craftsmanship (see pp. 132-3).

itself, this minimum of soul must absorb into the organism a fluid or dry nutriment which, though its contrary before absorption, becomes assimilated to the living tissue in the process which turns it into an actual constituent. The proximate efficient cause of this process, which is the analogue at a higher level of elemental transformation, is the vital heat of the heart.[1] This boils the food, absorbed as vapour from the stomach, into its final form as blood, though in so doing it functions as the instrument of the soul.[2] Aristotle describes the process with his usual type of illustration : " In all sanguinea the heart is formed first (cp. p. 100, note 3), and in the other animals the analogue of the heart. From the heart the blood-vessels extend throughout the body as in the anatomical diagrams which are represented on the walls,[3] for the parts lie round these because they are formed out of them. The ὁμοιομερῆ are formed by heat and cold, for some are put together and solidified by the one and some by the other. The nutriment then oozes through the blood-vessels and the passages in each of these parts, like water in unbaked pottery, and thus is formed the flesh or its analogues, being solidified by cold.[4] But all the particles given off which are too earthy, having but little fluidity and heat, cool as the fluid evaporates along with the heat ; so they become hard and earthy in character, as nails, horns, hoofs, and beaks. The sinews and bones are formed by the internal heat as the fluid dries, and hence the bones are insoluble by fire like pottery, for like it they have been as it were baked in an oven by the heat operative in the

---

[1] Though the nutritive soul *distinctively* characterises vegetable life, Aristotle generally treats it as it is exhibited in the animal, and in describing plants more often uses inference by analogy than direct observation.

[2] Though the soul too as efficient cause is posterior to the sun's dual movement.

[3] Presumably of any physiological lecture-room.

[4] Aristotle regards it as the function of the brain, the terminus of the blood-vessels, to cool the blood.

process of their coming-to-be. But "—Aristotle warns us that matter is necessitated by its form—" it is not anything whatever that is made into flesh or bone by the heat, but only something naturally fitted for the purpose ; nor is it made in any place or time whatever, but only in a place or time naturally so fitted."[1] " All the parts are first outlined and then acquire their colour and softness or hardness, just as if Nature were an artist, first sketching in the animal with lines and then putting in the colours."[2]

Though the nutrient matter is continually flowing in and out of its structure, the organism gradually increases with that uniform proportional expansion of every structural—i.e. formal—detail which is growth, the strict sense of αὔξησις. With maturity reproduction takes place, asexually and inevitably in plants, in animals by the occasional coitus of sexually differentiated individuals.[3] In animals, which " are like divided plants " (ibid. 731ª21), the surplus blood of the male is further developed into semen. In all organisms there must, it seems, be a matter more divine than the four elements, in which the soul is primarily embodied, and vital heat is occasionally promoted by Aristotle to the dignity of being an analogue of the aether, and termed spiritus (πνεῦμα) (cp. ibid. 736ᵇ29 ff.). And semen too contains πνεῦμα and is potentially " be-souled." In conception the semen unites with the female blood-surplus—the catamenia.[4] This also possesses πνεῦμα and even potential nutritive soul.[5] But

[1] GA 742ᵇ36–43ª22, abbreviated. See also note 2, p. 98.

[2] Ibid. 743ᵇ20–25, abbreviated.

[3] Coitus is occasional because animals have other things to do besides. Zoophytes and shell-fish, which are intermediate between plant and animal kingdoms, are generated spontaneously, i.e. " automatically " (cp. p. 92, note 1).

[4] Or their analogue. Aristotle often, instead of relying on direct observation, infers from man to animal, as he often infers from animal to plant ; i.e. from the more to the less perfect, and from the more to the less easily observable. If, as seems probable, he had never dissected the human body, to that may be due the rarer cases of inference from animal to man.

[5] As is proved by the production of wind-eggs.

its πνεῦμα is not strong enough to concoct it into semen, and in the subsequent growth of the embryo it contributes only the material element. Only the sperm contained in the seminal fluid is animal form. This initiates conception as proximate efficient cause,[1] and controls its plastic female complement throughout embryonic development, but contributes none of its own matter—" just as no material part comes from the carpenter to his material " (*ibid.* 730ᵇ12). It is thus that coming-to-be is perpetuated in the animate world (see p. 89). The revolution of the first heaven which, mediated by the sun's dual movement, produces incessant elemental transformation, is reflected at a higher level in an unending cyclic process of generation, viz., adult-sperm-embryo-adolescent-adult. The female provides the matter, and the final and formal cause of the process is the specific form ; for towards this the growing thing develops, and this in its maturity it embodies. And the species is also an efficient cause intermediate between the sun's heat and the sperm, for only an adult male in whom the specific form is fully developed[2] can secrete the sperm and initiate conception : Aristotle occasionally remarks that " it takes a man—and the sun—to beget a man."

Aristotle's theory of sex and heredity is difficult. Children resemble their parents because the semen, though secreted from one part only of the body, is like in kind to the blood which has nourished the whole body, and contains in a potential and undifferentiated state all the features of the offspring.[3] In embryonic growth generic characters appear before specific, specific before individual ; for the father begets *qua* a member of a kind as well as

---

[1] *I.e.* as the instrument of the male parent.

[2] See p. 92, note 1 end.

[3] In a brilliant discussion—GA 733ᵇ23–735ᵃ26—Aristotle develops his own theory against the pre-formationist " ontogeny " of the Hippocratean school, which he also rejects on perfectly sound evidence from observation.

qua individual, though it is *qua* individual that he is the main determinant factor. " In generation," says Aristotle, " both the singular individual and the kind are operative, but the individual is the more so of the two, for *it* is substance. And the offspring is produced indeed of a certain kind, but also as a singular individual, and *that* is substance."[1] If form prevails wholly over matter the child is a male resembling its father, " but if the impulse of change coming from the male principle prevails while that coming from the individual father does not, or vice versa, then male children are produced resembling the mother and female children resembling the father " (*ibid.* 768ª28 ff.).

Thus, since the father contributes the formal element, the variations in degree of masculinity which the offspring can exhibit will reflect only the degree of the mother's reaction and resistance to the controlling form : we may conclude that a daughter who takes after her mother is a walking criticism of her father's vital capacity.[2] The female, in fact, is " a stunted male " (*ibid.* 737ª27). Her physical conformation is (*a*) a sign that her function is mainly nutritive—to provide within her womb its whole material embodiment for the male form, and to nourish the new-born infant at her breast ; and (*b*)—as her smaller body, weaker veins, and comparatively anaemic pallor show—a symptom of her failure to be male. " Differentiation of sex," says Aristotle, " would seem to occur in living things for the sake of generation " (GA 732ª2). " Woman does not differ from man in species " (Met. 1058ª29). " Male and female are indeed properties

[1] *Ibid.* 767ᵇ32-35. It should be carefully noted that here Aristotle regards the singular individual, though concrete of matter and form, as primarily entitled to the name of substance ; cp. also 731ᵇ34. Sometimes he takes a different view ; see note 1, p. 102.

[2] If the individual impulse of both parents fails, the child resembles only its forebears—only varying degrees of generic character are transmitted.

H

peculiar to animal ; they are not, however, substantial
characters but are in the matter, *i.e.* the body."[1]

Thus Aristotle abandons Plato's view[2] that, though
woman is the weaker vessel, her function is the same as
man's : " Wherever it is possible and so far as it is possible,
the contrasted sexual characters are embodied in separate
individuals " (GA 732[a]6). He would certainly not, like
Plato, have admitted her to guardianship in an ideal
state ; for though within the household man, the natural
ruler, " hands over to woman the matters that befit her "
(EN 1160[b]34), yet " Women and slaves have not in them
the element fitted by nature to rule " (Pol. 1252[b]6).

3. ANIMAL SOUL : SENSE

When an animal sleeps dreamless and inert, only the
minimal, nutritive, soul is actual. Though digestion and
growth are then most active, sleep is essentially an inhibi-
tion and privation of the sentient life, punctuating it with
inevitable intervals of repose which diminish as the
animal becomes mature.

But with the advent of sense certain problems which
radically divide modern philosophy begin to grow
explicit. When we have climbed the *Scala Naturae* to the
beginnings of conscious life, we must wonder whether
Aristotle's assumption that each step exists for the sake of,
and finds its meaning in, the next, can still carry us forward

---

[1] *Ibid.* 1058[b]21 ff. See also p. 78. Observe (i) that male and female
are non-substantial, though necessary, characters because they (*a*) express material and not formal difference, and (*b*) exist for the sake of
change, male being the active contrary, female the passive ; (ii) that
Aristotle here regards as substance not the singular individual concrete
of form and matter, but its τί ἦν εἶναι or essence—*i.e.* the substantial
characters coalescing as a unity, the genus and differentia which together
constitute the definition of all the logically indiscriminable individuals
of the species. In short, substance on this view is not the singular
specimen but that which alone is eternal in the sublunary world, the
infima species. Cp. pp. 186 ff.

[2] Expressed in *Republic* V.

by orderly stages of analogy ; or whether we have perhaps
reached a chasm beyond which stands consciousness as
something wholly *sui generis*. Moreover, at least when
we reach beyond sense to thought, we cannot since Kant
refuse to consider the alternative suggestion that thought
has been all along presupposed in the earlier stages—that
we have been building up a merely phenomenal world.
And even if this difficulty—supposing it a real one—can
be met on the Aristotelian hypothesis, can we yet assume
that we may treat thought—or even, perhaps, sense-
perception—in a manner analogous to that in which we
treated the nutritive functions and the properties of
inorganic bodies, *i.e.* as the mere adjective of a singular
conscious individual ? If we abstract from the fact that
consciousness is that for which objects are, and treat
consciousness as itself an object, shall we be failing to rise
above the level we have already reached—substituting
mere repetition for genuine analogy ? Two thousand
years before Kant we can expect no more than the germ
of these problems, but here it must at least be said that
in his account of sense Aristotle neither always takes that
clear step beyond the physiological level which his own
hypothesis demands, nor distinguishes clearly between
mere feeling and sense-perception with an objective
reference.

Aristotle's exposition offers a further difficulty. In
elemental transformation and even in vegetable growth
the transition from potentiality to actualisation was a
simple continuous development, but at the point where
actualisation can be properly called activity a fresh stage
intervenes : for animal and human activity are intermittent. A permanent developed capacity, when not in
use, is in a sense actual, in a sense potential. Aristotle's
term for such a condition is ἕξις, and that this literally
translated is " habit " indicates his meaning. He most
often uses as an illustration the distinction between the

different senses in which a man can be said to possess the
capacity of knowledge.[1] Before he begins to learn, *e.g.*
geometry, a man, because by definition rational, is already
a potential geometer ; while a pupil his knowledge is still
largely potential ; but when he has mastered his subject
he possesses knowledge as a permanent condition which
he always can, but does not always, exercise in the actual
solving of a geometrical problem. Similarly a man may
be virtuous and a body healthy even when in sleep moral
activity and animal function are in temporary abeyance.
For Aristotle regards a ἕξις as positively qualifying its
possessor : " ἕξις means a disposition according to which
that which is disposed is either well or ill disposed, either
in itself or with reference to something else " (Met. 1022ᵇ10–
12). The important point is that the passage from ἕξις
to ἐνέργεια is held by Aristotle to be instantaneous—not,
like the preceding period of development, a process of
change, but a timeless supervening of activity.

These distinctions Aristotle draws in An. (417ᵃ21 ff.) as
a preliminary to his account of sense (αἴσθησις), but in his
use of them he is unfortunately not always unambiguous.

The purely physical preconditions of an act of sense-
perception are (i) a body possessed of certain properties ;
(ii) a sense-organ and a medium, both of which to some
extent share these properties.

If we take vision as the type of all the special senses[2] and
try to harmonise Aristotle's accounts,[3] the result is roughly
as follows. Transparency is a property which all bodies,
from the aether to those in which earth predominates,

[1] A distinction derived, no doubt, from Plato's *Theaetetus* ; cp. p. 51.

[2] Like most modern psychologists, Aristotle treats the other senses in
less detail. But we must bear them constantly in mind in order to
correct a dangerous tendency to think of the sensum as a static image,
which Aristotle's metaphors sometimes suggest.

[3] *E.g.* An. II, 7 and Sen. 2 and 3. Aristotle's debt to Empedocles
and Plato, and his advance upon them, will be obvious. His theory
of vision is an application of Plato's doctrine that the sun is αἰτία at
once of the existence and of the visibility of the perceptible thing ;
cp. p. 38.

possess in varying degree. To certain bodies such as air and water, which have no definite bounding surface, it attaches in a high degree, and their transparency, " when actualised by the agency of fire or of something resembling the aetherial body " (An. 418^{b}12), is light, the medium of vision. In opaque bodies with determinate surfaces their superficial transparency actualises as colour—or, we had better perhaps still say, potential colour, since strictly there is no colour without light.[1] The transparent actualises at the surface of bodies in a limited series of (potential) colours which vary in degree between two contrary extremes, of which white is the more positive, black the more privative (see note 2, p. 72). The genus taken potentially—colour, so to speak, in the dark—is an infinitely divisible continuum ; but each of the colours intermediate between black and white is actually determined, when it comes to light, as specifically distinct, and can be analysed as a μῖξις (see p. 74) of black and white in a definite proportion. This specific proportion of black to white is apparently in some way governed in its variation by the ratio of the elements blended by μῖξις to constitute the coloured body (cp. Sen. 440^{b}14–15), but we are not told how on this account a compound body can be pure white.[2] Colour has also a further character. When the necessary conditions are present, perception takes place ; and in perception (considered still as a merely physical event) colour occasions instantaneous qualitative change[3]

[1] When in An. 430^{a}16 Aristotle says, " Light in a sense makes potential colours actual colours," he is considering potential colour at a yet lower stage of actualisation. Colour actualised by light but as yet unseen is a kind of ἕξις.

[2] That the sun appears red through mist is the kind of fact from which Aristotle infers that black and white are the sole components of any colour. (Goethe revived the fallacy.) The whole discussion is obscured by failure to distinguish clearly between colour and luminosity.

[3] Aristotle wavers between regarding the act of perception as a timeless actualisation of a ἕξις and as a qualitative change—perhaps inevitably. It is a sign of the superiority of sight to the other senses that the act of vision is at least comparatively instantaneous ; cp. note 2, p. 108.

in the intervening light, and, mediately, in the visual organ.[1]

Aristotle does not so clearly describe the corresponding potential condition of the percipient. In potentiality—*i.e.* before the act of sense—the organ shares the object's perceptible character generically : in the act of vision, it appears, the organ "in a way" becomes specifically identical in colour with the object (*ibid.* 425[b]22). And the difference in potentiality may be too great to permit this identification ; very great excess on the side of the object may destroy the organ in the act of perceiving, and, in the case of touch, even the animal itself (*ibid.* 435[b]15–16). From these premises Aristotle seems to conclude that the organ is necessarily a mean between the extremes of the perceptible character : "When the object makes the organ actually like itself it does so because the organ is potentially like it. Hence it is that we do not perceive what is just as hot or cold, hard or soft, as we are, but only the excesses of these qualities : which implies that the sense is a kind of mean between the contrary extremes in the sensibles. That is why it discriminates, or judges, the things of sense. For the mean is discriminative ; relatively to either extreme it can put itself in the place of the other " (*ibid.* 424[a]1 ff.). But though Aristotle is no doubt trying— and failing,[2] as we still fail—to state what the physical structure of a sense organ must be if it is to serve as matter and instrument to actual awareness, yet we are probably justified in inferring from his analogous treatment of moral virtue (see pp. 141 ff.) that in calling it a mean, he is thinking rather of the organ as existing ἕξει—*i.e.* not as a mere physical structure but as already organic to the

---

[1] Aristotle regards light in the " free " transparent as the analogue of colour in the opaque body ; a view which may help to explain the change induced in light by colour.

[2] Probably Beare (*Greek Theories of Elementary Cognition*, p. 235) is right in saying that the pupil " is *per se* of no particular colour," but the case of touch does not seem to be precisely analogous.

living animal organism and capable of realisation at any
moment. Virtue is a mean because it is a soul's habit
of (a) feeling in any situation the precisely right degree
of emotion, and (b) making the precisely right response
to it in action ; and this right feeling-and-response necessarily lies between all degrees of excess and all degrees of
defect. So vision is a capacity to react rightly in just
discrimination of *this* precise colour from all others on
the colour scale. Aristotle expresses this precise adjustment of the scale of possible feeling to the scale of possible
response by saying that virtue is a mean determined by a
right ratio (λόγος) ; and, to describe the corresponding
adjustment of function and object, he frequently speaks of
sense also as a λόγος.[1]

Aristotle's analysis of the complete act of sense-perception is pregnant with suggestion. This act has two sides.
(1) " If the eye were an animal," he says (An. 412ᵇ18),
" seeing would be its soul, for seeing is the definable
substance of the eye." But (2) seeing is more than this :
the object does not merely stimulate actualisation, for
" A sense," we are told (*ibid.* 424ᵃ17–24), " is that which
is receptive of sensible forms without their matter, as

---

[1] " ' The mean ' is what possesses any two contrasting qualities in
equipoise " (note on An. 424ᵃ4 in the Oxford translation by Professor
J. A. Smith). In calling sense both a mean and a λόγος Aristotle is
perhaps referring not only to the right adjustment of function to object,
but also to the blending of extremes in a definite ratio which any act of
sense manifests, and which is analogous to the blend of black and white
in any colour. He may even intend us to regard as all equally a mean
and a λόγος (1) the organ, (2) the ἕξις, (3) the content apprehended,
(4) the percipient's self-adjustment to (and self-distinction from) the
object. These four are not so different as abstract analysis makes them
appear, and it is perhaps inevitable that within what Aristotle
is treating as in one aspect a system of quantitative relations we should
sometimes find it difficult to see what relations he regards as cardinal.
His general meaning seems to be well illustrated by Beare : " So a lyre
in tune is a mean or λόγος to the variety of chords or airs which may
be played upon it. It is capable of sounding high or low notes indifferently ; and has in its tension, or in the relative tensions of its strings
and of the frame on which they are strung, the due harmonic ratio to
all the sound solicitations to which it may be called upon to respond.
But until struck, the lyre is silent " (*op. cit.*, p. 233).

wax takes on the device of the signet-ring without the iron or the gold ; it takes on the golden or bronze device, but not *qua* golden or of bronze. Correspondingly, in the perception of each sensible, the sense is acted on by what is coloured or flavoured or sounding not in so far as each of those sensibles is called a particular thing but in so far as it is of a certain kind, *i.e.* in respect of its definable form." And—just as in its lower analogues, local change (see p. 87) and the assimilation of food[1]—the actualisation though it takes place wholly in the stimulated recipient subject, is nevertheless also the actualisation of the object : " The actuality of the sensible object and that of the sense are one and the same, though differently definable. Take for example, actual sound and actual hearing : one may have hearing and not hear, and the resonant does not always sound ; yet when that which can hear is actively hearing and that which can sound actually does sound, the actual hearing and the actual sound are merged in one—though one may call them, if one please, hearkening and sounding respectively. If the alteration, both the acting and the being acted upon, resides in that which is acted upon, then the sound as well as the hearing, so far as it is actual, must take place in that which possesses the capacity of hearing. . . . The same account may be given of the other senses and their objects " (An. 425[b]26 ff.).

We shall find the implications of this passage clearer if we first complete Aristotle's account of sense-perception. Like Plato he regards sight as the most developed sense ; and he implies a more or less definite order of development in range and dignity from touch (the fundamental sense, indispensable to life) through taste, smell, and hearing.[2]

---

[1] See p. 98. Both the form and matter of food are assimilated.

[2] Sight is superior at least in the sphere of practical life. But for the development of the intelligence, which depends on oral instruction, hearing takes precedence: Sen. 437[a]3 ff. Moreover the transition in the medium, which subserves the act of seeing, is the instantaneous actualisation of a ἕξις : hearing requires a process of local movement (of vibrating air). Smell requires ordinary qualitative change.

Only in the lowest animals is sensation confined to touch and taste : the vivipara, saving the mole, possess all the senses, and even he has eyes under his skin. Unlike Plato (cp. p. 37) Aristotle assigns a medium to every sense. This is always water or air, save that some earth is necessarily contained in flesh—the peculiar internal medium of touch which is connate with an organ in the region of the heart. " In the perception of tangible objects," says Aristotle, knowing nothing of the nervous system, " we are affected not *by* but *along with* the medium, like a man struck through his shield " (An. 423^{b}14). Touch also differs from the other senses, which discriminate only between a single pair of contraries, in that its sensible correlate cannot be reduced below the two contrarieties hot-cold and fluid-dry. To preserve the unity of the sense Aristotle urges that these are the sole fundamental qualities of body as such.

But sense-perception does not consist in five unrelated functions. As the capacity for vision or hearing actualises in the individual act of perceiving a single colour or sound, so the senses are special because in their specific activities the single generic nature of sense-perception is active. This unity in diversity of sense has its (somewhat obscure) physiological basis in the fact that " The special sense-organs have one common organ in which the senses when actually functioning must meet " (Juv. 467^{b}28). In fact they connect with the heart, the organ of touch immediately, the other organs through the bloodvessels : " Sense-perception is a single faculty, and the controlling organ is one, though as percipience " (*i.e.* as actualised) " it differs in relation to each genus of sensibles, *e.g.* sound or colour " (Somn. 455^{a}20–22).

The convenient and traditional term for this unspecialised function of sense is *Sensus Communis*, and its operation is fourfold :[1] (1) Its presence in all specialised sense-

---

[1] The doctrine which follows has its germ in the *Theaetetus* (see pp. 50 ff.), though Plato ascribes the synthetic function to thought and not to sense.

function is shown in the self-consciousness which always accompanies the latter. We are always aware, *e.g.* that we see ; and this awareness *is* sense-perception, though it is not the seeing of a colour. For, " To perceive by sight " does not always mean one and the same thing : even when we are not seeing, it is none the less by sight that we distinguish darkness and light, though not in the same way as we distinguish two colours (An. 425^{b}20–22). (2) It discriminates between the objects of two senses and between two qualities simultaneously perceived by one sense. We compare white and sweet, etc., with each other, and since they are sensibles it must be by sense that we do so. Nor can we judge their difference by separate organs : both must be clearly presented to a single faculty—otherwise the mere fact of your perceiving one thing and my perceiving another would make it clear that the two were different. The single faculty, then, must judge in a single instant ; for to judge that A differs from B is to judge simultaneously that B differs from A, and that A and B differ at the actual moment of judgment. How, then, can that which is simple and indivisible in its act experience in a simple and indivisible instant sensibilia which differ either generically (white and sweet) or as contraries (white and black) ? It relates to them, perhaps, as a point relates to two lines which it (*a*) divides, and (*b*), because common to both, conjoins :[1] in some such way it reflects either the numerical unity of two qualities in a single body (white and sweet), or the unity by analogy of, *e.g.*, white in one body and black in another.[2] (*c*) There are certain characters—alteration and quiescence, number and unity, figure, magnitude, and time—which are common to all bodies and perceived in the exercise of

---

[1] Aristotle regards the atomic " now," which at once links and separates past and future, as analogous to the mathematical point : it is no part of time, just as a point is no part of a line.

[2] See An. 426^{b}12 ff., and 431^{a}21–30—an obscure passage.

more than one special sense.[1]   But by the special senses
as such they are perceived only incidentally, and they are
not merely incidental characters of body.   Essentially
they are perceived by sight, *e.g.*, or by touch, not *qua* sight
or *qua* touch but *qua* sense—*i.e.* by *Sensis Communis* : " It
is by alteration," says Aristotle,[2] " that we perceive all
the other common sensibles.   Thus it is by alteration
(locomotion) that we perceive magnitude, and consequently
figure, which is a species of magnitude : while that which
is at rest we perceive by the absence of movement.
Number we perceive by the negation of continuity, though
also by the special sensibles."   Aristotle obviously implies
that alteration is presupposed in the object by the other
common sensibles, but the Greek commentators suppose
him to mean here that the alteration mediating perception
of the common sensibles is the process set up by them in
the subject.   This view is supported by the statement
that, " When the state of our own minds does not change
at all, or we have not noticed its changing, we do not
realise that time has elapsed " (Ph. $218^{b}21$), and by a
passage in Mem. ($452^{b}9$ ff.) : " It may be taken for
granted that there is something by which we distinguish
a greater and a smaller time, and presumably we distinguish them as we distinguish magnitudes . . . *i.e.* by a
proportionate (mental) alteration.   For there are in the
mind figures and changes analogous to the external
objects."   It is thus a psychical miniature which enables
us to gauge an external magnitude or duration, and the
implication is that we compare the two terms and infer
the outer from the inner.[3]   On the other hand, Aristotle's

---

[1] Aristotle sometimes treats them as perceptible by all the special
senses, sometimes only sight and touch.   Time, " the numerable character
of change " (see p. 83, note 2) clearly belongs to the list, though it is
not here included.

[2] *Ibid.* $435^{a}16$–19.   He is thinking primarily of locomotion.

[3] This psychical miniature, at once process and figure, is obscure.
Viewed physiologically it is perhaps a change occupying a certain area

usual and much sounder view is not that perception of the self as percipient mediates the perception of a sensible object, but that self-consciousness, everywhere but in the highest form of intelligence, is rather a by-product of the direct grasp of the object, and reached mediately through this : " Scientific knowledge, perception, opinion, and discursive thought have always something else as their object, and themselves only by the way."[1] We may suggest a partial solution : Aristotle does regard intelligence in its highest form as *essentially* self-conscious (see p. 171), and in the passages cited above from Ph. and Mem. he is discussing not animal but human perception, in which intelligence is already at work.[2] Possibly, then, self-consciousness plays a gradually more essential rôle as the scale is ascended. But whatever at any stage the order of transition in apprehension may be, the terms between which it takes place are not separate entities : the essence of Aristotle's teaching is the unity of subject and object.[3] (4) It is by sense unspecialised that we perceive such conjunctions of characters with objects as are only incidental to the special sense which is being exercised ; *e.g.* when we " see " that a white object is sweet, or is " the son of Cleon " (An. $425^{a}21$ ff.).

Thus sense is a real unity. *Sensus Communis*, though relatively unspecialised in the perception of common sensibles, is present as an uniting and discriminating capacity not only in the comparison of two special sensa, but also in every act of a single sense. The risk of error is absent, or at least minimal, in the acts of the special

in the special sense-organs and the heart. The difficulties of the doctrine are sufficiently obvious, but see p. 116, note 3.

[1] Met. $1074^{b}35$, and see pp. 115, 156. Cp. also pp. 243 ff. for Aquinas' interpretation of Aristotle's position.

[2] Measurement as opposed to vague differentiation of size is to Aristotle as to Plato (cp. pp. 40, 63) a function of intelligence and not of sense : cp. " Man is the only animal that knows how to count " (*Problems* $956^{a}12$. For this work see note p. 266).

[3] The doctrine of Aquinas should be compared. It is not easy to say how far he follows Aristotle, how far he develops him.

senses, and increases as *Sensus Communis* comes more
fully into play ; but *any* act of sense-perception is a
quasi-judgment—a single actualisation of subject and object
in which a sensum is at once united with and distinguished
from (*a*) a range of sensibilia and (*b*), secondarily, the self.
Aristotle seems in fact to recognise—or almost to recognise[1]
—that perception always implies a context, partly as a
more or less explicit background receding from the focus
of attention, partly as unrealised possibilities wholly
beyond the actual field of perception. Yet if sense-
perception is a *quasi*-judgment because it involves discrimination and the possibility of error, it is nevertheless
not rational judgment.[2] Man alone has reason, whereas
all the senses and all those further developments of sense-
function which have shortly to be discussed, are possessed
also by some sub-human animals. It may seem that
Aristotle virtually admits the presence of thought in all
perceptive discrimination, but he is perfectly clear that
these functions in some form belong to sense and not to
reason. No doubt in man all sense-function is rationalised,
and Aristotle, at least at his best, maintains that in man
sense-perception develops without a break into thought (cp.
§ 4 (A), (B), and (C)). But within a continuous developing
series he includes in sense all that is in his judgment a
sine qua non of sense as the higher brutes have it. It is
in fact the difference between these and man which decides
him where to draw the line, and his intention is not to
break the continuity of development at this point, but to
articulate clearly its phases.[3]

How are we finally to construe the single actualisation
of subject and object in the act of perception ? The clue
lies in Aristotle's statement that the sensum is the form

---

[1] He shows perhaps an occasional tendency to treat unspecialised
sense-function as if it were the composition of special sense-data.

[2] " Judgment implies conviction . . . but no brute is ever convinced "
(*ibid*. 428ª20).

[3] For the problem here involved see p. 119.

without the matter of the object. We saw that the form
of a chemical compound was the proportion, the λόγος, of
its constituents ; and though Aristotle often associates
shape with form in speaking of the form of perceptible
things, he always regards its λόγος, the intelligible
complex of essential characters embodied in it, as that
which makes a perceptible thing what it really is. We
may probably treat the simple sensum, in grasping which
a special sense is infallible, as a mere ideal limit. In every
actual case not only is sense-perception determined as a
mean on a scale by a λόγος, but the actually perceived
content is itself a λόγος : " If concord is a species of vocal
sound and if vocal sound and hearing are one, though
differently definable, and if concord is a λόγος ; then
hearing too must be a species of λόγος."[1] Aristotle no
doubt finds difficulty in the fact that an intelligible
complex of essential characters is universal and so far
not individual, a " such " and not a " this," no less an
abstraction from matter than the actualisation of matter ;
no doubt his association of shape with form expresses the
immersion of form in a matter which is at once mere
potentiality, opaque to knowledge, and at the same time
contributes that particularity without which there would
be no particular—in the sense of singular—thing perceived ; yet he does not regard the form received from the
object as a particular image or *quasi*-photographic copy,
a mere Empedoclean effluence. And to substitute a
cinematographic metaphor for a photographic would do
more justice to the fact that he conceives the *perceptum*
dynamically,[2] but it would still misrepresent his doctrine.
For sense-perception to Aristotle is not a continuous

---

[1] *Ibid*. 426[b]27 ff. Analogously the emotions, which are attributes of
the soul inseparably connected with the body, are defined by Aristotle
as λόγοι ἔνυλοι—perhaps " intelligible contents concreted in matter "
(*ibid*. 403[a]25). They can also be described abstractly from a purely
physiological point of view.

[2] It would perhaps be a fair account of it from a purely physiological
point of view.

moving picture presented to the percipient : though it is
the effect of the object, and a self-actualisation of the
object, it is at the same time a phase of the percipient's
activity—a part of himself. The Platonic metaphor of
signet and wax expresses only the universality of the
device in a multitude of waxen embodiments ; it does not
imply a static image, nor a doctrine of representative
perception. It is on Aristotle's view, as it was on Plato's,
a distinctive characteristic of the act of sense-perception
that a particular, a singular " this," is perceived ; but that
act entails, not the transference of a particular image,
but a re-actualisation in fresh matter of a form which
prior to, and in relation to, that re-actualisation *is* only
potentially. And the re-actualisation, it must not be
forgotten, is also a phase of the subject's activity. The
form achieves its destiny and receives its proper embodiment only in being perceived : the device is engraved on
the gold or the bronze only in order that it may impress
the wax.

One might conclude that the perceptible properties of
all " material " things exist only to subserve perception,
just as the edible properties of some of them exist to subserve nutrition—that in the end only as perceived can
anything be truly termed " this " or " that " ; but
Aristotle's teaching that a basis of identity underlies the
kinship of consciousness and its objects, and that the
problem lies in their separation rather than in their union,
is not fully developed. Against his predecessors' contention that without seeing and tasting there is no colour
and no flavour, he asserts the potential existence of the
substrata of perceptible characters (*ibid.* 426ᵃ20 ff.) ; but
elsewhere he well expresses the ambiguity of these
" permanent possibilities of sensation " : " When any
perceptible thing has passed out of the range of perception,
then, even if we have actually perceived it, we only know
it with the appropriate *universal* knowledge ; we do not

know it fully actualising our knowledge."[1] Yet in this doctrine of single and undivided actualisation there is a promise of something beyond that naïve realism of which Aristotle is sometimes accused, a promise which in his treatment of thought comes yet nearer to fulfilment.

4. FURTHER DEVELOPMENTS OF SENSE

(A) IMAGINATION

" Imagination " conveniently translates Aristotle's φαντασία, but φαντασία means primarily " appearance," and then the capacity for apprehending an appearance. Its emergence is thus described : " Though sense-perception is innate in all animals, in some the percept comes to persist, in others it does not. So animals in which this persistence does not come to be have no cognition at all outside the act of perceiving—no cognition of objects of which no percept persists ; animals in which it does come to be have perception *and* continue to retain the percept in the soul."[2] The physiological basis of this retentive faculty is not a fixed imprint (though Aristotle sometimes so describes it metaphorically), but the process of qualitative change set up in the perceptive act, which persists with diminishing vigour in the sense-organs—a kind of moving image :[3] in φαντασία the single activity of subject and object has weakened *qua* act of sense, but has not yet been developed to subserve something beyond the province of sense. The percept persisting as a φάντασμα appears in direct sequence

---

[1] An. Pr. 67ª39 ff. *I.e.* our knowledge remains a ἕξις, a merely *general* knowing of that *kind* of thing. On this sense of the word " universal " (καθόλου), see p. 219, note 1.

[2] An. Post. 99ᵇ36 ff. ; cp. Plato, *Sophist*, 263d ff.

[3] This is a vital point in Aristotle's doctrine. We cannot too often remind ourselves that he regards the sense-content (perceived, imagined, or remembered) always as dynamic, never as static—not as a cross-section of the psychical stream, but as that which persists through and in change. We might almost say that not only the common sensibles but even the special sensibilia are perceived " by alteration."

upon perception as an after-image (Somni. 459^{b}10 ff.) ; in sleep, when there are no fresh acts of perception to " extrude the persisting process and extinguish it as the greater fire makes the lesser to pale before it " (*ibid.* 461^{a}1), it re-emerges variously distorted as dream not distinguished from waking perception.

But imagination is illustrated only in its negative moment by dream and hallucination ; it is also a positive capacity, the next term beyond *Sensus Communis* in the developing series of sense-functions. Whereas *Sensus Communis* discriminates only between sensa and is universally present in the animal world, φαντασία is the power of distinguishing between an appearance as such and a sensum, and not all animals possess it.[1] A φάντασμα may even be present simultaneously with actual perception, as when " The sun appears only a foot in diameter, but we are convinced that it is larger than the earth " (An. 428^{b}2). In this instance, presumably, the content is (*a*) directly seen, (*b*) apprehended as only an appearance,

---

[1] An. 428^{a}1–11 cannot be otherwise interpreted without unwarrantable emendation. In Mem. 450^{a}10 Aristotle calls the φάντασμα " an affection of *Sensus Communis* " and seems actually to identify the two faculties. For this two reasons may be suggested :—(*a*) *Sensus Communis* apprehends time, and once this is admitted it is difficult to exclude φαντασία and even memory (cp. Mem. 451^{a}27 ff. I accept Beare's interpretation in the Oxford translation) from its activity. Aristotle tends to treat in terms of the lower faculty those activities which the lower faculty in fact always subserves save in the lowest animals ; just so he calls the vegetable soul nutritive, although nutrition is the lowest of its three functions. Moreover the organ of *Sensus Communis* is involved in all developed sense-function. But when he asserts that there are animals with *Sensus Communis* but without φαντασία, we may be sure that that is where he draws the line, just as he excludes any intellectual element from sense-discrimination. We learn in Mem. 450^{a}20 that *Sensus Communis* in some animals does not extend to a sense of time. (*b*) Aristotle's difficulty lies in the nature of the facts : it is only by contrast with waking life that a dream can be called mere appearance. If we could conceive as an ideal limit a rudimentary state of sense below all discrimination, this would be neither sense-perception nor φαντασία, but something for which the distinction between them is not yet explicit—mere presentation (*perhaps* Plato's εἰκασία). Hence all the developments of sense might just as plausibly be exhibited as developments of imagination, and a still better procedure would be to exhibit both sense and imagination as developing from mere presentation.

(c) related intellectually to the known size of the sun : perception is modified to subserve φαντασία, φαντασία is modified to subserve thought.[1] The intermediate stage is provided by " the sleeper who surprises the dream images as he wakes, and finds them to be mere movements in the sense-organs " (Somni. 462ᵃII), and by the semi-delirious patient to whom the pattern on the wall appears to be animals, while all the time he knows that it is not. We shall find that φαντασία continues to play a vital part in the subsequent stages of experience.

(B) MEMORY

The psychical continuity first apparent in the perception of time by *Sensus Communis* develops through imagination to memory : " Of the present there is perception, of the future expectation, of the past memory. Hence all remembering involves lapse of time " (Mem. 449ᵇ27 ff.). " When one actually remembers, he must consciously assert that he had previously heard or perceived or thought this thing " (*ibid*. 449ᵇ22 ff.). But memory, even the memory of intelligible objects, cannot exist without a φάντασμα, and that is " an affection of *Sensus Communis* (see note, p 117). Hence it belongs to the primary sense faculty and only incidentally to the intelligence. . . . If it were one of the functions of the intelligence it would not belong to any of the lower animals."[2] In a passage (*ibid*. 450ᵇI–12) which echoes Plato's *Theaetetus* (191d), Aristotle repeats the signet-ring metaphor to describe the physiological conditions of memory : to remember efficiently the organ must be neither too hard to receive,

---

[1] In the brutes and occasionally in man perception is modified only by imagination. How far perception without φαντασία—*i.e.* discrimination by *Sensus Communis* which does not involve discrimination between appearance and percept—occurs in animals not possessing φαντασία, Aristotle does not say.

[2] Mem. 450ᵃ10–20 condensed.

nor too soft to retain, the process imprinted on it. To the crucial question—" How is it that, though the affection (the φάντασμα) is present and the (related) fact absent, yet it is the absent that is remembered ? " (*ibid.* 450ᵃ27 ff.) —he replies unsatisfactorily that, as a portrait may either be seen merely as a picture or also referred to its original, so what is in itself a φάντασμα may as a moving memory-image (μνημόνευμα) be referred to the object of the initial perception. Here a representational doctrine does seem to be implied ; and it fails to explain the facts, for memory is not memory unless we are actually aware of the past when we remember. Yet Aristotle does at least show that it is because percept, φάντασμα, μνημόνευμα, are phases in which a single identity persists that memory is possible, and that this single persisting identity is the form, the universal.

(c) RECOLLECTION

We have found it not easy either to describe sense-perception without reference to judgment, or memory save as an inference from present to past on the basis of their identity. In fact we only know these functions as we find them in human rational experience, and any account of their analogues in the lower animals must be largely conjectural. That sense exists both as a moment distinguishable but not isolable within the human soul and also as the defining characteristic of the brute ; that just as some ὁμοιομερῆ remain inorganic so some animals do not develop rational function ; these are problems in the end no easier of solution than nature's occasional failures (cp. p. 92, note). Man is " not the best thing in the universe " (EN 1141ᵃ21), but at a mid-point on the scale ; and if he cannot know himself save in the light of what is above him, yet he knows what is below him only by an always hazardous inference from himself.

Recollection, however, is a capacity which man shares with no other animal. Like memory, but unlike simple sense, its development as a ἕξις is post-natal—habitual repetition of the act tends to increase the capacity—and the element of passivity present in all sense-function is here on the wane. For recollection involves a voluntary act of inference which is not, like memory, confined in respect of its starting-point to the content of present experience. This inference is closely akin to the also purely human function of deliberation with a view to action, and the principle of association upon which it works may be (a) contiguity, whereby the recollection of one event recalls another which in fact immediately succeeded it, and so on until revivification of the original train of experience reinstates the event which we desire to remember ; or (b) similarity ; or (c) contrariety. In all three cases "association marries only universals," for it is the form of the perceived object which in recollection emerges from a potential state ; and moreover Aristotle leaves us in no doubt when he says, "Things arranged in a fixed order, like the demonstrations of geometry, are easy to remember,[1] while things badly arranged are remembered with difficulty" (Mem. 452ª3 ff.). The physiological process underlying recollection is most readily stimulated when the association is by contiguity, though habitual recollection through purer logical connexions tends to modify the reaction of the organ. That is why reinstatement is easiest when contiguity and strict logical order coincide, as in recollection of a successively acquired chain of theorems. And there is further evidence that recollection has a sensory basis ; it may operate involuntarily on the same principles of association as those which govern deliberate search, and sometimes, when we have initiated the process, we cannot check our effort to remember.

[1] There is no difference in principle here between memory and recollection.

(D) APPETITE, MOVEMENT, PLEASURE AND PAIN

So far we have treated sense-function as if it were purely cognitive, and sense, it is true, is sometimes enjoyed by man for its own sake, and sometimes subserves higher and purely human cognitive faculties. But, though it was provisionally so described, the object of animal sense was never in fact a mere perceptible ; for frequently in man and invariably in all other animals the sense-stimulus is wholly spent in producing an equivalent purely practical reaction. Physiological analysis of this process shows that the stimulus causes variation of temperature in the heart and consequent expansion and contraction ; and " A small change at the centre makes many considerable changes at the circumference, just as by shifting the rudder a hair's breadth you get a wide deviation at the prow."[1] In the lowest animals reaction is vague and indeterminate (An. 434^{a}4), but in the higher brutes it takes definite shape as movement of the members and locomotion of the whole body. These movements are all directed towards the single end of self-maintenance and self-preservation, and so mutually inter-penetrant are the apprehension and the reaction that for a brute the object of sense is, as such, something to be pursued as conducive, or avoided as hostile, to this end : there is in fact for a brute no distinction between what a thing is and what action it demands.[2] The appetitive moment within this unitary practical consciousness—the reaction issuing in a movement of pursuit or avoidance—Aristotle calls ὄρεξις, and the words in which he describes its analogue in man vividly express the inevitable and immediate succession of stage upon stage in which animal sense-function is exhibited : " I want to drink, says appetite ; this is drink,

---

[1] MA 702^{b}25 ff. This work is possibly not by Aristotle, but its main contents seem to be Aristotelian.

[2] It follows that, if an animal could classify its sense-data, the result would differ *toto caelo* from a human classification.

says sense, or imagination, or thought : straightway I drink " (MA 701ᵃ32).

And sense, like all conscious activity, is also feeling— that is pleasure and pain. Now Aristotle regards pleasure as inseparably accompanying, if not actually identical with, free unimpeded activity, and pain as similarly con- nected with the obstruction of activity (see Chap. VII, § 6). Hence the feeling which all sense-apprehension also is, qualifies the subject not as passive but as active ; and, further, since successful self-maintenance is at once its proper function—its good—and its pleasure, a brute may be said to apprehend and pursue its end as something without distinction good and pleasant. Aristotle sums up as follows the three moments of cognition, feeling, and appetition, in terms of which the single undivided actualisa- tion of percipient and object develops : " To perceive is like bare asserting or knowing ; but when the object is pleasant or painful, the soul makes a *quasi*-affirmation or negation, and pursues or avoids the object. In fact to feel pleasure and pain is precisely to function with the sensitive mean (cp. pp. 106 ff.) towards good and bad as such, and avoidance and appetition in their actual exercise *are* this functioning : the capacity of appetite and the capacity of avoidance are not different from one another nor from the capacity of sense, though the three are differently definable."[1]

But it will easily be seen that appetition implies more than simple sensation : " An animal," says Aristotle, is capable of self-movement so far as it is appetitive, and it cannot be appetitive without φαντασία" (An. 433ᵇ27 ff.). Appetite in fact involves a rudimentary distinction between ideal and actual ; imagination appears in it as not merely the persistence of the past in memory, but also, as it were,

---

[1] An. 431ᵃ8–14. The intimate union of pleasure and ὄρεξις— " Where sense is there is pleasure and pain, and where these are ἐπιθυμία (the lowest form of ὄρεξις, dependent on touch and taste) is necessarily present " (An. 413ᵇ23)—often leads Aristotle to treat pleasure and ἐπιθυμία as equivalent terms ; cp. EN *passim*.

the insistence of the future in anticipation ; the form begins at length to manifest itself more clearly as a universal transcending its own embodiment in this and that fugitive act of perceiving a particular.

Thus the natural appetitive movement of an animal may be causally analysed as follows. As the Prime Mover moves, himself unmoved, so the object of ὄρεξις,[1] the imagined good-and-pleasant which appears to it, moves the animal's appetitive soul. This, through the connatural πνεῦμα therein (cp. p. 99), moves the heart, the pivot of the whole body, in the way above described. The heart moves the adjacent organs by pushing and pulling, and the whole physical process works on the principle by which a joint operates : one of the contiguous surfaces is stationary, the other moves, being both pushed and pulled. In this process the imagined good is (a) the formal cause, since the enjoyment of that good, the successful exercise of its proper function of sense-appetition, defines the animal in its real and full nature ; (b) in so far as it is merely ideal and not yet actual, the final cause ; (c) so far as its features, though merely ideal, are already present in detail to consciousness, the efficient cause. The material cause is provided by that basis of bodily change which has been already described. The serial analysis of change which Aristotle has formulated in the inanimate world is thus expanded and developed to embrace the animate. The sensory-appetitive soul is more truly initiatory than any term in sublunary causal series which we have yet had to consider, for the imagining of the good develops without a break from the reaction of the percipient to the perceptible, and the attainment of it is a single realisation of the animal in and as its proper end ; yet the appetitive soul is still a term in a causal series, still partially passive, moved ultimately by that which moves, itself unmoved.

---

[1] *I.e.* of ἐπιθυμία or in some animals also the nobler θυμός, impulse or anger : cp. Plato's θυμοειδές, p. 45.

NOTE

ARISTOTLE AS A BIOLOGIST

If soul is form and body is matter, the ideal classification of living beings would be one solely in terms of psychical function. Yet man lacks inevitably the complete insight for such an undertaking (cp. p. 123), and though Aristotle is true to his teleological principle and treats of matter only for the sake of form—though he is content with mechanistic explanation only when he can find no purpose —yet, like any modern biologist, he is constantly forced to infer to a psychical type from an analogue in physical structure and process.

Though Darwin spoke of Linnaeus and Cuvier as " mere schoolboys to old Aristotle,"[1] space permits us but the briefest reference to Aristotle's biological research. No botanical work survives, but he mentions about five hundred species of animals, and only uses second-hand evidence to supplement a mass of acute and obviously personal observation. Within the whole animal kingdom as it develops from the bloodless shell-fish that, still plant-like, rests head downwards, to man, warm-blooded and walking erect, Aristotle distinguishes three grades of likeness :—(1) The infima species—which Aristotle regards as immutable and not evolving—is a single identity. Difference between singular individual specimens serves no purpose ; it springs from the irregularity of matter, and is no part of nature's plan.[2] (2) Species of the same highest genus have identical bodily parts, which differ only in size and in the degree to which they possess the fundamental tactual qualities. (3) The highest genera are linked by analogy : " Bird and fish . . . only agree in having analogous organs ; for what in the bird is feather, in the fish is scale " (PA 644^{a}21).

[1] Darwin's *Life and Letters*, III, 252.
[2] See p. 92, note 1 ; p. 102, note 1.

He is fully conscious of the difficulties of classification and the absence of scientific tradition : the Platonic method of division by dichotomy allows only one differentia to each infima species.[1] It therefore cuts across obvious natural groups which possess several common characters, and it even produces fewer differentiae than the number of known species. Moreover one of the divisions at each stage is purely negative, and therefore not further specifically determinable. His solution is not to desert the principle by introducing fresh differentiae *ad hoc* and *ab extra*—this would result in a mere agglomeration and not in a system—but to accept several *fundamenta divisionis* from the start : " We must try to recognise the generic groups, following the lead given us by mankind in general, who have distinguished, *e.g.* the genus bird from the genus fish. Each of these groups combines many differentiae, and is not defined by a single one as in dichotomy."[2] This admirably flexible method results in the following classification,[3] which stood until the time of Linnaeus :—

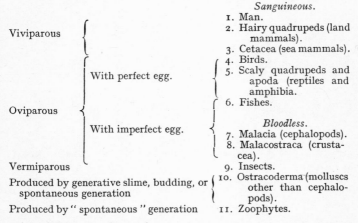

Sanguineous.

Viviparous
1. Man.
2. Hairy quadrupeds (land mammals).
3. Cetacea (sea mammals).

Oviparous — With perfect egg.
4. Birds.
5. Scaly quadrupeds and apoda (reptiles and amphibia.
6. Fishes.

Bloodless.

Oviparous — With imperfect egg.
7. Malacia (cephalopods).
8. Malacostraca (crustacea).

Vermiparous
9. Insects.

Produced by generative slime, budding, or spontaneous generation
10. Ostracoderma (molluscs other than cephalopods).

Produced by " spontaneous " generation
11. Zoophytes.

[1] See PA I, 2–4 ; also p. 58.
[2] PA 643^{b}10 ff. Aristotle is of course well aware that the traditional groups require supplementation ; cp. An. Post. 98^{a}13. See also pp. 218 ff.
[3] Taken from Ross, *Aristotle*, p. 117.

VII

PRACTICAL MAN

1. HAPPINESS

GREEK ethical theory starts from what is, not from what ought to be : it does not postulate a categorical imperative, but deduces man's duty from his nature. From the conviction that what is fully real is fully good sprang a broad conception of morality, which has since too often incurred the contempt of a perverse Puritanism. Plato and Aristotle believed—every Greek, indeed, took it more or less consciously for granted—that the standard of value in human life is both immanent and single ; that though moral goodness differs from the lesser excellences of man, it differs only as a whole, which is also a supreme part, differs from its remaining parts ; [1] and, finally, that to call man, an essentially active being, good, is to imply that he is good at doing something.

Aristotle accordingly claims general consent for the view : (1) that what all men seek is a single self-sufficing experience, which they call happiness ($\epsilon\dot{v}\delta\alpha\iota\mu o\nu\acute{\iota}\alpha$) ; a *summum bonum* and ultimate satisfaction, " which in itself alone makes life desirable and lacking in nothing " (EN 1097^{b}14) ; a final end comprehending all subordinate virtues and activities ; (2) that happiness is the criterion of excellence in these means, or relative ends, [2] which at once subserve and constitute it, and is therefore itself

---

[1] See Ch. VIII, § 4. Aristotle's distinction of art from conduct is not really an exception; see the next section.
[2] See p. 90, note 1.

above the praise which we bestow on them : " No one praises happiness as he does justice, but rather calls it blessed, as being something more divine and better " (*ibid.* 1101ᵇ26). Yet, when it comes to defining happiness more narrowly, men differ *toto caelo*. Is pleasure the final end ? Or wealth ? Or honour ? In words which echo Plato, Aristotle offers his own solution[1] in terms of specific function : " As for a flautist, a sculptor, or any artist, and, in general, for all things that have a function or a work to do, the terms " good " and " well done " are thought applicable to the function, so it would seem to be for man, if he has a function. Have the carpenter, then, and the tanner their functions, their work to do, and has man none ? Is he born with nothing to do ? Or as eye, hand, foot, and in general each of the parts has a function, may one lay it down that man similarly has a function beyond all these ? "[2] Man's function, and there-fore his happiness, is not, he concludes, any mere ἕξις of virtue or excellence,[3] but " an ἐνέργεια of soul which implies a rational principle " (*ibid.* 1098ᵃ7).

But Aristotle proceeds to amplify this definition in terms which foreshadow a breach with Platonic doctrine : " Human good turns out to be activity of soul in accordance with excellence or virtue, and, if there are more than one excellence, in accordance with the best and most com-plete " (*ibid.* 1098ᵃ16 ff.). Plato, of course, had already in the *Republic* placed the end of human life in the develop-ment of specifically human—*i.e.* rational—function. But he had treated the life of reason as essentially a unity : speculation and conduct are for him no more than the alternating phases of a single activity at once intellectual and moral. He had held the ideal of rational function—as

---

[1] It is of course originally Platonic.
[2] *Ibid.* 1097ᵇ25-33. Cp. *Republic*, 352d ff.
[3] There is no " virtue " in the distinction : the Greek word ἀρετή, usually translated " virtue," is simply the noun of the adjective ἀγαθός, " good."

exhibited by the philosopher guardian—to be a philosophic insight into the Form of the Good, manifesting itself primarily as disinterested speculation, but also secondarily as the necessary principle of practical life, as the intelligence which conduct must embody if it is to be termed fully good. Aristotle maintains on the contrary that the Form of the Good is unsound in theory, and that, even if it were not, it could afford no guidance for conduct (see *ibid.* I, 6). He distinguishes sharply between the speculative and practical forms of the good life, regarding philosophic insight not as the basis of virtuous action—he would not have the state ruled by a philosopher-king—but as a higher and wholly self-justifying activity which comes to birth only in the flower of mankind, and constitutes for those few a supreme happiness that is beyond and above the lesser happiness of practical men. Hence he divides man's rational activity into two separate functions : " The end of speculation is truth, that of practical wisdom ($\phi\rho\acute{o}\nu\eta\sigma\iota\varsigma$) action " (Met. 993^{b}19). This distinction he commonly bases on a difference in the object upon which thinking is directed. Perfect substance such as God and the astral intelligences, and even the objects of mathematical study, are immutable ; and for that reason the knowledge of them has no practical end to seek beyond the truth which it grasps. The world of nature changes, but the laws of its changing do not, and there again man can contemplate only for the sake of truth. Yet the natural world does afford some scope for human interference. Species is immutable, and the laws by which particular individuals develop their specific form are universal ; but from the irregularity of their matter arises a diversity among the individuals—an indeterminateness, or potentiality of alternative determination, in this or that inanimate thing, a caprice in the action of this or that living being. This renders their behaviour amenable only to general rules—even forces us sometimes to ascribe it to chance as to a real agency, for Aristotle, despite his subordination of the automatic to intelligence and nature,[1] seems to hold that the possibility of voluntary action demands some real absence of determination in things. He argues[2] that we can always in principle trace a causal series necessitating an event which has occurred, yet deliberation, which implies some power of initiation and control in the appetitive soul, would not be possible if this series could be extended into the future : " There will necessarily either be or not be a naval battle to-morrow ; but there will not necessarily be a naval battle to-morrow, and there will not necessarily be no naval battle " (Int. 19ª30 ff.). The knowledge of this indeterminate object will accordingly possess three characteristics : (a) it will be of an inferior kind, for knowledge as such is knowledge of the cause, and the partially indeterminate is that which is partially uncaused ; (b) it will not be developed very far beyond sense-perception, which is *par excellence* the apprehension of a particular ; (c) it will be knowledge embodied in, and almost one with, desire that issues in action, for the knowledge of an object *qua* indeterminate is *eo ipso* both the knowledge of it *qua* determinable and the active determining of it.

Yet we must not press distinction into discontinuity. Man's practical thinking is rational and not so utterly one with impulse as a brute's perception ; for man deliberates and chooses, whereas a beast does not. Deliberation, no doubt, is for a particular practical end, but even if it implies no disinterested knowledge of objects beyond their character as ends or means to ends, it does at any rate involve more than a cognition which issues without remainder in action. We may perhaps even say that in the suspension of action there is already an element—though not a pure element—of contemplation ; for despite Aristotle's sharp distinction between practice

---

[1] Cp. p. 92, note 1.   [2] Cp. Int. 9, Met. VI, 3.

and speculation, at least we may safely infer from his whole theory of consciousness as an ordered hierarchy of functions that man as a practical being is not what he would be if he were not also by nature speculative.[1]

2. THE ARTS[2]

Speculation is the fruit of leisure. History dawns with the struggle of natural man to exist, and continues with his successive efforts to rise above nature. Sense and imagination grow rational, and man begins to calculate : " Sensory imagination is found in all animals, but deliberative imagination in those alone which can calculate rationally. For the task of deciding whether to do this or that already involves calculation, and man's pursuit of the greater (good) necessarily implies that he has a standard unit to measure by. It follows that he can construct a unity out of several φαντάσματα."[3] It is from memory and recollection that anticipative imagination arises : " In man out of memory develops experience (ἐμπειρία) ; for the several memories of the same thing produce finally the capacity for a single experience. And experience seems pretty much like science and art, but really science and art come to men *through* experience. . . . Now art arises when from many empirical notions one universal judgment about the similars as such has sprung. For to have a judgment that when Callias was ill of this

[1] How far this developing series of conscious functions retains its character as it approaches its culmination is, as we shall see, part of the crucial problem of Aristotle's philosophy ; but his interpreter must allow for the fact that Aristotle's emphasis is always on difference where Plato's was on identity.

[2] In what follows "art" (τεχνή) means technical skill—practical thinking which is not divided from the making in which it issues. Aristotle does not clearly distinguish what would be now called "the fine arts" from the useful (see p. 136, note 1). He generally has the useful arts in mind when discussing τεχνή.

[3] *I.e.* he can partially elicit the universal from sense ; he can imagine a general situation which serves him as a norm (An. 434ᵃ5 ff.).

disease this did him good, and did good to Socrates and similarly to many other individual men, is a matter of experience ; but to judge that it has done good to all persons of a certain constitution, marked off as of one kind, when they were ill of this disease . . . this is a matter of art " (Met. 981ª5–12). " We think that knowledge and understanding belong to art rather than to experience . . . because artists know the cause, but men of experience do not. . . . Hence we think also that the master-workers in each craft are more honourable and know in a truer sense and are wiser than the manual workers, because they know the true causes of the things that are done. . . And we think art more truly knowledge than experience is ; because artists can teach, and men of experience cannot " (*ibid.* 981ª24–ᵇ9). Thus, as Mr. Ross puts it,[1] " What is revived by memory has previously been experienced as a unit. Experience, on the other hand, is a coagulation of memories ; what is active in present consciousness in virtue of experience has not been experienced together. . . . Experience is a stage in which there has appeared ability to interpret the present in the light of the past, but an ability which cannot account for itself ; when it accounts for itself it becomes art."

Art is something less than moral conduct, for it is only man's first conquest of nature : " It is as the poet Antiphon wrote," says the writer of the *Mechanics*,[2] speaking of discovery in mechanics, " ' Man's art reverses nature's victories.' " But art must appropriate nature's function : " Nature is a source of internal change in things, art is a source in things of change in something else " (Met. 1070ª7), and man conquers with his adversary's weapons : " Art achieves some things which nature cannot, but in others art imitates nature " (Ph. 199ª15). Nature neither

---

[1] *Aristotle, Metaphysics,* p. 116.
[2] 847ª19. This work is probably not by Aristotle, but its doctrine seems to be Aristotelian.

utilises the power of the lever nor builds houses—the matter for these processes does not contain the source of such change—but nature and the physician alike aim at producing health. In fact the lines on which art and nature work (*a*) are closely parallel, and (*b*), where they diverge, the advantage rests with nature. (*a*) In natural generation the species is formal and final cause, and also, as embodied in the sperm of the adult male, efficient cause. The concomitant secondary changes conform to the same law. In the process of building a house (i) the formal cause is the form, the structural principle, which the house will exhibit as its real nature when it is completed. And this form is also (ii), as the aim ideally present to the deliberative imagination of the architect, the final cause ; and again (iii), inasmuch as the imagined aim is also an end desired, the form is the efficient cause which initiates the actual construction of the house.[1] Correspondingly, when the sick man is cured, health is (i) the form which is actualised in his healed body, (ii) the aim ideally present to the physician, and so the final cause, (iii) the efficient cause initiating the process of healing. Thus, Aristotle explains, the deliberation of the physician starts from his conception of health : " The healing of the patient implies that the physician's train of thought has been as follows. *This* is health ; hence if the patient is to be healthy there must first be x, *e.g.* uniformity of temperature in the body ; then, if there is to be x, there must first be y, warmth ; and the physician's thinking continues thus until he brings it to a final term, that is to something [*e.g.* massage] which it is in his power to produce " (Met. 1032^{b}6–9). Comparably to the stages of natural development, these successive means to health, which the physician then proceeds to execute in the reverse order to that in which he has discovered them, are the constituents into which he has analysed the end : " The warmth in the process [*e.g.* of

---

[1] Pp. 121 ff. should be compared.

K

massage] has produced warmth in the body, and this warmth *is* health, or a part of health " (*ibid.* 1034ᵃ26). But (*b*) nature alone can effect substantial change : the change of which art is a source is secondary. An artefact is not a true creation. The skill of the architect and the sculptor can do no more than alter in quantity and quality the material upon which they work.

As the source of change immanent in a natural product is its nature and form, so his technical skill is the " nature " of the artist, the form which makes him what he is *qua* artist. It is also and at the same time the very form which the artist endeavours to actualise in the material before him ; his deliberative thinking is one with himself, with what it analyses, and with what it makes. " Health," says Aristotle, " *is* the λόγος, the knowledge, in the soul " (*ibid.* 1032ᵇ5). " The art of healing *is* the λόγος[1] of health " (*ibid.* 1070ᵃ29), for " The art *is* the form " (*ibid.* 1034ᵃ24). Whereas in perception the object actualises its potential nature in the percipient, in art the agent actualises his skill in the object ; but equally in perception and in art subject and object actualise in a single activity.

But production and action, like sense-perception, are concerned *par excellence* with the particular ; technical knowledge without experience effects less than the mere irrational knack of the empiric : " Experience is cognition of individuals, art of universals, and actions and productions are all concerned with the singular individual ; for the physician does not cure *man*, except incidentally, but Callias or Socrates, or somebody else, who happens to be a man. If, then, a man has the λόγος without the experience, and recognises the universal but does not know the particular in it, he will often fail to cure ; for it is the particular individual who is to be cured " (*ibid.* 981ᵃ15–19). The final term, in fact, of the physician's analysis is a particular. And again, as sense proper is inseparable

---

[1] " Definition " ; but see p. 14.

from appetition of a particular object, so art produces
nothing without wish.[1] The ideal in the artist's mind is,
though rationalised, still a φάντασμα, and in the practical
sphere imagination cannot be parted from appetition.
Aristotle never quite explains how the form, which is
universal, is particularised in appetition and action,[2] but
his whole doctrine of art and conduct becomes unintelligible
if we forget that despite his sometimes misleading language
his problem is not with a universal and a particular which
are first separate and then fused. For Aristotle—and
mutatis mutandis this is true of Plato too (cp. pp. 128–9)—
practical thought is one with the desire and the ability
to effect an end : it is not a purely theoretical knowledge
of what *is*, not a rule of which the purely intellectual grasp
leads without more ado to its application. No doubt the
union of thinking, desiring, and making, which τεχνή
essentially involves, is menaced by the threat of divorce,
as its precursor and lower analogue, the immediate oneness
of sense-appetition and reaction in the brutes, is not. For
the thinking of the artist is deliberative, and therefore
liable to error and disappointment. And the menace is
no doubt greater the more architectonic the art. But,
though it is grasp of a universal, the knowledge of the
master-craftsman, who does not work with his hands but
can teach his art, is something wholly different from the
mere theory of the man who " has the λόγος without the
experience." It implies as its inseparable complement
a trained insight—a kind of αἴσθησις—into the needs of a
particular situation, and a trained habit of eager and
effective response. And in that again, if art is compared
not with the theorising of the mere doctrinaire but with
true theoretical thinking, lies the limitation upon which
it depends. Barred from the realms of free speculation, the
artist dwells amid particulars that come to be and perish,

---

[1] Βούλησις, the highest and purely human form of ὄρεξις.
[2] See pp. 147 ff. and note 3, p. 211.

his thinking sunk in sense and enslaved to desire : but, if he renounce his masters, he is impotent.[1]

3. GOODNESS OF CHARACTER AND THE MEAN

Aristotle frequently compares and contrasts making and doing. In fact he treats moral conduct largely as the final stage of practical activity, which art exists to subserve. The relation of the two is easily intelligible if we remember that for Aristotle as for Plato ethics and politics constitute a single study. For them the distinction between individual, social, and political action is minimal. In the Greek democratic city-state civic tradition controlled the general lines of education, and every citizen, whatever his trade, was economically a shareholder in the commonwealth, and divided with his fellows the burdens of military service and of political and judicial office. Finding full scope in the state, he looked neither beyond it to a wider community, nor to any loosely affiliated body within it—neither, for example, to a catholic church nor to a purely professional association—for the exercise of his practical activities. There was nothing to occasion a conflict of loyalties, to hinder a nearly complete co-incidence of the man and the citizen. It is this ideal which Aristotle is interpreting when he maintains that

---

[1] On the whole, Aristotle does not distinguish the artist, in the modern sense of the term, from the craftsman. He does not conceive of an aesthetic activity which is self-justifying and *sui generis*. The sculptor, the composer, even the poet, are not to him men who actualise a universal vision in imaginative creation of the individual—in *free* imaginative creation, which has not, at least as its immediate aim, the altering of an object other than itself. Perhaps the reason—or it may be but a symptom—is this. Aristotle conceives imagination as that into which sense-perception develops. He does not, on the whole, think of both sense-perception and imagination as arising out of mere presentation (see p. 117, note 1), and of imagination as therefore capable of an aesthetic development not in immediate connexion with sense-perception.

The reader will judge for himself how far Aristotle's theory of poetry requires the modification of this criticism ; see Appendix (B).

the state is a creation of nature—prior in fact to the family and to the individual as the whole is to the part. Man is a social animal by nature. He who cannot live in a community is a beast and not a man ; he who has no social need, because he is sufficient unto himself, is a God (see Pol. I, 2). Hence Aristotle regards the function of the statesman, because its end is the happiness of man, the political (social) animal, as at once the highest manifestation of moral conduct and the master art. Almost at the beginning of the *Nichomachean Ethics*[1] he writes : " It is the art of politics that ordains which of the sciences should be studied in a state, and which each class of citizens should learn and up to what point they should learn them ; and we see even the most highly esteemed of the arts to fall under this, *e.g.* strategy, household management, rhetoric ; now since politics uses the rest of the practical sciences, and since, again, it legislates as to what we are to do and what we are to abstain from, the end of this science must include those of the others, so that this end must be the good for man. For even if the end is the same for a single man and for a state, that of the state seems at all events something greater and more complete whether to attain or preserve ; though it is worth while to attain the end merely for one man, it is finer and more godlike to attain it for a nation or for city-states. These then being the ends at which our inquiry aims, it is political science."[2]

But when Aristotle abstracts and considers the basis of moral conduct in the individual, he tends perhaps to over-emphasise its difference from art. Up to a point they are closely analogous. Both can be taught, because both, unlike sense-perception, imply a habit acquired post-natally. In both this habit—ἕξις—develops from an

---

[1] Which is taken as authoritative for Aristotle's teaching in these sections: see pp. 263-4 ff.

[2] EN 1094ᵃ26 ff. The passage is largely inspired by Plato's *Politicus*.

innate potency which Aristotle calls " a potency of contraries," or " a rational potency," because, unlike the
a-rational tendencies of natural bodies, it is capable of
alternative realisation in two contrary directions, the one
good, the other bad : " Neither by nature nor contrary
to nature do the virtues of character arise in us ; rather
we are adapted by nature to receive them, and are made
perfect by habituation. . . . We get them by exercising
them, as also happens in the arts. . . . It is from playing
the lyre that both good and bad lyre-players are produced . . . otherwise there would have been no need of
a teacher, but all men would have been born good at their
craft. So too with the virtues : by doing the acts that we
do in our transactions with other men we become just or
unjust, and by doing the acts we do in the presence of
danger, and being habituated to feel fear or confidence,
we become brave or cowardly. Hence it makes a very great
difference—in fact *all* the difference—what kind of habits
we form from our very youth."[1] Thus, at its rawest
stage, the material out of which virtue of character is
made consists in certain ranges of susceptibility to impulse[2]
with which nature endows the appetitive soul of man.
Man is born capable of experiencing any degree of feeling
on a continuous scale, the contrary poles of which are,
e.g., lust for, and indifference to, certain tactual sensations,
natural confidence and fear, anger and phlegm, love and
hate, the hoarding and the spending instinct, etc. The
more elementary of these feeling-ranges are much the
same in all animals, but the extent of appetitive response
to them, which is relatively constant and automatic in a
beast, in a man varies on a continuous scale and is subject
to deliberate control. And the repeated action of this
control both modifies the extent to which the feeling will
recur, and also, according as it is well or ill exercised,

---

[1] The substance of EN II, 1.
[2] Analogous to a range of sensibilia, see pp. 105 ff.

creates those habits, or ἕξεις, which Aristotle calls virtues
or vices of character (ἦθος). For this reason the capacity
for varied reaction, flexible under control, is a rational
potency.

It follows from this doctrine that the series of acts by
which a virtuous ἕξις is developed are formally of the
same nature as those in which that ἕξις is subsequently
actualised ; but a really brave or just action can only be
done from a confirmed and stable habit.

It is here that art and conduct diverge. Art develops
by habitual response to appetition, but it is not *par
excellence* an affair of the passions, as conduct is. It acts
upon an external object, whereas the moral agent reacts
to and upon his own impulsive self. In both cases the
actualisation of subject and object is single and resides
in the object, but the object in the one case is the agent's
own character, in the other a product beyond the artist's
activity.[1] The artist is therefore judged good or bad
solely on the merits of his work : his morals are irrelevant
(cp. EN 1105ª26 ff.). Aristotle accordingly contrasts the
artist's labour as a mere process towards an external end
with conduct as a true activity throughout which the end
is always fully immanent (cp. p. 86). Yet, if this distinction is made more than relative, it is not really consonant
with Aristotle's view of conduct ; nor is it a wholly
plausible account of art. No doubt a good cobbler may
be a thorough scoundrel, and technical skill may be
perverted to a villainy the more effective ; but the more
a man's talents and interests are absorbed by the steady
direction of his energies in an important profession, the less
chance there is of his being a bad man.[2]

We shall only understand what conduct is when we

---

[1] Thus nature is a source of immanent but involuntary change, art
of change in something else, conduct of deliberate self-change.

[2] For a modification of this sharp opposition between art and conduct
see note 1, p. 163.

know precisely how reaction to feeling is controlled and habituated. But we must first observe the further development of the material which exists for the sake of this control. To begin with we must remember that those ranges of feeling that human flesh is heir to are feelings of pleasure and pain (see pp 122 ff.). " Pleasure is engrained in our life," says Aristotle (EN 1105ª3), and " The whole concern both of virtue and of political science is with pleasures and pains " (*ibid.* 1105ª10 ff.). Now one reason he adduces for the latter statement is that " It is on account of the pleasure that we do bad things, and on account of the pain that we abstain from noble ones " (*ibid.* 1104ᵇ9). In short, the good and the pleasant, identical as pursued by the beast, are for man divergent, and between them as a third possible object of pursuit appears the useful—that which is sought not for itself but as a means to the good or the pleasant. And the problem of conduct is set by the fact that these three objects of appetition may conflict. But we shall not solve it if we forget that the good and the pleasant have developed from a single germ. Pleasure for Aristotle necessarily accompanies all unimpeded activity, and it is a vital tenet of his ethic that conflict, when it occurs, is between ends which are never simply duty and pleasure, but always on the one hand a duty that, successfully performed, will inevitably be pleasant, and on the other a pleasure which will accompany some other suggested activity (cp. § 6). In fact Aristotle's other reason for the concernment of virtue with pain and pleasure is as follows : " We must take as a sign of ἕξεις of character the pleasure or pain that ensues on acts ; for the man who abstains from bodily pleasures and delights in this very fact is temperate, while the man who is annoyed at it is self-indulgent, and he who stands his ground against things that are terrible and delights in this, or at least is not pained, is brave, while the man who is pained is a coward " (*ibid.* 1104ᵇ4–8).

Indeed this is inevitable if reaction modifies the nature
of subsequently recurring feeling.

The material of conduct, then, as we now see it, is a
continuous range of pleasure-pain feelings, which covers
all degrees of intensity on a scale between certain limits
set by human nature. These feelings are subject to the
formative control of response in action, and this response
too varies on a scale. Hence any degree on the one scale
can be correlated with any degree on the other. Now
the ἕξις of the appetitive soul—the soul which feels
and reacts—will be virtuous if it is such as to issue
in acts in which a right ratio (λόγος) correlates response
and feeling, and so renders the degree of response-and-
feeling a mean between excess and defect. But the agent's
task is not simply to correlate response and feeling rightly,
but to do so in relation to his own particular circumstances
and nature. And this he can only do by looking to the
ideally wise agent as his norm of conduct. Hence the
rule of conduct which Aristotle teaches may be thus
expressed : " So act that you, a man of a certain nature
faced with a particular set of circumstances, may relate
your response to your feeling in the same ratio as that in
which the ideally wise agent would relate his response to
his feeling in analogous but ideal circumstances." This
is the essence of Aristotle's famous doctrine that virtue of
character is " a habit of decision, consisting in a mean,
which is (a) relative to us,[1] and (b) determined by a λόγος,
i.e. the λόγος by which the man of practical wisdom
would determine " (ibid. 1106ᵇ36). A single precisely
right action lies between all degrees of excessive feeling
and response in one direction, and all degrees of corresponding defect in the other.

This is not the doctrine of *aurea mediocritas* into which
it was later misconstrued, but merely Aristotle's expression
of that symmetry or measure which the Greeks associated

---

[1] *I.e.* determined by the agent's individual nature and circumstances.

with all values.[1] Aristotle's illustrations from diet and the arts (*ibid*. II, 6), and his statement that " Though virtue is by definition a mean, yet with regard to what is best and right it is an extreme " (*ibid*. 1107ᵃ6), leave no doubt as to his meaning. Nor is it an attempt to treat morality in purely quantitative terms. For a good state of character—of man's appetitive soul, which Aristotle doubts whether to call rational or irrational (cf. *ibid*. I, 13) —never exists by itself. It is either : (*a*) an abstraction for purposes of exposition from within the completely good soul of the ideally wise man of action ; or (*b*) a state of obedience to more or less external authority, which characterises every adolescent and some men for all their lives. Thus it always presupposes a virtuous habit of the rational soul, either (*a*) in the mature agent himself, or (*b*) in his preceptor. In the first part of EN Aristotle, who writes to aid the statesman in the business of moral education, is thinking chiefly of (*b*).[2] Hence he describes the proportion governing the mean as a right rule (λόγος) which youth takes on trust from the mature wisdom embodied in its teachers. At present we see this wisdom as a merely assumed external efficient cause. Until the pupil has become his own master, and his actions freely express his own whole nature—until, that is, he has grasped the reason for the rules that he has so far taken for granted as facts, and practical wisdom has become immanent in him—we cannot learn from him what moral conduct is. In short, the doctrine of the mean is not, as has been often supposed, Aristotle's last word on morality. It is a definition of conduct taken at an immature or an abstract level—a definition of something which *is* only δυνάμει, or so far merely as it *is* only δυνάμει.[3]

---

[1] It is also the inevitable sequel of his doctrine of sense, see pp. 106 ff.

[2] Though he is sometimes ambiguous.

[3] See also p. 107, note 1.

4. PRACTICAL WISDOM AND MORAL RESPONSIBILITY[1]

Virtue of character is a good ἕξις of the appetitive soul, and appetition is inseparable from sense. Practical wisdom (φρόνησις) is a good ἕξις of the practically rational soul, which is concerned with human good and evil; and consequently it is not something added to, or even fused with, virtuous character, but its completion and culmination. Therefore φρόνησις will be a more complex development of those two inseparable moments, each all-pervasive of the whole, which constitute the soul of sense and appetite. Accordingly φρόνησις is, or implies,[2] (a) an intuitive grasp by νοῦς (see p. 213), involving developed φαντασία, of what is the life of good action—practical happiness—as a whole; and (b) a desire (βούλησις) for that happiness. Moreover, for animal sense the end was simple and the reactive movement immediate, but for practical man the end is a complex ideal not immediately feasible as a whole. Hence φρόνησις is also (a i) a deliberative activity analogous to the thinking of the physician : it analyses ideal happiness into constituent means, which, the order of discovery reversed, become successive stages of actualisation. Now this deliberative process develops the universal from a comparatively indeterminate and general ideal towards a concrete and practicable conclusion ; and mere theory, technical or moral, effects nothing, since all acts are particular acts done here and now. Hence the deliberative analysis must (a ii) terminate in a particular ; the man of practical wisdom must descend, as the experienced physician descends, into the sphere of discriminative sense-perception. And that is to say that the general wish for happiness will (b i) grow gradually determinate as deliberation proceeds, finally become concrete in (b ii) the appetition

---

[1] See particularly EN III, 5.
[2] See following note.

of an immediately feasible singular, and issue in a particular act.[1]

Thus the wisdom of his teachers, which as a right rule directed the adolescent, becomes immanent in the mature φρόνιμος, the man of perfected practical wisdom. As the complete plan of the good life for himself and his circle— for all his fellow-citizens, if he is a statesman—it is at once the final and the efficient cause of his activity and the form which makes him what he is. And the object in which his activity and its object singly actualise is not the external product of an art, but himself and his fellows, with whom he is one in substance.

But there are certain comparatively external advantages which are yet indispensable means to practical happiness ; and these are not wholly within the control of the moral agent. Some measure of virtue can be achieved by all who are not born morally impotent. Virtue is durable ; the good man is steadfast amid the vicissitudes of life. Vice and virtue depend on the use rather than the possession of external advantages—"Where virtue is, these are more virtuous," as Othello says of Desdemona's graces. Yet if a man die too young, or live hopelessly diseased—even hideously ugly ; if he suffer the misfortunes of a Priam, misfortunes beyond that

---

[1] Though in 1143[a]8 Aristotle says " φρόνησις issues commands, since its end is what ought to be done or not done," he generally defines it in cognitive terms. For its three cognitive moments cp. 1142[b]33 : " The end of which practical wisdom is the true apprehension " ; and 1141[b]13– 16 : " The man who is without qualification good at deliberating [i.e. the φρόνιμος] is he who is capable of aiming according to calculation at the best for man of things attainable by action. Nor is φρόνησις concerned with universals only—it must also recognise the particulars ; for it is practical, and practice is concerned with particulars." Aristotle attributes grasp of the definition of the good—i.e. of the end which forms the premiss of the deliberative thinking—to practical νοῦς (rational intuition). Practical νοῦς is thus the moment of immediacy within φρόνησις from which deliberation starts, and the term νοῦς is sometimes even loosely extended to cover the perceptive grasp of the particular in which deliberation terminates ; cp. 1143[a]35. See also p. 213.

adversity through which nobility shines the brighter ; if, though through no fault of his own, he be too poor to be generous, too humbly situated to win honour, too much isolated to enjoy the friendship of other men ; then he cannot be said to experience the full activity of practical happiness. Hence the categories of morality—the sphere of particulars and of merely general rules—are not absolute. Right is what furthers happiness, wrong what hinders it ; but happiness may be beyond a man's reach, and it may even accrue to him in a measure more than proportionate to his effort. Aristotle—and all sound moralists have followed him—faces the fact that moral judgment upon the individual can only be relative and approximate, because it is passed upon a subject which does not contain within itself all the conditions of its own being. Moral conduct is a man's making of himself, and the stuff he fashions is never wholly his own creation. The line dividing a self, which perpetually expands and contracts in a social and material medium, from circumstances which we choose to regard as external to it, can never be rigidly drawn. We can never finally distinguish within the active life that commands our admiration as a whole the agent's own contribution, for which moral praise is due, from the gifts of fortune—or, if we prefer it, from the grace of God. Hence Aristotle, writing primarily not as a theorist but to aid the practical statesman, falls back in his treatment of responsibility upon the particular act to find the test of moral merit. Yet in doing so he is perfectly consistent with his general principles, for it is the ἐνέργεια and not the mere ἕξις of virtue that is crucial : " As in the Olympic Games it is not the most beautiful and the strongest that are crowned, but those who compete (for it is some of these that are victorious), so those who act win, and rightly win, the noble and good things in life " (*ibid.* 1099ª3 ff.).

The agent, then, is responsible, and the fit subject of

praise and blame, so far as the source of his particular act
lies within himself, *i.e.* so far as it is done from deliberate
decision (προαίρεσις). When Aristotle defines choice as
" either appetitive reason (νοῦς), or ratiocinative appetition," and adds that " such a source of action is a man "
(*ibid.* 1139ᵇ4), προαίρεσις seems to be equivalent to
φρόνησις, taken in the broad sense given it above, but
defined with special reference to the particular act. When
he limits προαίρεσις within the wider sphere of wish
(βούλησις), calling it " the deliberate appetition of things
within our power,"[1] he is further emphasising the necessity
of making the test of moral conduct a man's reaction to
the particular moral situation rather than the whole
general plan, which governs his life, but remains always
in large part unfulfilled. And the same motive inspires
his opposition of προαίρεσις as choice of means to βούλησις
as wish for ends.[2]

Yet Aristotle's attitude to the famous paradox of
Socrates is enough to show that he intends no ultimate
divorce between particular act and governing ideal. He
replies to the Socratic generalisation that vice is ignorance
by narrowing the scope of its application. Socrates is
right, inasmuch as in the vicious man the whole plan of
his life is wrong, his whole vision of the good obscured :
" The originative causes of things done are the ends they
are aimed at ; but the man whose moral nature has been
corrupted by pleasures or pains forthwith fails to see any
such cause—to see that for the sake of this, or because of
this, he ought to choose and do whatever he chooses and
does ; for vice is destructive of the originative cause of
action."[3]

It is true, in short, that a man may be helplessly bound

[1] Thus making it almost equivalent to volition : *ibid.* 1113ᵃ10.
[2] Despite the fact that means in the sphere of conduct are for him
essentially constituent of their ends ; see *ibid.* II, 3 and 4. He does not
elsewhere so confine προαίρεσις.
[3] *Ibid.* 1140ᵇ16 ff.   See also 1144ᵇ17 ff. and 1145ᵇ23 ff.

in this ἕξις of immoral ignorance, wherein the end is totally
perverted, and evil has become his good and his pleasure.
But, on the other hand, the ἕξις itself has been built up
by a succession of particular acts which *were* deliberate,
and it is only of these formative acts, which do not yet
characterise a man as fully bad, that we can ask how a man
can know the right and do the wrong. Here alone is the
sphere of moral conflict.

5. MORAL CONFLICT

Aristotle analyses the particular act of sin against
knowledge in the single but typical case of ἀκρασία, incontinence, or lack of self-control in the sphere of tactual
pleasures and pains (*ibid.* VII, 1–10). He meets the
contradiction, which seems implied if we admit, as in some
sense we must, that a man can do evil while knowing[1]
the good, with his distinction of knowledge as a mere ἕξις
from knowledge as an ἐνέργεια (see p. 104). Where the
end is fully known and fully desired—*i.e.* known and
desired as a universal end concrete in a singular instance
which is a feasible means to its realisation—action must
follow immediately and without question. *E.g.* if I know
in general that solid food is good-and-pleasant for man,
and in general desire it as such ; and if I also know in
particular that this I have before me is solid food, and
that I am a man requiring food ; then I immediately eat
it. Action follows immediately as the conclusion of this
practical syllogism, because its major premiss is the object
not of theoretical thinking, but of a thought that is one
with wish : " Thought by itself alone moves nothing, but
only the practical thought that aims at an end " (*ibid.*
1139ª36). But the good and the pleasant may diverge ;
i.e. what, if unqualified, is good, becomes bad in the

---

[1] It must be remembered that " knowing " throughout this discussion
means *practical* knowing.

presence of a greater good with which it competes as an alternative end. It then retains of its goodness only the pleasant character, and it may even rob the greater good of its own attendant pleasure. If this occurs, the major premiss becomes dual : *e.g.* sweet things are (*a*), *qua* injurious, to be avoided, but (*b*) *qua* pleasant, to be tasted. And the minor bifurcates accordingly : this sweet thing is (*a* i) *qua* injurious, to be avoided, but (*b* i) *qua* pleasant, to be tasted. Here the ἕξις of appetitive knowledge in which the major consists can actualise in only one of the minor premises. (*a*) and (*b*) are not mutually exclusive alternatives either as wish or as knowledge, but (*a* i) and (*b* i) are. Hence when the incontinent man eats the sweet thing, he acts against (*a*) and not (*a* i)—against what is only a ἕξις and not an ἐνέργεια of knowledge.

This account of incontinence is still based on analysis of the particular act,[1] but in the light of Aristotle's theory of evil it is tolerably clear. He holds, as we saw, that perfect substance is perfect form, whereas in composite things their matter—though it is that in them which is potential and unreal—stands out inevitably as not a mere privation but a positive constituent, which complements form within the composite (see p. 11). To be a harmony of form and matter is the best that a particular thing can attain. Now if form and matter do not harmonise, the resulting imperfection differs at different levels. When nature errs, her work is simply something undeveloped and incomplete. When the artist fails to conquer his medium, and the form of the statue does not fully actualise the bronze, the material element merely remains so far dead and external to the form. But when the moral agent fashions himself, the material he works upon is already vitalised, even already in some degree rationalised ; and

---

[1] Precisely how the universal fuses with the particular in the practical syllogism is not very clear—in fact it may seem doubtful whether Aristotle was well advised to treat practical thinking syllogistically ; cp. Chap. X, § 2 (B) and especially note 3, p. 211.

if he fails to conquer it, it will rise against him in active opposition, a self within the self. And if the incontinent man gives up the struggle, the lower self becomes dominant: no longer a mere rival, it subordinates to its own form the capacities which goodness has developed. *Corruptio optimi pessima* : the really bad man is a perverted, not simply a defective, moral agent.[1] The last words of this section of EN are : " Brutishness in degenerate animals is a less evil than vice, though more alarming ; for it is not that the better part has been perverted, as in man—they have no better part. Thus it is like comparing a lifeless thing with a living in respect of badness ; for the badness of that which has no originative source of movement is always less harmful, and reason (νοῦς) is an originative source. . . . A bad man will do ten thousand times as much evil as a beast " (1150ᵃ1 ff.).

On the whole, then, Aristotle is neither a determinist nor a libertarian. It is hard to know how much to stress his view that there is a real indeterminacy in things—he had not full insight into the problem—but at his best he interprets freedom as self-determination : " In a household the freemen are least at liberty to act at random, but all things or most things are already ordained for them, while the slaves and animals do little for the common good, and for the most part live at random."[2]

6. PLEASURE

In the main, Aristotle's treatment of pleasure[3] accords with this doctrine. He mediates between the hedonism of Eudoxus and the asceticism of Speusippus, developing

---

[1] Cp. also pp. 160–1. Plato's doctrine of evil and conflict is the same in principle ; cp. p. 45. In *Republic*, IX, he describes the tyrannical man as a precise perversion of the man who is monarch of himself.

[2] Met. 1075ᵃ19 ff. Cp. p. 172.

[3] See EN VII, 2–14, and X 1–5. The two accounts are not perfectly consistent.

L

but also criticising the teaching of Plato's *Philebus* (cp. pp. 59 ff.). Pleasure inseparably accompanies unimpeded activity, " supervening upon it as the bloom of youth does upon those in the flower of their age."[1] *Per se* pleasure is utterly indeterminate. It has no quality of its own and cannot be abstracted from activity. Hence pleasures are good or bad solely according to the specific difference of their activities, and an activity is intensified by its own proper pleasure, hindered by the alien pleasure of another activity. But activity is not a process of change,[2] and all pleasure, because it is inseparable from activity,[3] is complete at any and every moment of itself: " Pleasure is a whole, and at no time can one find a pleasure whose form will be made more complete if the pleasure lasts longer. Hence, too, it is not a process of change. For every process (*e.g.* building) takes time and is for the sake of an end, and is complete only when it has made what it aims at. It is complete, therefore, only in the whole time or at that final moment. In their parts and during the time they occupy, all processes are incomplete, and are different in kind from the whole process and from each other. For the fitting together of the stones is different from the fluting of the column, and these are both different from the making of the temple " (*ibid.* 1174^{a}17 ff.). Similarly, " It is not possible to move save in time, but it *is* possible to be pleased ; for that which takes place

---

[1] *Ibid.* 1174^{b}31–33. Activity is already by definition perfect, and Aristotle may perhaps mean that pleasure is not, as Plato had made it, an ingredient—a matter to be informed—of a whole in which pleasure and activity are combined, but just what unhindered experience is so far as it is immediately felt, and not analysed in terms of its objective features.

[2] As Plato had supposed ; see pp. 61–2. Cp. also p. 86.

[3] The real basis even of the abnormal pleasures, which are subject to intensification by contrast with pain—those, *e.g.* which accompany gradual restoration to health, or a course of debauchery sought as an escape from pain—is a real pleasure inseparably accompanying the normal, still unimpeded, function of the sound remainder of the organism. They are only false and bad so far as they qualify the diseased organism as a whole (EN VII, 12 and 14).

in the ' now ' is a whole " (*ibid.* ᵇ8). " We may *become*
pleased quickly . . . we cannot *be* pleased quickly "
(*ibid.* 1173ᵃ34).

Aristotle then raises a further question : " How is it
that no one is continuously pleased ? Certainly all human
things are incapable of continuous activity. Therefore
pleasure also is not continuous " (*ibid.* 1175ᵃ3–5). " There
is no one thing that is always pleasant, because our nature
is not simple, but there is another element in us as well,
inasmuch as we are perishable creatures ; so that if the
one element does something, this is unnatural to the other
nature, and when the two elements are evenly balanced,
what is done seems neither painful nor pleasant ; for if
the nature of anything were simple, the same action
would always be most pleasant to it. That is why God
always enjoys a single and simple pleasure ;[1] for there is
not only an activity of movement but an activity of
immobility, and pleasure is found more in rest than in
movement. But " Change in all things is sweet," as the
poet says, because of some vice ; for as it is the vicious
man that is changeable, so the nature that needs change is
vicious ; for it is not simple nor good " (*ibid.* 1154ᵇ20 ff.).

Yet this doctrine of pleasure and activity hardly stands
criticism. No doubt all human experience takes the form
of a " specious present," a diversified lapse or duration to
some extent held together and grasped as a unity. Doubtless, too, there are moments in life which seem to transcend
time, to lie between no past and future. Yet if conduct
approaches this divine consummation more nearly than
craftsmanship, and speculation than conduct, none the
less there can surely be no human activity in which the
end is fully immanent throughout—*i.e.* no activity which
is human only because it is intermittent and not because
it is in some degree a process. And there is one very weak
spot in Aristotle's argument. He distinguishes a " whole "

---

[1] *Per contra* Plato ; see p. 61.

from a mere " collection," as a totality in which the order
of constituents is necessary and not indifferent (Met. V, 26).
Hence he presumably regards the atomic " now " as a
whole, because it contains an end and a beginning in one.[1]
But the atomic " now " can have no possible content :
it cannot be made equivalent to that which is not in time
at all.   Aristotle is in fact confusing it with the specious
present, within which analysis *would* reveal duration.

7. THE PARTICULAR VIRTUES [2]

Plato had allotted four cardinal virtues to the soul and
analogously to the state, which reflects the structure of
the soul : courage belongs to the spirited part, wisdom to
the rational ; temperance in the desiring part makes
possible that harmonious co-operation of the three parts
(cp. p. 45) in diversified function, in which justice consists.
Aristotle counters the Platonic emphasis on the unity of
reason in all virtue, first by dividing reason in two
(cp. pp. 128 ff.), and then by analysing Greek civilisation
and the human types[3] which express it.   Φρόνησις is a
single jewel of many facets, but analysis necessitates
abstraction ; it is a loosening of the elements within the
whole that significantly links them.   It is, then, not
surprising to find that Aristotle treats the particular
virtues, not with special reference to the intelligence which
they involve, but as virtues of character which illustrate
the doctrine of the mean.

Only a rough order can be traced.   The materials of
courage and temperance are those susceptibilities to
pleasure and pain in the crude and general form in which
man shares them with the beasts.[4]   Courage, the mean

---

[1] And presumably a mathematical point would be a " whole " for
the same reason (see p. 110, note 1).   Unfortunately neither has a
middle ; see p. 228.

[2] EN III, 6–V, 11.

[3] Taken largely from the New Comedy.

[4] It is not obvious why courage precedes temperance.

between cowardice and rashness, is displayed in its normal (ideal) form by the officer in the citizen army who faces death, the supreme pain, for honour's sake—the honour of his own deed, even if it bring him present pain and the loss of his life, of which he well knows the value, and the honour of his country, with which he is one in substance even if he does not live to see her glory vindicated. The other ranks of the citizen army, who fight for fear of public disgrace or even merely of their officers, have a less degree of this courage, and there are four inferior types which deviate from true bravery : in the courage of the professional soldier, and the confidence inspired by blind pluck, a sanguine temperament, or actual ignorance of the situation, grasp of the true end gradually fades and disappears. Aristotle has been criticised for exalting a merely " physical " courage, but to him the truest bravery is the most intelligent, and if courage is to be distinguished from higher virtues which imply it, he is probably right in seeking its differentia where he does. He is bound to find his ideal types in the full and healthy excellence of man's moral nature rather than in the *tour de force* by which the spirit overcomes the weakness of a flesh that gives it no support. Less plausibly does he confine courage to the battlefield ; yet that is consistent with his view that virtue depends partly upon opportunity.

Temperance, lying between profligacy and a seldom found insensibility, is again narrowly confined to pleasures of touch and taste. The " mean " doctrine has been said to break down here,[1] but insensibility is an obvious defect in potentiality for happiness, and in a less normal people than the Greeks self-repression may easily become a vice.

The materials of the next virtues, liberality and munificence, belong to man as a legal owner of property. Here pleasure and pain depend on the distribution of material possessions. But at the next level honour is concerned,

---

[1] Cp. Ross, *Aristotle*, p. 207.

and man's aim is the maintenance of social position and
dignity. The appropriate virtues are greatness of soul
(μεγαλοψυχία)[1] and the proper attitude to ambition. The
former is " a sort of crown of the virtues." The great-
souled man " thinks himself worthy of great things and
is worthy of them, being good and marked by greatness
in every virtue. Chiefly he claims honour, but in accordance with his desert, and at great honours conferred by
good men he will be moderately pleased, accepting them
because they have nothing greater to bestow ; but honour
from casual people and on trivial grounds he will utterly
despise. He will be little moved by good or ill fortune,
for not even towards honour does he bear himself as if it
were a very great thing. He does not run trifling risks, but
in great danger he is unsparing of his life, knowing that
life may be too dearly bought. He confers benefits—the
mark of a superior—but is ashamed of receiving them and
apt to confer greater in return. Though he never asks a
favour or recalls a wrong, he remembers the service he
has done, but not that which he has received.[2] He is
dignified towards the great, but unassuming towards the
middle classes. Open in hate and love, and dependent on
none save a friend, he tells the truth bluntly save when he
speaks in irony to the vulgar. His possessions will be
beautiful rather than useful, for he suffices to himself.
His step is slow, his voice deep, his utterance level."[3] The
portrait is not wholly pleasing. Yet it fails artistically
rather than in psychological penetration. Plato might
have drawn it and embodied the same essential truth

---

[1] Or perhaps " proper pride," since it lies between vanity and humility.
[2] See EN IX, 7. A benefactor loves those he benefits more than he is
loved in return ; every man loves his own handiwork more than he
would be loved by it if it came alive, and the beneficiary is the benefactor's handiwork, beloved by the benefactor because to him it is the
actualisation of himself—also because to him it is both something
noble, and loved, as a mother loves her child, for the labour it has cost ;
whereas to the recipient of the benefit it is merely advantageous.
[3] EN IV, 7 and 8, abbreviated.

without giving offence. If it seems a caricature, we must
remember that the magnificent man has full self-knowledge
and is at the same time wholly without self-consciousness
in the bad sense of the term.

Good temper brings us to the virtues of social intercourse,
in which pleasure and pain are further refined—friendliness,
truthfulness, and ready wit—and with a glance at bashful-
ness, a virtue only in youth, we pass to justice. In a
broad (Platonic) sense justice is another name for the
whole of virtue, with special emphasis laid upon the
relation between man and man. For Aristotle conceives
that, ideally, the law would enforce in every situation
the action appropriate to virtue. As a particular virtue
justice means, roughly, honesty in the sphere covered by
Attic civil law,[1] and covetousness is the relative excess.
Aristotle's treatment is elaborated rather obscurely in
terms of mathematical proportion. In his zeal for concrete
fact he tends to forget that the Law has a curious history,
and that the details of legal procedure require a great
deal of interpretation before they can become data for
the moral philosopher. He appends an essay on economic
" justice " with no obviously moral bearing, in which he
traces the origin of currency and the dependence of price
upon demand,[2] and with some remarks upon equity (*ibid.*
V, 10), which corrects the inevitably universal and abstract
letter of the law in the spirit of the legislator, he passes
to friendship.

8. FRIENDSHIP

Friendship,[3] the binding force of states, is an activity
implying virtue. It is even beyond virtue, for in perfect

[1] Which covered much now assigned to criminal law. Hence honour
and personal safety are among the external goods—called by Aristotle
" divisible " in the sense that more for A means less for B—which
provide particular justice with its materials.

[2] He ignores, however, the cost of production. See *ibid*. V, 5.

[3] Φιλία at its highest is love : it covers all attraction between two
human beings. It is discussed in EN, VIII and IX.

friendship, which exists for the sake of " the Good," the relation of man to man, the especial mark of justice, is transcended. The whole of each related term—the whole character and personality of each friend—is involved, and relation passes into identity. A true friend is a second self, and in his friendships the good man expresses his relation to himself.[1] Loving life, and living in consistent sympathy of aim with himself, he desires and does what is good for the sake of his true self, *i.e.* the thinking element in him which makes him the individual man he is.[2] Such a self is not exclusive, and such self-love is not selfishness : " If a man were always anxious that he himself above all things should act justly, temperately, etc., and in general strove always to secure for himself scope to act honourably, no one would call him selfish or blame him " (*ibid.* 1168^{b}25 ff.). In friendships not fully reciprocal the lover actualises himself in the beloved, who is relatively passive (cp. p. 154, note 2) ; but in perfect friendship each friend enjoys the other's love as a common effort to secure a common good, an activity undivided from his own. Moreover, to be happy is to be aware of an activity which is good and therefore intrinsically pleasant, and to be aware of it as one's own activity. But self-consciousness in practical life is still a by-product (cp. p. 112) ; it is easier to be fully aware of others and their actions than to divide oneself into agent and spectator. Hence, though the good man is self-sufficing, his self-sufficiency is extended and strengthened, not diminished and made dependent, by friendship. But he cannot so love many people.

Friendship for the sake of advantage, and friendship for

---

[1] This is Aristotle's criticism of the analogy of individual and state which Plato had worked out in terms of justice ; cp. p. 152.

[2] See *ibid.* 1166^{a}22 ff. Φιλία thus helps to bridge the gulf between practical wisdom and the speculative life in which man fully realises himself in loving and knowing God. For that doctrine and its difficulties see the next chapter.

pleasure's sake, are inferior approximations to the perfect type of φιλία. Neither is possible between utterly bad men, but both are relatively impermanent because less of the friends' personality is concerned : union becomes again mere relation of terms, and little more than justice is involved. Both may be extended to several people at once, but friendship for the sake of pleasure is the less sordid, and it does at least, like perfect friendship, necessitate a life spent in common.[1]

9. POLITICS

Aristotle's *Politics* contains several sets of lectures, and some of them are fragmentary.[2] But no other work of his displays more clearly the vast masses of fact which he mastered and analysed in order both to criticise and to complete the broad outline of Platonic theory. In history and politics he is as acute and comprehensive an observer as he is in the animal world. We can here only sketch his political views as a part of his whole system, but scarcely a chapter of the *Politics* has failed directly or indirectly to influence subsequent political thought.

We have already seen (pp. 136 ff.) that for Aristotle as for Plato the state exists by nature as the real *prius* of the individual, and that in consequence the main function of government is to promote the εὐδαιμονία of the citizens by making them virtuous : " Those may be expected to lead the best life who are governed in the best manner of which their circumstances admit " (Pol. 1323ᵃ17).

Aristotle, like Plato, conceives political philosophy as normative, and the construction of an ideal state as an

---

[1] Aristotle's account of the three types of φιλία derives from Plato's *Lysis*.

[2] And probably written at different periods of his life and thought. The *a priori* and empirical elements do not seem in complete harmony, and Books VII and VIII on the ideal state were very likely composed before IV–VI, which deal with actual constitutions : see pp. 265 ff.

essential part of its task. He agrees too that in the ideal
state the naturally better[1] rules the naturally worse for
the good—and the freedom—of the whole state. But he
distinguishes sharply the statesman's activity from the
philosopher's (cp. pp. 129 ff.), and he takes the view that
Plato has over-simplified the structure of the state. To
give to the state the unity of the sentient organism,
which feels as its own the pains and pleasures of each
several member, Plato had allowed no differentiation below
the three classes of husbandmen, warriors, and rulers ; and
within the two latter classes he had abolished the family
and private property as a menace to the loyalty of the
citizen. In the *Republic*, justice, scarcely distinguished
from friendship, culminates in a single φιλία in which
love of self, kinsman, friend, and city is one undivided
passion. Aristotle replies that the strength of love depends
on limitation, and that the extension of family feeling to
coincide with patriotism could only result in its proportionate dilution. The state is " a community of com-
munities." Man takes to himself a wife and a slave, being
fitted by nature to rule both of them ; his wife as his
delegate within the household, for she can deliberate ; his
slave, who can only obey, as " a living tool for the conduct
of life," whose inferior natural function is to serve a master
for their mutual benefit. Several families unite to form a
village, several villages to constitute a state, which
" comes to be for the sake of life, but *is* for the sake of
the good life."[2] The state is like all works of nature and
man : its quantitative proportions must be precisely right.
It must be neither too small to be self-sufficient, nor too
great to be controlled : " Of an exceeding great multitude

---

[1] The reader of the *Politics* must always remember what human goodness means to Aristotle.

[2] Pol. 1252^{b}29. Aristotle is here describing the genesis of the state
within history as we know it. In *reality* the state, in which alone the
individual is actualised, is prior to him. Aristotle maintains that
ultimately the actual is prior to the potential temporally as well as
really ; see note 1, p. 92.

who shall be the general, or who the herald save a Stentor ? " (*ibid.* 1236^{b}5). The ideal territorial conditions can be determined accordingly.

The classes necessary to the proper functioning of the state are the serfs, the husbandmen, the mechanics, the traders, the warriors, the rich who bear costly public burdens, the rulers and officials, and the priests. But the warriors are those who are to become officials and rulers in middle age, and priests when they grow old ; and they alone are to own the land. Hence the four latter classes, which are thus genetically one, are the sole organic parts of the state ; the remainder, though they differ in degree of importance, are mere *sine quibus non* of the well-being of the citizen community.[1] Aristotle implies that the happiness of the state requires an order of external goods, which descends through the slave—" the living tool "—to the physical features of the city's locality. This order is analogous to that according to which within rational man the nutritive ranks below the sensory-appetitive soul, and itself requires an external nutriment. Some men in fact are by nature inferior in virtue to others, just as in different degrees obedience is the virtue of children and women. Aristotle does not regard their common rationality as qualifying men for political equality, though he concedes that the son of a natural slave need not be one himself, and he condemns enslavement by right of conquest.

He does not, like Plato, favour a communistic system. Private property affords an extension of personality, and is not only a source of legitimate pleasure but also a means to generosity. Its *use*, however, should be common, and its excessive accumulation is an evil. But the remedy for this evil is not to equalise property by legislation which the mere increase of the population will nullify ; the

[1] The doctrine is that of the *Republic*, save that the rulers do not lead the speculative life in old age. Presumably Aristotle's priests do not know God as the philosopher knows him : cp. Ch. VIII, § 1.

solution is "rather to educate the nobler natures not to desire more, and to prevent the lower from getting more" (*ibid.* 1267^{b}5). Sharing the usual Greek view of trade as an illiberal pursuit, he even regards barter as less natural than use, though inevitable up to a point. The exchange of goods for money, which leads to usury, seems to him definitely unnatural, despite the convenience of currency. It must be remembered that economic organisations with large resources of invested capital were no more necessary than representative government in the small city-states of Greece. The public spirit of a few rich individuals could take the place of the one, and primary self-government of the other, to an extent impossible in the cumbrous nation-states of our day.

In actual states qualification for citizenship varies, but in general—and reasonably—the citizen is he who can claim a share in legislative and judicial functions. Yet if a man greater and better than his fellows should arise, it were well that he alone should rule. The ideal state is in fact monarchical, and the monarch's care of his subjects reflects paternal love. But the ideal monarch, as Plato had held in the *Politicus*, will rule as the embodiment of law. Though Aristotle distinguishes the legislative, the judicial, and the executive elements in the state, Athenian politics had taught him how dangerous the process of particularising the law's generality by *ad hoc* enactment could become, and he minimises the executive function.

Monarchy perverted becomes—as in Persia—tyranny, which is analogous to a dominion of master over slave for the sole benefit of the master. Failing the wise autocrat, let the best men of the state form an aristocracy, reflecting the household ruled by a wise master partly through his wife. Aristocracy perverted becomes oligarchy, the rule of a rich minority, sometimes found in actual fact ameliorated by good breeding and education ; and this answers to the rule in a household of a master who interferes by force where he should not, or of an heiress who rules by " virtue " of her wealth. The most practicable ideal for actual states is polity—government by a large middle class, based on free birth and a moderate property qualification. This reflects the friendship of brothers, and its perversion, democracy, is like a family where the head of the house is weak, and all the sons claim an equal share of control irrespective of age or merit.[1]

Thus polity is the worst of the good constitutions; tyranny the worst, and democracy the least bad, of the perversions. Polity is possible where " there naturally exists a large warrior class able to rule and to obey in turn according to a law which gives office to the well-to-do in proportion to their desert."[2] If a large middle class holds the balance between rich and poor, they will mistrust each other too much to combine against it, and polity thus has the merit of " consisting in a mean."[3] To democracy, which is based on the idea of liberty and equality for all, Aristotle grants the possible advantages that a number of ordinary men may be collectively better than a few good ones, and less liable to be all moved by passion at once; and, further, that if the people are allowed to choose and dismiss their rulers, it is at all events the consumer who is made the judge. On the whole, his view of democracy, which elaborates Plato's rather than differs from it, is that it illustrates the resistance of matter to form—it is something indeterminate rather than actively vicious—and his contention that democracy is the least bad, tyranny the worst, of the perverted constitutions, accords with his own theory of evil in EN and with Plato's (see pp. 148 ff.).

---

[1] With this order of constitutions and their domestic analogues compare the order of constitutions and corresponding *individuals* in *Republic*, IX. See also *Politicus*, 297c ff., where Plato is nearer to Aristotle.

[2] Pol. 1288ª12. Aristotle has in mind the Athenian constitution of 411, in which the 5000 hoplites dominated.

[3] That the worst of the good constitutions illustrates the mean *par excellence*, confirms the view of the mean taken in Chap. VII, § 3.

In an unfinished sketch of ideal education (Pol. VIII), Aristotle observes that the training of youth is commonly left in private hands, and that opinion differs as to whether it should be intellectual, moral, or utilitarian. His own view is that the education of the ideal citizen will be the concern of the state. For the citizen belongs not to himself but to the state, and education is a training for the practice of virtue—the sole end for which the state exists. Sparta, despite her wrong-headed militarism, has rightly taken this view. The citizen is to be trained for leisure—neither, that is, to make a living, nor for war and politics as ultimate ends, but for self-sufficing rational activity. But Bk. VIII ends without a discussion of intellectual training, and only treats of eugenics and of the earlier stages of a liberal education. Of these the principle is that a boy must learn to obey in order that he may learn to rule. Of the subjects customarily taught Aristotle allows the need of some gymnastic—since the body must be trained before the soul ; of reading and writing ; of drawing, because it teaches one to appreciate the beauty of the human form. To music, a very important factor in Greek education, of which he speaks at some length, he accords a recreational, a moral (cp. pp. 224 ff.), and even perhaps (cp. 1341ª40) a specifically aesthetic pleasure. But the type of melody must be carefully selected on moral grounds, and, though boys should be taught to play an instrument well enough to become tolerable critics of skill in execution, to be a professional player is vulgar.

For Aristotle's analysis of actually existent constitutions (Pol. III) and the right methods of governing even the worst of them by a " mean " policy (Pol. VI), and for his diagnosis of the causes and cure of revolution (Pol. V), we have no space but to say that he puts at the disposal of the practical statesman a knowledge and insight which have never been approached.

VIII

MAN AND GOD

1. DIVINE PHILOSOPHY

MAN may rise above the beasts, dominating his passions and developing the full flower of his practical capacities ; he may be blest in friendship and in ruling his fellows wisely for the single good of them and of himself ; but he has not yet touched the top of human destiny. Practical happiness is after all secondary : its unresting activity has still an end beyond itself. " Happiness," says Aristotle, " is thought to depend on leisure ; for we are busy that we may have leisure, and make war that we may live at peace. Now the activity of the practical virtues is displayed in political or military affairs, and these are unleisurely. Warlike actions are completely so . . . but the action of the statesman is also unleisurely, and—apart from the political action itself—aims at power and honours, or at all events happiness, for him and his fellow-citizens : a happiness different from political action, and evidently sought as being different.[1] . . . But the activity of contemplative reason is regarded as superior in serious worth and as aiming at no end beyond itself. It is thought to have its proper pleasure augmenting the activity, and to have too self-sufficiency,[2] leisureliness, unweariedness—so far as this is possible for man (cp. p. 151) ; and all the

---

[1] This to some extent modifies the sharp antithesis of τεχνή as process to conduct as pure ἐνέργεια (cp. p. 139).

[2] The philosopher is not wholly independent of external goods ; virtue too he must have and even friendship ; but even in solitude he can contemplate truth : see *ibid.* 1177ᵃ29.

other attributes ascribed to the supremely happy man are
evidently those belonging to this activity. It follows that
this will be the complete happiness of man."[1] Yet the
nature of this happiness is not simply deducible as a
complement within human life demanded by the unrest
of practice : " We assume the gods to be above all other
things blessed and happy ; but what sort of actions must
we assign to them ? Acts of justice ? Will not the gods
seem absurd if they make contracts and return deposits,
and so on ? Acts of a brave man, then, confronting dangers
and running risks because it is noble to do so ? Or liberal
acts ? To whom will they give ? And what would their
temperate acts be ? Is not such praise blasphemous, since
they have no bad appetites ? If we recounted them all, the
circumstances of action would be found trivial and unworthy of gods. Still, every one supposes that they *live*
and therefore that they are active ; we cannot suppose
them to sleep like Endymion. Now if you take away
from a living being action, and—as we must *a fortiori* if
that being is God—production, what is left but contemplation ? Therefore the activity of God, which surpasses
all others in blessedness, must be contemplative ; and of
human activities, therefore, that which is most akin to this
must be most of the nature of happiness " (EN 1178^{b}8–23).
Can man, then, share this beatific vision ? The passage
first quoted continues, " But such a life would be too high
for man ; for it is not in so far as he is man that he will
live so, but in so far as something divine is present in him ;
and by so much as this is superior to our composite nature
is its activity superior to the exercise of the other kind of
virtue. If reason is divine, then, in comparison with man,
the life according to it is divine in comparison with human

---

[1] *Ibid*. 1177^{b}4–24 abbreviated. Thus the statesman's ultimate aim is
to facilitate man's sole self-justifying activity—the exercise of reason,
for the sake of truth only, upon the best of knowable objects : cp.
pp. 128 ff.

life. But we must not heed those who bid us, being men, think the thoughts of men, and, being mortal, think of mortal things : we must, so far as we can, make ourselves immortal, and do all things to live by the best that is in us ; for even if that be little in bulk, much more does it in power and worth surpass everything. That little would seem, too, to be each man himself, since it is the ruling and the better part of him. It would be strange, then, if he were to choose not the life of his self but that of something else. . . . Reason more than anything else *is* man " (1177^b26-78^a7).

To discover what is speculative reason—this best in man, " whether it be itself divine or only the most divine element in us " (*ibid.* 1177^a15)—we must first pick up the thread of man's purely cognitive development ; and the problem before us will clearly be whether man's theoretical reason completes or transcends his humanity. Already we have evidence on both sides. But it is at least clear from the passages quoted that the philosopher lives no life of otiose contemplation, nor of cold intellection. His leisure is not rest that alternates with toil ; he strives not, because he possesses, and not because he is " unpractical " ; he is passionless because he is fully active. Aristotle fears no charge of intellectualism. Speculation is to him " the unimpeded life of the soul."[1] It is an apprehension of the ultimately real, which is fully one with its object ; and if we conceive it as excluding some element in experience which we oppose to knowledge, and its perfection as thereby lessened, then it cannot be one with its object. Aristotle's ideal is still that of Socrates, and, as Burnet finely and unanswerably remarks, " Intellectualism, if there is such a thing, can have no martyrs."[2] Yet no more than Plato's *Republic* does Aristotle's ideal state picture a society which has so mastered economic

---

[1] Bosanquet, *Science and Philosophy*, p. 142, and cp. *ibid.*, Essay XXI.
[2] *Thales to Plato*, p. 13.

M

and political conditions that every man has leisure to philosophise. To the suggestion of such a millennium must he not have answered that nature will for ever renew the temporal show, the cyclic manifestation of her eternal species ; that universal leisure could only sap the vitality of speculation, for philosophy is rooted in practical wisdom, and total differentiation of function has still its basis in a common citizenship ?

2. SENSE AND PASSIVE REASON[1]

Already in the animal world a rudimentary universal begins to transcend the fugitive acts of perception : we have seen the persistence of the sense-content as a φάντασμα unite past and present, and even lead to anticipation of the future (cp. pp. 122–3). In human practice reason is present over and above φαντασία, but the partially indeterminate object of practical thought is hardly less the object of imagination and desire than of rational knowledge : even the thinking of the statesman is distinctively characterised by its concern with realising an ideal in particular actions. On the other hand, the objects of theoretical knowledge are exempt from change and time. But in man such knowledge still rests on a basis of sense. Hence a φάντασμα is always present to subserve thinking, but present as an adjunct (cp. An. 432ª12) : φαντασία is not wholly and indistinguishably absorbed by thought, any more than in an animal sense absorbs nutrition without trace.

Reason, like sense, implies a moment of passivity. For both functions consist in the reception of form : as sense receives in its organs from sensible things their forms without their matter, so reason receives in itself from φαντάσματα forms that are *per se* fully intelligible, and, says

---

[1] Noûs, here used in a broad sense to cover at least all speculative activity. " Mind " is a possible alternative translation.

Aristotle, "knows them in φαντασματα" (*ibid.* 431^{b}2). And as the ἕξις, *e.g.*, of vision is stimulated instantaneously to activity by the visible thing, and in this activity seeing and seen object actualise singly and without division—so the capacity of reason is stimulated by the φάντασμα to an activity which constitutes it one with the form it knows : reason is therefore "the form of forms." Moreover, whereas self-consciousness in sense-perception is a by-product, so utterly one is reason, when actually knowing, with its object, that its knowing is as such a knowing of self.[1] Hence (*a*) before the act of seeing, the ἕξις of vision is potentially capable of seeing any colour within certain limiting extremes, and its organ, though it is of no particular colour (cp. note 1, p. 106), does possess other sensible characters ; but (*b*) reason in its passive moment must be *sheer* capacity : it must be as utterly unmixed with, and devoid of any character belonging to, its potential objects as it is utterly one with them in its activity. If it had any such character to start with, the intrusion of its own specific nature would prevent its complete identification with its object : it could not be the form of forms. Hence, too, it is unmixed with the body, of which it is ultimately the form, and uses no organ : its passivity is not that of sense,[2] for whereas intensity in the perceptible object tends to incapacitate sense (cp. p. 106), a higher degree of intelligibility in the intelligible object renders reason the more capable of apprehending the less intelligible.

The object which reason, stimulated by the φάντασμα, knows in the φάντασμα, is the form of the thing, its τί ἦν εἶναι, or essence, its substantial definable nature and not its matter : "We discriminate flesh and the definable form of flesh either by different faculties or by the same faculty in two different states. For flesh necessarily

---

[1] Analogous to the transcending of relation in perfect friendship.

[2] *E.g.* in its transition to actuality it does not pass between contraries ; its nature does not suffer change, and Aristotle therefore even calls it "impassible."

involves matter . . . it is a particular form in a particular matter. Now it is by the sense-faculty that we discriminate the hot and the cold, *i.e.* the factors which combined in a certain ratio constitute flesh. But we discriminate the definable form of flesh by something different, either wholly separate from sense[1] or related to it as a line bent back at an angle is to the same line straightened" (An. 429ᵇ12 ff.). Hence, "As the hand is a tool of [*sc.* for using] tools, so reason is the form of forms and sense the form of sensible things" (*ibid.* 432ᵃ1). Aristotle's meaning would seem to be as follows. Sense actualises singly with the form of the sensible thing, and does so as matter and instrument of reason. Reason operates reflectively upon sense, of which it is the form, just as the hand uses the tools which it has itself shaped and endowed with their true nature and significance. Reason is thus continually perfecting the achievement of the inferior psychical faculties—perfecting, that is to say, at once its lower self and the object of its own less developed experience. For these two *together* are reason's undeveloped self which it fulfils and informs, and in the complete union of reason with its object culminates that relative and imperfect union of the lower faculties with their objects, in which the thing apprehended remained partially external to the apprehending subject, and self-consciousness was present only as a by-product :

> " For speculation turns not to itself,
> Till it hath travell'd and is mirrored there
> Where it may see itself."

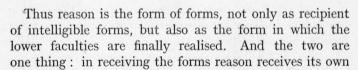

Thus reason is the form of forms, not only as recipient of intelligible forms, but also as the form in which the lower faculties are finally realised. And the two are one thing : in receiving the forms reason receives its own nature.

[1] In particular from φαντασία.

3. EFFICIENT[1] REASON

But thought to Aristotle is not decaying sense. To actualise passive reason, comparable in its total privation of character to primary matter and to Plato's omni-recipient, more is needed than a mere φάντασμα. Passive reason implies an active reason, above and beyond its own actualised self, as efficient cause of its actualisation : " Since in every kind of things, as in nature as a whole, two factors are involved : (1) a matter which is potentially all the particular members of the kind ; (2) a cause which is productive in the sense that it makes them all (the latter standing to the former as, *e.g.*, an art to its material), these distinct elements must likewise be found within the soul.

" And in fact reason, as we have already described it, is what it is by becoming all things, while there is another reason which is what it is by virtue of making all things : this is a sort of positive state, like light. For in a sense light makes potential colours into actual colours. *This* reason is separable, impassible, unmixed, since it is in its substantial nature activity (for always the productive is superior to the passive factor, the originative source to the matter which it forms).

" Actual knowledge is identical with the thing known : in the individual potential knowledge is prior in time to actual knowledge, but in the universe as a whole it is not prior even in time (cp. p. 92, note 1 end). But this reason is not at one time knowing and at another not. When it is set free from its present conditions it appears as just what it is and nothing more : this alone is immortal and eternal. Yet while *this* is impassible, passive reason is perishable : therefore we do not remember. Without *this* nothing knows " (An. III, 5).

---

[1] Ποιητικός. The traditional rendering is " active," which is not incorrect ; but it is agency rather than activity which Aristotle wishes to emphasise—agency as a moment of activity. He never actually uses the phrase ποιητικὸς νοῦς.

These few enigmatic sentences not only begot the most famous controversy of medieval philosophy (see Chap. XI, § 2), but have also been the germ of many diverse metaphysical systems. The main difficulty is this. In all other relevant passages Aristotle speaks simply of reason, and does not, at any rate explicitly, discriminate between a passive and an efficient reason. And much of the passage just quoted is grammatically so ambiguous that one cannot say with any confidence whether the intended distinction is between two reasons or between two discriminable moments of reason ; and one can hardly translate the Greek without prejudging the question. Aristotle is evidently attempting—as Plato in his doctrine of " reminiscence " (cp. p. 30) attempted—to interpret the essential twofold character of thought :—On the one hand, there is no truth that is not truth for a thinking subject, and our thinking is our own activity. On the other hand, the truth we seek is objective : in asserting truth as our own judgment we assert it as holding beyond that or any individual's judgment.[1] So much seems clear, but beyond this no explanation appears possible without guess-work. That of Zabarella (see p. 249) is, up to a point, a fair conclusion from the evidence. Rightly connecting the doctrine with the *Republic*,[2] he holds that efficient reason informs and perfects the φάντασμα, making it a pure intelligible form and no longer a confused sensuous whole, just as sunlight actualises colour in the material body. As light and colour together constitute a single thing which stimulates vision, so efficient reason and the φάντασμα unite as the single efficient cause stimulating passive reason to the activity of judgment upon the intelligible forms which it receives. Efficient reason acts thus upon the φάντασμα, and, united with the φάντασμα, upon passive

[1] The antithesis is ultimately the same as that of empirical to *a priori* knowledge.
[2] Compare closely pp. 37 ff.

reason, not *qua* intelligent, and also not *qua* itself known—so the sun acts not *qua* itself visible—but merely as the cause of intelligibility (cp. p. 173, note).

Zabarella's final conclusion is that passive reason is the form of man ; efficient reason is God. This is open to grave doubt, but we shall do best to consider first what Aristotle says of God *eo nomine*.

4. GOD AND MAN

It will not surprise us to learn that the being of God, who is pure form and perfect substance, is the enjoyment of a pure and perfect contemplative activity. Man's thought rises intermittently upon a basis of φαντασία, and this betokens a residue in him of unabsorbed potentiality[1] —signifies that his activity is still in some sense only adjectival to his nature ; but " If the divine reason thinks, but this depends on something else, then (since that which is its substance is not the act of thinking, but a potentiality) it cannot be the best substance " (Met. 1074^{b}19). In short, man is *active*, but God *is* activity. Moreover, because to have any meaner object than itself would degrade it,[2] Aristotle concludes that God's thought finally overcomes the difference of subject and object : " Since thought and its object are not different in things that have no matter, the divine thought and its object will be the same—the thinking will be one with the object of its thought " (*ibid.* 1075^{a}3 ff.). " God's thinking is a thinking on thinking " (*ibid.* 1074^{b}34). The object of this thought is not composite—" if it were, thought would change in passing from part to part of the whole " (*ibid.* 1075^{a}6)—but single and indivisible ; and the thought is timeless.

Are we to conclude that this eternal self-revelation, which

---

[1] Corresponding to a residue in the object of matter and potentiality which eludes thought.

[2] Reason apart from its object has no character ; see p. 167.

is God, subsists in isolation from a world which it utterly transcends ? God is said by Aristotle to be " a substance eternal, unmovable, and separate from sensible things " (*ibid.* 1073ᵃ4), but if the divine thought merely excludes and transcends the world, the world loses all intelligibility, and God's thought becomes merely abstract and formal, a singleness below and not above distinction. If we sever utterly the developing series of actualisation from its culmination, then at every lower stage too a chasm opens, and the system disintegrates.

But Aristotle does not, it seems, intend this conclusion : " We must consider also whether the nature of the universe contains the good, *i.e.* the highest good, as something separate and by itself, or as the order of the parts. Probably in both ways, as an army does ; for its good is found both in its order and in its general, and more in the latter ; for he does not depend on the order, but it depends on him. And all things are ordered together somehow, but not all alike—fishes, fowls, and plants, for example, are ordered together, but are unlike. Yet this does not mean that they stand in no relation to one another—there *is* a relation. For all things are ordered together in a common relation of contributing to a single end, since the nature of each of them is a source of activities of this contributive kind. But the manner in which they are ordered together is [not that of an order of like elements, but] analogous to the order of a household, within which the freemen are least at liberty to act at random, but all or most of their duties are already ordained for them, while the slaves and animals do little for the common good, and for the most part live at random. I mean in short that (*a*) all things must be sufficiently differentiated for each to have its own peculiar function, but (*b*) there are other *common* functions in which they all participate, thus contributing to the organisation of the whole " (*ibid.* 1075ᵃ11–25). Aristotle concludes the chapter with a criticism of theories which " make the substance of the universe a mere series of episodes. . . . The world refuses to be governed badly : ' Ill is the rule of many ; one ruler let there be.' "

God, then, it would seem, is immanent as well as transcendent, and if we apply the causal analysis to the universe at large, we get some evidence for the same conclusion. God, as we saw (Chap. V, § 5), is, as unmoved mover, the ultimate efficient cause of the world. This—for natural science a mere postulate—means in the end that God so moves the world as the object of love and desire : in God efficient and final causes coalesce. Of God as final cause Aristotle says : " It is the object of desire and also the object of thought which move, themselves unmoved. But the primary desirable and the primary intelligible are the same. For while what *seems* good is an object of appetite, only what really *is* good (and nothing short of that) is an object of rational wish (βούλησις). But desire is consequent on judgment, rather than judgment on desire : for the thinking is the starting-point."[1] Now if God is ultimate final cause of the world, he should be also its ultimate formal cause, the form which is not only the standard of perfection by which alone all lesser things can be judged and defined, but also the *forma informans* of the world as a whole. But Aristotle, though he is clearly aware of the problem, does not reconcile immanence and transcendence. Man's contemplation of the divine, which if complete knowing is one with its object, must be at once a consciousness of and a love for his own best self, for the reason which makes him what he is (see p. 156, note 2) ; the yearning of the natural order to assimilate itself to God by incessant cyclical becoming ; do these imply mere imitation of the divine nature, or real self-

[1] Met. 1072^a26 ff. The doctrine seems to be that since God in himself is good because his self-intelligence is complete reality, hence in relation to the world his primary character is his intelligibility (cp. p. 170). That is why desire, which in animals is one with awareness, is in man already corrigible by knowledge.

identification with it ? Does God rule the world as the
general commands his men, expressing himself through
the disciplined functions which they perform for love of
him, and taking constant thought for the welfare of his
whole army ? Or does he rule as the beloved, unconscious
of the passion he inspires and himself unmoved, rules the
life of the unconfessed lover ? The latter seems the apter
metaphor, for indisputably, when Aristotle speaks in
detail, the balance of emphasis falls upon transcendence,
particularly when he denies God all knowledge of evil.[1]
And yet the ultimate final cause of the universe must
surely also be its formal cause.

The problem inevitably repeats itself in man, and again
the emphasis in detail is upon transcendence. Even if the
efficient reason is God immanent in man for a lifetime,
yet its presence is more often described as the miraculous
transient lodgment of an alien thing than as that which
distinctively characterises the individual man. In GA
736^b28 it is suggested that at conception reason " enters
from without and alone is divine." In An. I we are told
that reason comes to be in us as an imperishable substance,
and its apparent enfeeblement in old age is ascribed to a
decay of " something within " (presumably the physical
basis of φαντασία), analogous to the decay of the sense-
organs.[2] " Discursive thinking," Aristotle there continues, " loving and hating, are affections not of the
reason but of that which has reason, in so far as it has it.
That is why, when this vehicle decays, memory and love
cease : they were activities not of reason, but of the
composite which has perished. Reason is, no doubt, something more divine and impassible " (An. 408^b25 ff.).

---

[1] Cp. An. 430^b22 ff.: " How is evil apprehended, or black ? In some
fashion by its contrary. But that which apprehends must potentially
be, and must contain within itself, the contrary which it apprehends.
Yet, if there be something which has no contrary, then it is the object
of its own knowledge, is in actuality and is separately existent."

[2] An argument which seems to prove too much.

According to this account the reason which survives is not a human personality,[1] but we can hardly infer that it is God. It is true that efficient reason, as it appears in An., seems to be in psychology somewhat the analogue of the unmoved mover in physics—a postulate which the psychologist, who treats of reason only as the thinking of the individual, must assume but cannot examine. Here, we might suggest, are the two points of contact between God and the natural world ; God plays, perhaps, a dual rôle as efficient cause, moving the heavens to generate mankind, and moving also the mind of man that he may know. But such speculation verges on mere fancy. We are told that to the metaphysician the unmoved mover is God ; but of efficient reason no more is said.

It is perhaps more likely that Aristotle conceives a less direct relation between man and God. It may be that efficient reason is a pure substance, identical in all men, and itself intermediate in the developing series between man and the astral intelligences—themselves sufficiently obscure. The latter, like God, move their spheres as the object of love, and possibly efficient reason actualises passive reason in the individual through the love that each man bears, not directly to God, but to this divine spark within him.[2]

But the clues conflict and no solution satisfies. Aristotle is striving with a fundamental problem, which begins in psychology with Plato's analysis of the soul, and in

[1] It must be observed that the question here is not primarily whether the particular soul as such survives death. To this Aristotle, who held that the source of all plurality, and therefore of the distinction between men as singular individuals, is matter, must have replied in the negative. The real point at issue is whether or not reason really characterises the individual man.

[2] One might be tempted to take the distinction of efficient and passive reason as that of substance and essential accident (see pp. 78 and 197 ff.) —to view the modes of discursive thinking as capacities of change necessarily inherent in reason *qua* embodied, but as not elements in its substantial nature. But if efficient reason is a pure substance, it can have no essential accident (see p. 194).

metaphysics with the Platonic Forms : if the best element in a complex is that which most truly characterises it, how does that element relate to the rest of the complex ? φρόνησις, for example, is the best of practical life, and gives their significance to the external good things which the moral life includes ; yet φρόνησις should lie wholly within man's power, and external goods do not. The truth man seeks to win in speculation proclaims its independence of any individual possessor. The more the complex becomes hierarchical in character, the more its highest stage tends to appear no longer a *forma informans*, but a transcendent *forma assistens*. But the germ of the problem is already present wherever there are matter and form. As against Plato, Aristotle does his best to preserve immanence for the human soul, and if Forms are to be transcendent, he will nevertheless not allow transcendence and self-subsistence to mere abstract and general universals such as he believes Plato's Forms to be. Yet in the end his God seems scarcely less remote than the Platonic Form of the Good as he conceives it. He does not press the implications of his own conception of self-consciousness, and he does not so develop the anti-thesis of form and matter, actual and potential, as to distinguish between a single universe seen *sub specie temporis*, and seen again *sub specie aeternitatis*. His God, if not Epicurean, is certainly not Spinozistic.[1] Aristotle is a monist in so far as his universe is a single ordered hierarchy. But, despite his ceaseless effort to link its analogous phases and his astounding success in so doing, he cannot rise above this comparatively linear hierarchical conception of the real to envisage it as a hierarchy which is *totum in toto et totum in qualibet parte*. Often he relapses into pluralism, isolating elements within the whole to save them from that dependence and imperfection which relation to the rest would seem to entail.

[1] Yet see p. 222.

IX

BEING AND KNOWLEDGE: THE CATEGORIES AND SUBSTANCE

So far we have looked on the universe through Aristotle's eyes as a scale on which consciousness appears only midway. We treated the emerging stages of consciousness as essentially characterising the ascending grades of conscious substance, and we ignored at first the fact that we can in the end say nothing of the whole ordered universe, the whole *Scala Universi*, save as the object of knowledge (cp. pp. 102–3). But we learned at last that in God—and perhaps at moments in man—knowledge is completely one with its object. And the problem of efficient reason should at least have warned us that if we are to maintain this ultimate identity of subject and object without embracing the relativism of Protagoras, we cannot continue to treat knowledge as no more than the adjective of an individual thinker.

Aristotle, as we saw, does not develop these results, nor reach beyond the conception of a single hierarchy of beings. But he does supplement this conception by reflecting explicitly from two points of view upon the universe as the object of thought. In Met. VII and VIII he discusses the nature of substance as such, laying emphasis on the object. In the *Organon*—the name afterwards given to the group of logical works—he treats of thought itself, not as the function of an individual subject, but in terms of truth and falsehood and with special reference to its form. This systematic separation of aspects conspicuously differentiates him from Plato, but he is held by his view of the relation between, and the ultimate identity of, mind and its object from pursuing methodological distinction so far towards divorce of form from content as did some of his successors. In the doctrine of the categories, which gives its title to the first book of the *Organon*, the two points of view are somewhat ambiguously combined.

1. THE CATEGORIES

A doctrine of categories is fundamental in Aristotle's philosophy, but its origin and development are so obscure that the *Categories*, where alone it is formulated in detail, has been attributed both to the beginning and to the end of Aristotle's career.[1] Moreover, at least its latter half is probably not Aristotle's work.

In a phrase which aptly links the Socratic conversation with his own philosophic dialectic, Plato speaks of thought as " the soul's conversation with herself " (*Theaetetus*, 189e ff.). The implied view of language, developed in the *Cratylus*, reappears in Aristotle as a rather crude correspondence theory of word and thought : " Spoken words are the symbols of experiences in the soul, written words the symbols of spoken words. As all men have not the same script, so not all have the same speech sounds, but the experiences, which these primarily symbolise, are the same for all, and so are the things of which our experiences are the likenesses " (Int. 16a4 ff.). *Prima facie*, at any rate, Aristotle deduces the categories from an analysis of linguistic forms.[2] He proceeds roughly thus :—(a) He divides language into " things said without combination " and " things said in combination," *i.e.* simple terms (nouns and verbs) and prepositions ; (b) he classifies the

---

[1] The *Categories* gives the impression of being an elementary course of lectures, whatever the date of its composition may be. See also p. 268.

[2] Cp. pp. 34, 51, 53. He ends, however, by cutting across grammatical distinctions.

senses in which ordinary usage predicates one term of another—hence the name " categories," which means " predications " ; thereby (c) he reaches a classification of being.

(a) All terms will be found to fall under one of ten categories :—

> Substance (e.g. " Socrates," " man ").
> Of a certain quantity (e.g. " two cubits long ").
> Of a certain quality (e.g. " white ").
> In a relation (e.g. " double," " greater ").
> Somewhere (e.g. " in the Lyceum ").
> At some time (e.g. " yesterday ").
> Being in a position (e.g. " reclines ").
> Being in a state (e.g. " is shod ").
> Doing (e.g. " cuts ").
> Suffering (e.g. " is cut ").

(b) The singular individual—the τόδε τι, or " this somewhat," as Aristotle calls it—is primarily entitled to the name of substance.[1] It is par excellence the subject of predication, and itself neither predicable " of " a subject (i.e. as a universal of a particular), nor predicable as " inherent in " (i.e. as an accident which cannot exist apart from) a subject. Species and genus are " secondary substances," predicable only " of " a subject - genus of both species and singular, species only of singular. All other terms fall under the remaining categories, and are accidents predicable only as inherent in substance.[2]

(c) But the subject of a proposition need not be a substance, and the categories are not only the main heads of predication : they also classify all nameable things in

---

[1] Cp. note I, p. 101. Substance to Aristotle is always a τόδε τι, but though he more often applies the term to the singular individual, yet he frequently speaks of form (εἶδος) as a τόδε τι (see Bonitz, Ind. s.v. ὅδε). This shows how his view of what really is substance wavers.

[2] Elsewhere, however, Aristotle commonly speaks of accidents as predicable " of."

respect to the precise character of their reality.[1] If we take any definitory judgment, and ask what kind of essential being is predicated of the subject, the answer is bound to be one of the categories. Thus, for example, if we define Socrates as essentially a man, a cubit as essentially a measure, white as essentially a colour, four as essentially twice two, we are predicating respectively of these four subjects as their essential being, substance, quantity, quality, and relation.

The list of categories seems somewhat arbitrary. Aristotle apparently assumes that the accidental categories, which, because substance alone is self-dependent, are all logically posterior to substance, themselves too form some sort of logically developing series in which each succeeding term presupposes and depends on its predecessor (cp. EN I, 6). But he never works out such a series, and the efforts of his commentators to do so do not convince. In the *Categories* only substance is treated with any care, and in the lists given outside that work position and state only once appear. At best the categories constitute a system surprisingly comprehensive if one tries to apply it, despite its empirical character.

Before we consider difficulties arising from Aristotle's formulation of the doctrine, it may help us to ask what are its probable antecedents. As a theory of how the real is reflected in the forms of judgment, it seems to presuppose Plato's *Sophist* (cp. pp. 52 ff.) but the list bears no obvious relation to the common characters of the *Theaetetus* and *Parmenides*, or to the inter-participant forms of the *Sophist*.[2] Nor are the categories put forward as all-pervasive characters of the real such as we seemed to detect when we followed Plato's more dialectical line of thought (cp. pp. 55 ff.). On the other hand, Plato's distinction of self-

---

[1] Aristotle implies but does not state this corollary.
[2] Sameness and difference, however, is a principle pervading all the categories (cp. p. 181, note 2). Most of the notions which the categories express find incidental mention in various Platonic dialogues.

subsistent from dependent being is possibly the source of
Aristotle's conception of substance and accident, and in
shaping it he may be following Plato's second line of
thought in the *Sophist* (cp. p. 57). Yet, if he is doing so,
he takes as his corner-stone what Plato seems merely to
suggest in passing. We found that in the *Sophist* the
introduction of this distinction increased a tendency to
confuse being as the minimal characterisation of all that
is, with being in the sense of the real as a complete whole
(cp. p. 57). Aristotle, as we might expect (cp. Chap. VIII,
§ 4), makes no attempt to work in logic with the notion of
an absolute whole, and reduces the four terms of Plato's
antitheses to three : substance, accidental being, and
being as a minimal character of all that is. Minimal being
is not a kind, or genus, of which the categories are the
subgenera. For, according to Aristotle,[1] classification
by genus and species implies division into co-ordinate
groups. Strictly speaking, it classifies only substances,
and at all events it can apply only within each several
category. But the categories are not co-ordinate ; they
exhibit a logical order. Hence there is only being as
substance, being as *quantum*, *quale*, etc. The categories
are highest genera, and minimal being is analogous to a
grammatical stem present in, but not apart from, the
inflected forms in which it is conjugated or declined.[2]

On the whole, then, Aristotle seems to follow Plato's
second line of thought. He does not offer the categories as
a dialectical system in which the real as a whole develops
and grows concrete through an ascending series of partial
definitions. On the other hand, the categories do not

---

[1] Inspired *perhaps* by Plato's second line of thought.

[2] Not-being is declined correspondingly (Met. 1089ᵃ16 ff.) ; unity and
plurality also (of which same and different, like and unlike, are species),
bearing a different sense in each category, characterise all things that
are. Good and evil, too, are found in each category with a different
sense. In EN I, 6, Aristotle founds an attack on the Platonic Form of
the Good largely on the ground that goodness is predicated in several
categorially different senses ; cp. also p. 129.

N

directly reflect the stages of that ordered universe of which we have watched the gradual construction in Aristotle's thought. So far as they classify real things, those real things are not precisely the members of the *Scala Universi* as such. God and the other perfect beings are pure substance, but *quanta* and *qualia* are not, as such, things of a lower grade on the scale. For all the members of the *Scala Universi* are, as such, substances, albeit less and less perfect—more deeply immersed in matter—as the scale descends ; and they are classified, where classification is possible, by genus and species.[1] The *Scala Universi* and the categories are two systems which coincide at their summits inasmuch as God is perfect substance, but do not coincide elsewhere.[2] Rather the various categories serve to order and determine that diversity of accidental characters whereby imperfect things reveal their changing natures,[3] their various degrees of failure to be divine.

But the position thus reached is an ambiguous compromise ; for Plato's first line of thought—or something like it—is not altogether without its influence, since the earlier categories, at all events, might, with modification, take their place in a philosophical dialectic as partial definitions of the real as a whole. What happens is perhaps this : Aristotle discovers certain all-pervasive characters of the real, but he cannot set them out as a series of partial definitions of reality as a whole, because of reality as a whole he has no genuinely operative conception beyond the *Scala Universi*, which he has reached empirically. He aims at Monism, and his central doctrine

[1] Of course only a world of generation and decay can be classified by genus and species, for genus as such is something merely potential (see pp. 186 and 198). This becomes more obvious when we watch the exhibition of it *in concreto* ; cp. pp. 100 ff.

[2] Their respective bases, primary matter and minimal being, might seem to coincide, inasmuch as both are devoid of all positive character. But they are the pure potentialities (the sheer privations) postulated by different systems, and cannot be equated.

[3] All accidental characters express some potency of change ; cp. p. 78 and p. 102, note 1.

of causation demands it ; but he fails to rise above a more
or less pluralistic system. The scheme of things entire is
to him a hierarchy of substances and not a whole of
dialectical moments. Hence the categories have to classify
characters which belong to a plurality of substances
already empirically systematised, and, so far as they
constitute a developing series, they order and determine,
not reality as a whole, but the degrees of imperfection in
those substances.[1] Thus, because Aristotle regards the
complete and perfect as that which is finite and limited
(cp. p. 83, note 2) ; because he does not equate perfect
being with being that is all-comprehensive, the two
systems in the main diverge. But because the highest
members of the *Scala Universi* are perfect beings, they
coincide at the summit.

The categories are the highest universals of a pluralist
system, and the universals of a pluralist system are
inevitably empirical. They tend to become mere abstract
common characters which classify externally. Universal
and particular make claims that pluralism cannot reconcile.
The universal cannot genuinely characterise its particulars,
nor they afford the universal its proper articulate content.
Pluralism refuses to recognise that all judgment has
ultimately a single subject—that the very claim of the
universal to *be* universal is a claim to characterise reality
as a whole and a criticism of the pluralist universe.[2]
Lastly pluralism tends gradually to treat the universal
as a mere mental concept, and to oppose it to " external "
real things.

Though Aristotle reaches the categories through the
reflexion of the real in words, the symbols of thoughts,

---

[1] While certain other all-pervasive characters which cut across the
categories and appear in different senses in several categories (cp. p. 181,
note 2) are left outside the system in unexplained isolation.   These
were called by the schoolmen *Transcendentia*.

[2] A criticism which is manifest in that residue of characters which
remain outside the categories.

yet on the whole he refrains from this final step.[1] The real and the intelligible remain for him ultimately one. He does not embrace that realism which a pluralist metaphysic in the end involves. Yet, when the theory of substance as singular individual breaks down (see § 2), he is forced to seek an alternative within the limits set by Plato's second line of thought, and his field is further narrowed by his resolute rejection of the Platonic Forms as he conceives them. The universal must be individualised in what it characterises, not divorced from that and then given a fresh individuality in a new world of its own.

2. SUBSTANCE

In the *Categories* the essential characteristics assigned to substance are three. It is always a subject and never a predicate. It has no contrary, and admits of no degree : there is no contrary of Socrates or man, and a man cannot be less or more man. It persists identical, while accidents vary between contrary poles : the same man is now hot, now cold, etc. As the ultimate subjects of predication, which " underlie everything else " (Cat. 2^{b}15), singular individuals fulfil these conditions more adequately than species, species than genera.[2] Hence in the first book of

[1] Though he tends somewhat in that direction in An. Pr. See pp. 210, 211.

[2] Thus Aristotle seems to formulate the " primary substance " as a precise antithesis to the Platonic Form. But, though it is a " this somewhat," a primary substance is not merely anything called " this " or " that " in common speech. Primary substances are the individuals of which reality consists ; those which timelessly *are*, and those which by natural processes have come to be. They are, so to speak, born and not made. Nothing which owes its unity to art or to chance is a primary substance. God, the astral intelligences, and the efficient reason are primary substances, and so is any member of an animal or vegetable species. But a statue is not—the shape which turns the block of marble into a Hermes is predicable under quality, not substance—nor is a dead portion of an organism separated from the whole. Among inanimate things the title clearly belongs only to the heavenly bodies, the four elements, and the whole bulk of each mineral species : a mountain, *e.g.*, or a river, would not be a primary substance.

the *Organon* the categories are chiefly considered as a means of classifying all the predicates applicable to an individual subject : *e.g.* Socrates *qua* substance is a man, *qua* quantified is tall, *qua* qualified snub-nosed, *qua* related a husband, etc. They thus exhibit the varying degrees of intimacy with which its various possible predicates attach to a subject. But the main distinction is between substance and the accidental categories. Accidents may change— even, if they qualify superficially, disappear[1]—whereas substance abides, unvarying in degree. But if any substantial character be removed, the individual itself disappears.

Nevertheless Aristotle's formulation of the theory leads to contradiction. (1) Since the categories classify being exhaustively, the category of substance will contain not only the substantial characters such as animal, man, etc.— the secondary substances—but also the singular sensible substances of which these are predicated. And this Aristotle maintains. Yet (2) if the categories classify universal predicates, the singular substances to which they apply—those at all events which are sensible—must remain outside all the categories.[2] But (3) if the singular substance is isolated from the substantial predicates which define its essential nature, it becomes simply nothing.[3] Hence (4) all its essence, all that you can say of it in defining it, does turn out to be contained in the category of substance—except its individuality, its unique " thisness." But (5) even if the singular *qua* a unique particular is apprehended by sense and not by thought, yet a substance must be individual.

Another route leads to the same difficulty, but also to a

---

[1] It must be remembered that the term " accident " covers all non-substantial characters, whether superficial or necessarily inherent. " Co-incident " would perhaps more nearly render the Greek original, συμβεβηκός.

[2] This difficulty arises only in the category of substance. White *is* a quality, but it is *eo ipso* a predicate. Socrates, however, is a substance, but he is not a predicate.

[3] In fact, Locke's " bare substratum," which Berkeley had no difficulty in exposing.

possible solution. The substantial characters predicable of the sensible singular are the genus and differentia which together constitute its definable form. The genus is conceived by Aristotle as a universal which by itself is abstract and potential, no more really existent than is minimal being apart from the categories. This mere potentiality begins to actualise in the first subgenera into which the genus is divisible ; but actualisation continues until the genus receives its final logical differentiation into infimae species. Genus and differentia are thus the termini of a process of logical actualisation.[1] Together they sum up a group of substantial characters, which form an indissoluble unity, just because they are the stages of a development and are only significant as actualised in the culmination of that development (cp. Met. VIII, 6). So Aristotle appears to follow that second line of thought contained in the *Sophist* which led Plato from true dialectic towards division. For though the genus, like minimal being apart from the categories, is abstract and potential, yet the subgenera through which, and the infimae species in which, it actualises, are regarded by Aristotle as sets of co-ordinates, and not as presenting a developing series.[2] The *Scala Universi is* a developing series, but within its lower stages development is apparently superseded by a scheme of co-ordinate groups : " An individual man is no more truly substance than an individual ox " (Cat. 2^{b}28).

Now below the infima species there are only logically indiscriminable singulars ; multiplicity signifies the presence of matter, and the singular " this " or " that " is, as such, that which belongs to sense and eludes thought and definition. If you define Socrates as animal-terrestrial-rational-man—or, more shortly, rational-man—you have in effect defined no more than the infima species man.

---

[1] For a manifestation of it in the concrete, see pp. 100 ff.

[2] *I.e.* regarded laterally, so to speak, within the genus, the subgenera and again the species are merely co-ordinate.

But if you try to define him more closely, you are met with a mass of accidents, which are (*a*) inexhaustible, and (*b*) essentially liable to change ; and any change in them will immediately render your definition untrue. Hence in Met. VII, where Aristotle debates with masterly penetration how to meet the claim of substance to be at once universal, intelligible, and definable, and at the same time unique and individual, the singular is at length superseded on the throne of substance by the infima species.[1] That is to say the genus is taken to be fully actualised in its infimae species, and its further differentiation into singulars is treated as irrelevant. Singulars— so runs the thread of Aristotle's thought—are not intelligible, but the infima species *is* intelligible ;[2] and is also, in contrast to the genus, individual[3]—it is, in fact, the nearest approximation to a true individual which thought can grasp in the lower stages of the *Scala Universi*. In the light of this change not only the superficial peculiarities but all the accidents inherent in sensible singulars are treated as differences due to the material element which is the principle of their plurality.[4]

If this solution is intended by Aristotle as metaphysical

[1] Or " materiate form," as Aristotle also calls it because it attains existence in a material embodiment and cannot be defined without reference to matter, though matter is itself indefinable. The discussion is interspersed with criticism of the Forms. Aristotle attacks the theory as a purely arbitrary individualisation of universals, and the detail of the polemic, as well as the context, suggests that he is attacking Plato not for divorcing infimae species from singulars, but for separating and re-ifying genera taken apart from species. Plato seldom distinguishes clearly between genus and species. Cp. Stenzel, *Zahl u. Gestalt, bei Platon und Aristoteles*, 133 ff., and Taylor, *Plato*, 515.

[2] Of course on the view that the singular individual is primarily substance, we should have to say that the actualisation of the genus only becomes complete when the infimae species are further differentiated into singulars ; *i.e.* that singular substances *are* logically discriminable. This Aristotle sometimes seems to maintain; cp. Met. 1071ª17–29, especially 24–29.

[3] It can hence be called τόδε τι ; cp. note 1, p. 179.

[4] See p. 102, note 1, and p. 129. In Cael. I, 9, Aristotle states that even when an infima species has but one member, as in the case of the whole heaven, the essence and existence of this unique individual do

we must regard the *Scala Universi* somewhat as follows. God, the astral intelligences, and efficient reason will not be affected. In them the clash of universal and particular does not arise ; for they are individuals, not as units of a plurality actual or possible, but as each utterly unique in its kind, because a pure and not a materiate form. In them essence and existence are one. But in the sphere of sensible substance thought can distinguish as fully real only genera as articulate in systems of co-ordinate infimae species. Plurality and superficial differentiation must be ascribed to an indeterminacy, which is real, but real with a reality not as such intelligible (cp. p. 92, note 1). Between the two, however, there are certain accidents, which inhere necessarily in a genus or a species, characterising in some degree all its singulars (cp. p. 78). And though the indissoluble unity of substantial characters which constitutes the infima species is that which is primarily real and intelligible in this sphere, yet these accidents too, because they attach necessarily, are permeable to thought. But they inhere dependently in substance, and this dependence is their essence. Their *esse* is *inhaerere*, because this is the essential nature of all that is classified by the accidental categories. They all express capacities of variation, and are marked as belonging to the world of change. They attach only to infimae species, or materiate forms, for in perfect substance no accident inheres, superficial or necessary.[1]

not coincide. The whole heaven, because perceptible, is a particular, its species a materiate form which might, though in fact it does not, possess other embodiments. It is unique, not because its essence and existence coincide, but for other reasons. Yet Aristotle leaves the impression that this single embodiment of a form in a comparatively perfect matter provides at least a nearer approximation to pure form than the several constituents of the perceptible world : *e.g.* an astronomical demonstration which had for its subject the whole heaven, or the sun, or the moon, would be superior to a demonstration of which the subject was some sublunary natural species (cp. pp. 197 ff.).

[1] The Scholastics distinguished between the (substantial) attributes and the propria of God, but Aristotle does not at any rate explicitly do so, and it is hard to see how it can be done consistently with his doctrine of pure substance.

It has, however, been maintained that classification by genus and species and the conception of the materiate form as substance are formulated by Aristotle not as ultimate metaphysical notions, but only as a necessary postulate of the special sciences. On this question the following chapter may throw some light, but we shall find that either view presents very great difficulty.

X

BEING AND KNOWLEDGE: THE THEORETICAL SCIENCES AND LOGIC

1. THE THEORETICAL SCIENCES

WE have seen how Aristotle divides thought according to the nature of its object (pp. 129 ff.), and, since " All thinking is either practical or productive or theoretical " (Met. 1025^{b}25)—since the division is exhaustive—there can be no thinking in respect of art or conduct save that which is embodied in, and one with, the variable objects which in those spheres submit to man's power of intelligent alteration. Rules and principles of conduct may be formulated, but the rough and indeterminate nature of the subject-matter yields only that inferior truth of which action is the further end (cp. p. 130) ; and moral character, formed for action and by action, is a prerequisite for the understanding of them. Such principles may aid the statesman and the teacher, but to the young man, though he may have progressed far in, *e.g.*, geometrical studies, they will mean very little : " For he is inexperienced in the actions that occur in life, and political science starts from these and is about these ; and further, since he tends to follow his passions, his study will be vain and unprofitable, because the end aimed at is not knowledge but action " (EN 1095^{a}3 ff.). There is, in short, no theoretical science of art or conduct.

It does not seem obvious why conduct should not be studied for the sake of knowledge. In fact no man has contributed more to the *theory* of ethics than Aristotle, and his doctrine of art and conduct is vital to his theory of the universe. Yet he maintains firmly that the theoretical sciences, or " philosophies," are three and three only—" first philosophy," natural science, and mathematics—and none of these has the practical world for its object.

(A) FIRST PHILOSOPHY

First philosophy, or metaphysics,[1] is " the science which investigates being *qua* being and its essential attributes "[2] (Met. 1003ª21). To expand and interpret this definition, Aristotle indicates a threefold contrast between first philosophy and the special sciences, which latter are grouped exhaustively under natural science and mathematics. Metaphysics (1) investigates the absolutely real, that which in the fullest sense *is*; and since the crown of the *Scala Universi* is God, metaphysics claims the title of theology. *Per contra* the special sciences study the lower beings of the natural scale, for " There are as many parts of philosophy as there are kinds of substance " (*ibid.* 1004ª2). But (2), because the absolutely real is pure substance,[3] metaphysics again contrasts with the special sciences, inasmuch as the latter all study being as declined in one of the accidental categories. (3) Metaphysics is a universal science which inquires into being as a whole, whereas all the special sciences " mark off some particular being—some genus, and inquire into this, but not into being simply nor *qua* being. Nor do they offer any discussion of the essence of the things of which they treat; but starting from the essence . . . they then demonstrate more or less cogently the essential attributes[4]

---

[1] Originally an editorial term (=" The problems subsequent to those of Physics "). It heads the treatises on first philosophy which appear in the *Corpus Aristotelicum* immediately after those on natural science.

[2] N.B.—Not accidents.

[3] *I.e.* because *Scala Universi* and categories coincide at their summits.

[4] *I.e.* necessary accidents; cp. p. 188.

of the genus with which they deal."[1] To the question how these various definitions relate—" Whether first philosophy is universal, or deals with one genus, *i.e.* some one kind of being "—Aristotle replies, " If there is no substance but those which are formed by nature, natural science will be the first science ; but if there is one immovable substance, the science of this must be prior, and universal just because it is first" (*ibid.* 1026ª27 ff.). He means, presumably, that metaphysics is universal because to all things substance is the cause and principle of their fundamental nature.

We are thus enabled to expand the account of man's speculative activity given in Chapter VIII, § 1. Self-identification with the divine nature is the supreme reward of the speculative life ; but this beatific vision gives the metaphysician a standard by which to judge the degrees of derivative reality which the lower stages of the universe exhibit. The detail of this applied metaphysic is hard to determine, but if we look to the actual contents of Met. and to Aristotle's scanty and not wholly consistent statements and implications, we can again trace roughly two lines of thought which coincide imperfectly. (1) Descending the *Scala Universi*, the metaphysician will ask in what sense the essences assumed without proof by the special sciences are real. *E.g.* he will relate the unmoved mover of physics to God as final cause, and criticise the notions of a natural body and of a mathematical entity. And in so doing he will discuss conceptions such as matter and form, potency and actuality, causation. (2) He will consider being, and also not-being. For opposites always fall under a single science, and being *qua* being, having no genus, can only be defined by its negative limits—in opposition, *i.e.* to its own negation. As definitions of being *qua* being he will formulate the laws of contradiction

[1] Met. 1025ᵇ8 ff. N.B.—(1) and (3) assign the same rôle to the special sciences.

and excluded middle :—whatever *is* cannot be also other than itself ; whatever *is* must either possess or not possess a given character. These laws are thus formulated " ontologically," but they are also axioms implied in the demonstrations of special science.[1] He will treat of those principles which fall outside the categories : one and many, with their species same and other, like and unlike ; good and evil, beautiful and ugly,[2] true and false. And he will study the declension of being through the categories.

To fit himself for this task the metaphysician must himself have studied the special sciences,[3] but his method as a metaphysician is not demonstration. If it were demonstration, presumably God and the other pure substances would be the subjects which it assumes to be real (*i.e.* would constitute its ὑποθέσεις), and the features of the perceptible world would somehow appear as essential accidents inhering in them. But Aristotle does not, and could not, so relate pure substance to the world of change ; for pure substances are not unities of genus and differentia, and they have therefore no essential accidents.[4] The metaphysician's method is in fact dialectical. Yet it is not the dialectic of Plato's *Republic*. The assumptions of special science are apparently not in the strict sense proved by first philosophy—not, *i.e.*, exhibited as no longer isolated groups but at length altogether fully transparent within an articulate system united and illuminated by the divine nature. On the whole, Aristotle seems to hold that there is in the assumptions of special

---

[1] *I.e.* they are formulated as definitions of being *qua* being, and it follows necessarily from this that they are also " Laws of Thought," governing all reasoning about anything which is any sense real.

[2] Better perhaps " fair and foul " : the Greek words equally mean " noble and base."

[3] Aristotle himself had done so with a thoroughness even beyond that demanded by Plato of the philosophic ruler in his preliminary mathematical studies ; for he had practically created zoology and psychology. His metaphysician is not the modern specialist.

[4] See, however, p. 188, note 1.

science something in its own nature insusceptible of proof, and the object solely of immediate intuition (cp. p. 212). He only explicitly displays this dialectic at work in establishing the laws of contradiction and excluded middle. These can only be " demonstrated by refutation " (Met. 1006ᵃ11) and *ad hominem* (*ibid.* 1062ᵃ2) ; *i.e.* any single statement of one's opponent or pupil can be shown to involve them. Hence the metaphysician's dialectic is rather a method of instruction and disputation than of logical proof (see pp. 215 ff.). In Aristotle's own *Metaphysics* his method is largely aporematic : he is often more concerned to elaborate a dilemma than explicitly to solve it.

(b) THE NATURAL SCIENCES

" Second philosophy," or natural science, covers the whole sphere of change where change accords with necessary laws. It treats, *i.e.*, of natural bodies whose essential nature is possession of an innate source of movement and rest.

Aristotle's works on natural science present a series which ascends the *Scala Naturae* from general to particular.¹ In *Physics* I and II he discusses the fundamental principles of natural body, *i.e.* matter and form, privation, nature, and cause ; the later books treat of alteration with special reference to locomotion, the primary kind of change, and the attendant problems of space, time, continuity, etc. He concludes by establishing the hypothesis of an unmoved mover. The remaining works treat various species of natural body and their essential accidents, *i.e.* their specific modes of change. Thus *De Caelo* discusses all the five elements, and so contains both a cosmology²

¹ The order is retained in the *Corpus Aristotelicum* (see p. xi), and will be already fairly clear to the reader from the references given in the text and notes.

² Aristotle sometimes adumbrates a special science of substance that is sensible but eternal (Met. 1069ᵃ30, and cp. p. 187, note 4) ; sometimes

and—in the modern sense of the term—a physics. *De Generatione et Corruptione* returns to treat of substantial change, and of alteration other than locomotion ; but it treats them with special reference to the formation of ὁμοιομερῆ . Very roughly speaking its subject is chemistry. The *Meteorologica*[1] concerns phenomena of (*a*) the fiery region, (*b*) the air and water constituting the atmosphere, and (*c*) the earth. It is in fact a study in elemental transformation closely connected with *De Caelo*. The psychological works, *De Anima*, etc., profess to give a general account of the " be-souled body " as a species of natural body, though the peculiar nature of soul extends the scope of *De Anima* somewhat beyond these limits. Thus they prepare the way for biology, which Aristotle necessarily regards as closely linked with psychology. The *Historia Animalium* collects facts from which the other works of this group—as their titles indicate (see p. xi)—deduce theories ; but the essential accidents of animate substance would remain obscure were these works not supplemented by the *De Anima*.[2]

These treatises vary somewhat in method as the scale is ascended. They are primarily lecture-notes, and Aristotle writes as a teacher, usually striving to establish principles by dialectical argument which starts from his predecessor's theories. In the *Physics* he assumes on the whole the critical attitude of the metaphysician rather than demonstrates from assumptions. He is not so much teaching natural science as instructing an audience, which will in time come to study first philosophy, what natural science is. In biology, both because he was himself a specialist,

he assigns the study of the spheres to astronomy as a branch of mathematics. Compare Plato's attitude in the *Republic*, p. 40. In An. Post. Aristotle states that there is an " observational " as well as a strict mathematical treatment of the subject-matter of astronomy (cp. 78^{b}34 ff.).

[1] Doubt has been cast upon its authenticity.

[2] Zabarella regards An. as dealing with the form of the " besouled body " only, the biological works as concerned only with its matter.

and because the impossibility of identifying *a priori*
principles with " fact " is more obvious here than at a
more abstract level, he gives us a mass of fact in the
Historia Animalium, and a good deal of demonstration
in the other treatises. Nevertheless he has a very definite
view of what the specialist in each department of natural
science studies, and of his method in so doing. Method is
a logical inquiry (see Chap. X, § 2), but it is time to consider the subject-matter of natural science as it presents
itself to the specialist.[1]

To the layman, who as a rule has not reflected much
upon his sense-perception, the world presents a confused
whole of singular things and their properties. The general
preliminary function of science is to reflect upon these
singulars, and to discard as unintelligible any merely
superficial accidents which qualify them only as members
of a plurality of percepta ; to distinguish their substantial
characters from their necessary accidents ; and, finally,
to group the infimae species so reached under separate
genera. From this process results a world of genera linked
to one another by relation of analogy, and possessing in
Aristotle's view a real and not a merely provisional fixity.
Each genus is a substantial character,[2] merely potential if
taken in abstraction, but actually existing concretely
articulated in and as a number of different infimae species,
which are at once universal and individual. And to this
genus attach a number of necessary accidents, or co-
incidents, the status of which within the genus constitutes

---

[1] The reader should consult GC, ed. Joachim, Introd.

[2] Exactly how Aristotle would work out his rule that one genus is
the subject-matter of one special science is far from clear. Within
mathematics (the subject-matter of which is only *quasi*-substantial ;
see § (c) below) arithmetic, plane geometry, solid geometry, etc., are
separate special sciences, each having its separate subject-genus.
Within nature, which in Met. 1005^{a}34 is called a single genus, we
might perhaps distinguish psychology, physiology, and botany as special
sciences, each having a separate subgenus for its subject-matter. But
Aristotle does not precisely articulate the branches of natural science,
and it seems hard to avoid cross-classification. See also p. 203, note 3.

the next problem for science. In order to solve it, each genus is made the province of a specialist ; for " A single science is one whose domain is a single genus, viz., all the subjects constituted out of the primary entities of the genus—*i.e.* the parts of this total subject—and their essential accidents " (An. Post. 87ª38 ff.). Thus, so soon as he is free from the preliminary task of distinguishing his own genus, the specialist has before him several infimae species, which, though " parts " of the genus which groups them, are the " primary entities," or fundamental constituents, in which alone the genus exists articulate and actualised. He has also a mass of essential accidents, " which inhere in the simple infimae species, and in the genus only in virtue of these " (*ibid.* 96ᵇ23). The essential accidents differ from the substantial characters—genus and differentia—which together constitute the simple (indivisible though concrete) unity of the infima species. For their *esse* is *inhaerere*, and, while they do not enter into the definition of the species, they are themselves indefinable (because non-existent) without the species.[1] The causal link between the essential accident and the infima species which supports and defines it is always ultimately, if not proximately, a single one of the substantial characters of the species : *e.g.* in the infima species man the capability of laughing and weeping inheres in virtue of the differentia rational, not in virtue of the genus animal. Now the task of the specialist is to show in detail precisely how these accidents really—*i.e.* causally—inhere, and therefore the assumptions peculiar to his own science[2] with which he starts will be (1) that certain infimae species are thus and thus definable, and (2) actually exist as

[1] Cp. *ibid.* 73ª34 ff. and p. 188.

[2] He assumes also as " common axioms " the laws of contradiction and excluded middle. These underlie his demonstration as principles, but are not among its peculiar assumptions. The assumption by the mathematician of certain quantitative axioms creates a difficulty which we cannot here consider ; see An. Post. 75ª38 ff. and 76ᵇ14 ff. and also p. 202 below.

substances ; (3) that certain essential accidents, at present only nominally definable, inhere generally in (*i.e.* in some infima species or other within) the genus. The existence of these accidents and the real causal definitions corresponding to them, he cannot assume ; for the existence of accidents is their inherence, and the precise nature of this will appear only in the conclusion of his demonstration. *E.g.* the propensity to laughter and tears can only be defined as " an essential accident inhering in man *qua* rational," and that definition is precisely the conclusion of the proof that man is capable of laughing or weeping.[1] When the specialist has thus proved and defined an accident which inheres directly through a substantial character, he will prove a second accident as flowing directly from the first, a third as directly consequent upon the second, and so on ; but the ultimate causal link connecting the whole chain of accidents with the infima species will be a single substantial character of the latter.

Thus substance, at all events for special science, is the infima species. It is no more the concern of the specialist that genera are linked analogically upon a scale than that the species is manifest to sense as a multiplicity of singulars. What is real to him—the real counterpart which his system, so far as completed, will reflect—is (1) a group of infimae species linked as differentiations of a genus which is actual only in and as its species ; (2) for each species a chain of accidents, merely potential in their generic, or *quasi*-generic, forms, but in actuality connected each to the next by an immediate causal relation, and forming a

---

[1] Aristotle illustrates definition of essential accidents (cp. *ibid*. 93^{b}7 ff.) with an instance which shows it to be analogous to definition by genus and differentia : " Thunder is a noise (genus) caused by the quenching of fire in a cloud (differentia)." The example of laughter and tears is Aristotelian though not actually used by Aristotle, but his favourite instances—*e.g.* " either-odd-or-even " as an essential accident of number —show that the normal form of the essential accident is a disjunctive couple expressing the contrary poles which limit a capacity of variation. The underlying thought is that accidents express change.

series ultimately supported by, and deriving its meaning and being from, the infima species, which is alone substantial.

The question whether to first philosophy the infima species is ultimately real we must still postpone. But even as a conception of special science there are grave objections to Aristotle's view. It depends on opposing the genus and species relation to the relation which consists in analogy—*i.e.* the relation of terms in a developing series (cp. p. 186). Now no doubt it is not surprising that Aristotle should attribute an ascertainable fixity to natural genera and species, whereas modern science regards its classifications of nature's endless diversity rather as provisional, and, at least in the case of biology, as makeshifts which prepare the way for a system exhibiting evolutionary development. Yet Aristotle himself is no conservative, but the greatest of all pioneers in special science. It is abundantly clear that he conceives an order of development[1] in the species of the animal kingdom, and he himself admits in two crucial cases a subject-genus in which the infimae species do form a developing series : " The cases of figure and soul are exactly parallel ; for the particular specific types subsumed under the common name in both cases—figures and living beings—constitute a series, each successive term of which potentially contains its predecessor, *e.g.* the square the triangle, the sensory capacity the self-nutritive " (An. 414^{b}28 ff.). If, however, the prior species exists potentially in the posterior, just as the genus actualises through its subgenera, the self-dependence of the infima species is ruined. Either there will in the end be a science for every infima species, or substance will become a matter of degree.

It might be urged that science is bound to classify provisionally by co-ordinate species—that in science as in philosophy there must remain imperfectly coincident systems. But Aristotle seems to conceive special science

---

[1] Or rather of " developed-ness."

as moving towards co-ordination and away from the developing series. He is very sure that the infima species is the most real thing within the ken of the specialist. The ideal type of scientific demonstration, as we shall soon see more clearly (§ 2 (B)), works with species whose self-dependence is not to be sacrificed to inter-relation.

Within the limits of one infima species and its accidents the difficulty recurs. The atomicity which isolates the single species shows itself to be a self-dependence achieved by mere mutilation, and results in a quite untenable "one way" relation between species and accidents. Aristotle attempts in vain to establish a materiate form indefinable without reference to matter and change, and then to exclude from its essential nature—its nature as substance—the characteristic phases in which this change is manifested.

(C) MATHEMATICS[1]

If we remove from natural bodies the primary property of change, and with it natural place (cp. p. 82), time, and all further concrete determinations of their perceptible nature, we leave them characterised only by certain essential accidents predicable under the category of quantity. These we may treat in separation from the substances in which they actually inhere, and, since upon the primary quantitative accidents depend series of derivative accidents, we can then demonstrate the inherence of the latter in the former, just as natural science demonstrates the inherence of accident in substance. In short, these primary accidents—which are the objects of mathematics—can be treated as if they were substances—as analogous, i.e. to the materiate forms of natural science.[2] And the matter to which their definition will have refer-

---

[1] See Ph. II, 2 and Met. XIII, 3.
[2] E.g. triangularity abstracted becomes for the geometer triangle, and he demonstrates as its essential accident that it possesses angles equal to two right angles.

ence will be an intelligible, not a sensible, matter. In arithmetic it will be the bare principle of plurality, in geometry sheer extension in two or three dimensions; but always it will be a matter more abstract and potential than the perceptible matter of locomotion.[1]

These *quasi*-substances fall into two main *quasi*-subgenera : discrete quantity, the object of arithmetic, and continuous quantity, the object of geometry. " Arithmetic, which proceeds from fewer assumptions, is more exact than and prior to geometry, which requires additional elements ; *i.e.* a unit is substance without position, while a point is substance with position."[2] Hence accuracy decreases as we ascend through the more concrete sub-genera of geometry to the ambiguous science of astronomy.[3] In some passages Aristotle seems to imply a general mathematics logically prior to arithmetic, the principles of which also serve as common axioms implied in all

[1] See p. 80. Save that mathematical entities are not conceived as really separate, the doctrine seems akin to that attributed by Aristotle to Plato ; see p. 41, note 1. For intelligible matter see Ross, *Aristotle, Metaphysics*, on 1036ª9–10. If we compare the natural scale of substances and the series of types of matter (cp. p. 78), both of which ascend from primary matter as their logical postulate, we get fresh light on Aristotle's cross-classifications of the universe.

[2] An. Post. 87ª34 ff. Numbers have only order, but the continuous quanta of geometry are determined in position as well by their mutual relations (cp. Cat. 4ᵇ21 and 5ª32). Position presupposes only extension and is therefore not the same as natural place, but an abstraction from it—nothing but a purely quantitative implication of it.

[3] See p. 88. Met. 1069ª30 ff. adumbrates a special natural science of substance which is sensible but eternal. Met. 1077ᵇ23 ff. : " There are many propositions about things merely considered as in motion, and it does not follow that there should be a mobile separate from sensibles "—suggests a special mathematical science obtained by abstraction of essential accidents and perhaps equivalent to the astronomy of the *Republic*. It is interesting to observe how Aristotle distinguishes special sciences (*a*) categorially and by abstraction of accidents, and (*b*) by types of substance. On the whole he uses the first method to define the mathematical sciences, and the second to define the natural sciences, and it is not surprising that some ambiguity should occur at the point where these two closely approach one another. Met. 1078ª5, however, even seems to imply that any essential accidents might be legitimately abstracted as *quasi*-substances : *e.g.* male and female might be made the subject of a science of sex.

special mathematical proof.[1] But the peculiar assumptions of the special sciences, mathematical or natural, are not transferable as premises of demonstration from one subject-genus to another, save when an applied science concerned with observation of facts—such as optics— goes to pure mathematics for its theory.

Aristotle, then, is convinced that numbers are not substantial things, and he contemplates no creation by dialectic of a universal mathematical philosophy. Yet, though he does not seem to have been a specialist in mathematics, Platonic influence has left its mark. Not only is his cosmology based on the opposition of the circle and the straight line (cp. p. 81), but the *Republic* clearly originates his view of procedure in all special science. Geometry, with which he was evidently familiar as systematised in a form closely resembling Euclid's *Elements* is, in fact, his ideal type of special science, and he tries, with very moderate success, to accommodate the natural sciences to this norm. He accordingly treats all types of causal connexion as equivalent to the relation of ground and consequent—a relation, moreover, which by his theory of substance is already restricted to inherence of attribute in subject.[2] In An. Post. II, 11, he offers a strange classification of cause, by which he apparently groups final, efficient and material causes under the head of formal cause, and explicitly defines the material cause as " an antecedent which necessitates a consequent."[3]

2. LOGIC

Philosophic opinion has wavered long and still wavers between two extreme views of logic :—(1) Logic is a purely

[1] Met. 1077ª9–12 ; An. Post. 74ª17–25.
[2] To observe this inevitable restriction is vital for the understanding of Aristotle's logic, and of the whole subsequent development of logical theory ; cp. also p. 207.
[3] 94ª21. See footnotes to the Oxford translation.

formal study of validity, a theory of thought in abstraction from all but the barest minimum of content. (2) Such abstraction would leave thought featureless, a passive reason totally devoid of character. Logic therefore studies thought only as expressing the character of the real, for this expressive activity is precisely the nature of thought.

The germ of both views can be found in Aristotle, and he may perhaps on the whole be counted a supporter of the second. But his support can be claimed only subject to important reservations. The second view leads towards the conclusion that if thought expresses the nature of the real, then thought is an essential character of the real—*is* the real *qua* intelligible. And logic thus tends towards absorbing the whole of metaphysic, and distinguishes itself from any other philosophical investigation only by an inevitable difference of emphasis. But Aristotle is far from equating logic with first philosophy. Thought—so he seems to reason—is essentially an activity, and theoretical thought attains its full and true nature only in the actual direct apprehension of its object. Hence there is no fourth " theoretical science " with thought itself for an object, for thought apart from its own proper object is a mere ἕξις and not an ἐνέργεια. Thus there is intelligent practice, and there is theoretical thinking ; but there is, strictly speaking, no theory of either. But it does not follow that logic as a separate study simply disappears. A ἕξις is not a mere featureless potentiality, and it is possible to investigate with merely general and illustrative reference to their content the various forms in which the human mind organises its knowledge. Just as ethics is a by-product of practice, a formulation of principles to aid men to live the practical life, so logic is a by-product of active speculation, and an indispensable preliminary study for the future student of special science and metaphysic. This attitude is expressed in the title *Organon* (" instrument " of science), first given to the group of Aristotle's logical works in the sixth century, and Aristotle himself makes quite clear the status of logic as a propaedeutic : " The attempts of some who discuss the terms on which truth should be accepted are due to a want of training in analytics ;[1] for they should know these things already when they come to a special study, and not be inquiring into them while they are pursuing it " (Met. 1005[b]2 ff.).

The close-knit structure of his reasoning, which the Scholastics delight to analyse in terms of Aristotle's own logical forms, shows him a master in the use of the instrument which he had forged to replace the old dialectical method. Nevertheless in most of the *Organon* Aristotle does not write as a purely formal logician. He deduces the forms of thought from the features of its object, and he seldom forgets the real source of their distinction.

(A) SIMPLE APPREHENSION AND JUDGMENT

We saw that Aristotle's view of substance leads him to restrict logical connexion to the inherence of attribute in subject (p. 203). The *De Interpretatione*, the second book of the *Organon* and closely connected with the first, formulates a theory of judgment dominated by the notion of singular substances, and by the crude representational theory which we met with in the *Categories*. " Things said without combination " are held to reflect simple atomic experiences, or " conceptions " (νοήματα) ; and the soul, so far as these are present in it only as units still uncompounded, is below the level of judgment : there is as yet no scope for truth and falsehood.[2] Judgment, it appears,

[1] The term " analytics," which refers to the analysis of reasoning into terms, propositions, and the figures of the syllogism, is the nearest Aristotelian equivalent to " logic." Λογική to Aristotle means dialectic ; see § 2 (c).

[2] *I.e.* these νοήματα are not manifestations of that activity whereby νοῦς apprehends pure incomposite substances (see p. 213). That activity is infallible because it is *above* discursive thinking.

consists in the combining and separating of these ready-made materials. Now it is hard to see how singular νοήματα, which must in some cases reflect universal characters only intelligible as inherent in substances, can be regarded as separate units of consciousness ;[1] and this theory of judgment is scarcely consistent with Aristotle's usual emphasis on the continuity of development at least throughout the lower stages of cognitive activity.[2] We might therefore be tempted to say that the νοήματα are a mere logical presupposition of judgment, just the moment of immediacy of which judgment is the mediation—or better, perhaps, of which judgment is the analysis and re-synthesis. But the νοήματα are *terms*, and we cannot regard the immediate moment of experience—that which experience is so far as it is merely " given "—as a collection of terms awaiting connexion. It is rather a something inchoate and indeterminate, a matter and potentiality which the developed judgment, the articulate unity of terms in a relation, compels us to presuppose.

Based on this notion of atomic conceptions, Aristotle's theory of judgment is bound to be crudely representational. The terms, isolated from one another, become isolated from the real. Judgment becomes the copying of an unrelated aggregate of reals, and in the end its combinations and separations could only turn out to be the vagaries of subjective caprice.[3] Aristotle here violates his own fundamental doctrine that in all forms of awareness subject and object actualise in a single undivided activity. For we must conclude from that doctrine that the mind

---

[1] In Cat. 1a29 Aristotle actually recognises *singular* qualities : the singular whiteness, *e.g.*, predicable as inherent in this particular body. But he makes the distinction nowhere else.

[2] Although his treatment of sense-perception sometimes suggests the same error ; see p. 113, note 1.

[3] The corresponding theory of language is equally crude. Words are conceived really to be as they appear in a pocket-dictionary, and not as they live in speech—not, *i.e.*, as identities concrete in a diversity of significant contexts.

and the real *qua* object of mind are the two inseparable factors in the development of a single and undivided reality.

But the *De Interpretatione* is possibly an early work (see p. 268, note 1), and Aristotle at his best does not so desert his own teaching as to the identity of subject and object. The doctrine of singular substances suggests that the universal designates ultimately a mere class or collection of individuals—that, if " man is mortal " is true, it is true because every single man is mortal.[1] Yet even in this book, in order to classify judgments according to quantity, Aristotle distinguishes individual and universal (primary and secondary) substances as genuinely different kinds of entity : (1) judgments in which the subject is universal, are (*a*) universal—" every man is mortal," (*b*) non-universal—" man is white," or " some man is white " ; (2) judgments about individuals—" Socrates is white "— are singular (see Int. 7). These three types are not three stages on a scale of lessening generality. The predicate is not here quantified so as to contain the subject within itself as in a class, but rightly taken as characterising the subject.

Aristotle distinguishes the various oppositions of affirmative and negative judgments which language allows, but he regards the categorical as the only true type of judgment. Hypothetical and disjunctive are not for him separate types : the possible is a predicate (cp. An. Pr. 32^{a}13 ff.), and the normal type of essential accident contains disjunction within itself (cp. note 1, p. 199). This ignoring of modal distinction follows logically from the Aristotelian theory of substance, and has its inevitable consequence in the ambiguous doctrine of a real indeterminacy.[2]

[1] Hence the nominalist doctrines of the Middle Ages : see Chap. XI, §§ 2 and 3.
[2] Cp. p. 92, note 1, and p. 130.

(B) INFERENCE

The syllogism was Aristotle's chief logical discovery (cp. SE 184^{b}1), and it is because he confines logical connexion to the subject-attribute relation that he comes to regard the syllogism as the single type of all inference. A general treatment of it occupies the *Prior Analytics*, but the syllogism was in fact constructed as the proper vehicle for scientific demonstration, and that is discussed in *Posterior Analytics* I.

We learn there that demonstration *par excellence* is a syllogism in the first mood of the first figure,[1] and Aristotle proceeds to lay down the conditions to which the basic syllogism—the syllogism which draws its premises from the first principles of the science—must conform. The minor term of this syllogism is an infima species, its major a primary essential accident, its middle an element in the definition of the species. Thus its premises are basic premises drawn from the fundamental assumptions of the science, and it directly and precisely reflects, and takes its peculiar form from, the features of a counterpart which, at least to the scientist, is fully real. Predication in premises and conclusion must be strictly universal and commensurate, and Aristotle enunciates minutely the conditions required to ensure this. P must (1) attach to any and every instance of S ; (2) be predicable essentially of S, either (*a*) as an element in the definition of S (middle term), or (*b*) as involving S in its own definition (major term) ; (3) be predicable as flowing from the nature of S ; (4) be predicated of S as of its primary subject ; and therefore (5) be predicated immediately and necessarily.[2]

---

[1] " Barbara " : both premises affirmative and universal.

[2] (1) is a mere corollary of necessary connexion, and does not really concern science. (3) seems added because an essential accident of the type (2) (*b*) need not conform to (1). (4) is illustrated as follows :—The attribute, *e.g.*, of possessing angles equal to two right angles is predicable of isosceles-triangular-figure. But to isosceles it attaches only in virtue

A further condition of the basic demonstrative syllogism is that the middle term, which reflects the real proximate cause of the connexion, must partially define both major and minor terms. For it is as knowledge of cause and definition that science differs from opinion, which is grasp of an unmediated connexion, *i.e.* of a bare fact in which terms capable of necessary connexion or disconnexion through mediation are merely conjoined.[1]

Had Aristotle exemplified the basic syllogism the result would presumably have been something like this :

	Major	*Middle*	
Major premiss :	Laughter inheres in the rational :		*i.e.* rationality immediately and necessarily (5) carries with it the essential accident of laughter and tears, as its primary subject (4) and as involved in its definition (2*b*).
	Middle	*Minor*	
Minor premiss :	Rationality inheres in man :		*i.e.* rationality as a substantial character (2*a*) immediately, necessarily, and as its primary subject, characterises the infima species man.
	Minor *Middle* *Major*		
Conclusion : (which also defines the major term)	In man *qua* rational laughter inheres :		*i.e.* in the infima species man, made commensurate through the middle term, laughter and tears inhere universally.

We have already seen how the chain of episyllogisms is developed when the basic syllogisms have been established, and we have by anticipation criticised this view of scientific procedure (pp. 200 ff.). Aristotle constantly insists that

of its genus triangle, which is prior to isosceles ; and to the wider genus, figure, as such it does not attach. Therefore triangle is its primary subject. Thus Aristotle has in mind a logically ordered series of characters differentiating a genus : these, beginning with the most concrete, are stripped away in thought until the subject becomes precisely commensurate with the predicate ; cp. 73^{b}33 ff.

[1] Aristotle holds that even a mediated connexion, if not recognised as such, is the object of opinion and not of knowledge ; see 89^{a}16 ff.

knowledge of the basic premises is prior to, and the causal condition of, knowledge of the conclusion (cp. *e.g.* An. Post. I, 2) ; and to escape an indefinite regress he urges that they must be known with immediate certainty as self-evident. But clearly, if there were such self-evident truths, they could be evidence for nothing else. Their virginal isolation would be inevitably barren. Had Aristotle recognised that *if* in premises and conclusions S and P are commensurate, they are therefore reciprocal— that in fact any character conceals a relation, and that in the end a reciprocal relation—his whole linear conception of inference, and his entire doctrine of substance, would have had to be recast. The basic syllogism would have been found to express, not the dependence of accident through defining character on substance, but the hypothetical connexion of characters attaching to a never fully expressed subject within a never completely explicit system.[1]

To reply that, unless limits are somewhere set, the special sciences cease to exist, would be only a partial defence. For, within any provisional limits that may be given it, a special science does not advance by a simple development of implication which adds to without modifying a stock of ascertained truth, but by constantly reformulating its assumptions, which are the structural outline of its whole system. It is not possible even in mathematics—though there the fact is less obvious—to isolate knowing from thinking, demonstrative truth from discovery.

We need not linger over the application of syllogism to all inference, which Aristotle elaborates in An. Pr. As the foundation—practically, indeed, the whole structure—of traditional formal logic this extension of the scope of syllogism is sufficiently familiar. The principle is this. In the ideal syllogism of demonstration *causa cognoscendi* is identical with *causa essendi*. Thought moves in a *natural*

---

[1] For Aristotle's ignoring of the hypothetical judgment see p. 207.

order from minor term through middle to major, and the middle term is subject in the major premiss, predicate in the minor.[1] In the second figure the middle is predicate, in the third subject, of both premises. Because they thus distort the real which they reflect, the second and third figures are imperfect and merely potential, and require conversion to the first figure. But Aristotle admits no fourth figure because, at least in An. Pr., he treats the terms as differing in extent,[2] and their relative width, not the position of the middle term, is his primary *fundamentum divisionis*. The effort to force all inference into syllogism in fact necessitates greater flexibility of form than the first figure allows, and Aristotle is moving towards the loose quantitative relations of formal logic. But he never teaches a logic of mere validity, and he nowhere admits in scientific syllogism a singular term.[3] Amid all the intricacies of conversion and modal distinction the first figure remains the norm of reasoning.

We are now in a better position to see what status the special sciences and their objects have for the metaphysician. If we still wish to maintain that the materiate form is real only for science, we shall urge that Aristotle's conception of demonstration derives from the *Republic*,[4] and that Plato there states quite clearly the partial and inadequate

---

[1] This movement is clearly seen if we enunciate the minor premiss before the major.

[2] Though he does not take them " in extension," *i.e.* regard them as classes which are collections of singulars.

[3] Moon, sun, etc., as subjects of astronomical demonstration, do not, I think, constitute an exception (see p. 187, note 4). The familiar example of the text-books—All men are mortal ; Socrates is a man ; therefore Socrates is mortal—would not have been regarded by Aristotle as syllogism, but merely as a making explicit by ἐπαγωγή (cp. p. 28) of what was already known potentially in the " major premiss " ; see Post. An. 71ᵃ17 ff., and footnote to ᵃ21 in the Oxford translation. The "practical syllogism " (see p. 147) is a hybrid produced by Aristotle's not very successful attempt to assimilate practical thinking to theoretical.

[4] See pp. 40, 41. Aristotle calls the assumption that the infima species, thus and thus defined, actually exists (see pp. 198-9), a ὑπόθεσις, and a great deal of his logical terminology is mathematical in origin.

nature of a thought which cannot examine its assumptions. Against the materiate form, which is an infima species, it will be useless to adduce Aristotle's frequent treatment of the genus as matter and potentiality, but we may find support in passages where he speaks of the universal as only actualised in sense-perception (cp. pp. 115–6), and also two occasions on which he offers the ὑποθέσεις of syllogism as an instance of the material cause.[1] The conception of premises as material cause—of deductive thought as moving to a conclusion in which potential premises are actualised—conflicts hopelessly with the notion of self-evident primary premises, but it is nevertheless consonant with the fact that Aristotle clearly regards the conclusion of demonstration as not eliding the middle term (see p. 209).

But the evidence against this case is too strong. Plato degrades scientific truth by contrasting it with dialectic, and, as we shall see (§ 2 (c)), Aristotle, though his position is ambiguous, holds a very much lower view of dialectic than his master, and exalts demonstration accordingly. He is convinced that demonstration implies a higher knowledge *in the demonstrator* than itself reveals : the assumptions of the scientist, which it is not his function to prove, are none the less known to him fully and certainly and in all their bearings by the immediate and infallible intuition of νοῦς. And when Aristotle asserts this doctrine, a certain stern intensity glows through the obscure and elliptical language of the *Posterior Analytics* : " Since the primary premises are the cause of our knowledge—*i.e.* of our conviction—it follows that we know them better—that is, are more convinced of them—than their consequences, precisely because our knowledge of the latter is the effect of our knowledge of the premises. Now a man cannot believe in anything more than in the thing

----

[1] Ph. 195ᵃ18, and Met. 1013ᵇ20. Aristotle seems, however, to be using the term ὑπόθεσις in these passages in a looser sense than that indicated in note 4, p. 211—to cover, in fact, all premises of syllogism.

he knows, unless he has either actual knowledge of it or something better than actual knowledge. . . . But if a man sets out to acquire the scientific knowledge that comes through demonstration, he must not only have a better knowledge of the basic truths, and a firmer conviction of them than of the connexion which is being demonstrated : more than this, nothing must be more certain or better known to him than these basic truths in their character as contradicting the fundamental premises which lead to the opposed and erroneous conclusion. For indeed the conviction of pure science must be unshakable " ($72^{a}30–^{b}4$). And " No other kind of thought is more accurate than scientific knowledge—except νοῦς " (*ibid.* $100^{b}8$).

In Met. IX 10, the intuitive grasp of νοῦς is explained as a direct contact identifying it with a simple incomposite object. Unlike discursive thought, which may reflect erroneously the composite (of substance and accident) which is its object, νοῦς is infallible, and to its truth the only alternative is sheer blank nescience : " Contact and ' assertion ' are truth (' assertion ' not being the same as affirmation),[1] and ignorance is non-contact " (Met. $1051^{b}24$). Νοῦς used in this, its strict, sense of immediate intuition (cp. p 166, note 1) is the form which thought takes in the metaphysician's grasp of the pure substances which are essentially incomposite, viz. God and the astral spirits. The object of νοῦς need not, it seems, be perfect save in its kind—even the practical ideal of the good man is said to be the object of νοῦς [2]—but it must be completely real and of self-dependent simplicity, since it is known as self-evident. The materiate form, then, is fully real, and as it is known by a kind of thought that is higher than

[1] *I.e.* not implying significant negative judgment as its correlate, πάσις, here translated " assertion " for want of a better word, does not imply predication : the deliverance of νοῦς is not judgment.
[2] See p. 143 and p. 144, note 1. But the relation of practical to theoretical νοῦς is obscure ; see Chap. VII, § 5.

P

scientific knowledge, we cannot but conclude that, despite its immersion in matter, it is not amenable to any metaphysical reconstruction.[1]

This conclusion is enforced when we observe the devices to which Aristotle is driven to maintain the full reality of the materiate form amid a world of change, and the immediate certainty with which it is grasped. He states frequently (cp. *e.g.* Met. VII, 8) that as when, *e.g.*, a brazen sphere is constructed, the total composite of matter and form comes to be by a process, but the brass and the spherical form do not ; so form and matter in general do not come to be, but the form supervenes timelessly upon its appropriate matter. Correspondingly, the apprehension of the form itself, which is incomposite, is a timeless act : " That which is not quantitatively but qualitatively simple[2] is thought in a simple (indivisible) time and by a simple act of the soul " (An. 430^{b}14 ff.). Now to explain this timeless character in the form and in the thought of it, Aristotle often resorts to the analogy of the mathematical point : " Some things are and are not, without coming to be and passing away, *e.g.* points, if they can be said to *be*, and, in general, forms " (Met. 1044^{b}21 ff.). And he conceives apprehension of the form to be an act which occurs in a moment of time—in the atomic " now," which is at once division and union of past and future, just as the point is the limit which joins two lines.[3] But here Aristotle betrays himself. Despite his conviction

[1] In which case it seems to follow that, at all events to the metaphysician, the world of nature will present itself as a sheer plurality of unconnected forms. For genera, which for the man of science link species, are as such only potential and therefore must be absent from the metaphysician's intuitive grasp of pure form ; cp. note 1, p. 182. Nor does it seem an adequate defence to retort that the suggestion of a plurality of forms implies that the forms as such contain a material element. The implication is rather a part of the self-contradictory position to which Aristotle is reduced.

[2] *I.e.* the infima species.

[3] Compare the discriminative function of *Sensus Communis* : p. 110 and note 1 *ibid.*

that a point is not a constituent of a line (cp. p. 72, note 3),
he is evidently assuming that a point and a moment of
time, because each indivisibly unites an end and a beginning, are wholes indivisible as the infima species is indivisible. We meet again here the confusion which we
criticised in connexion with Aristotle's doctrine of pleasure
(Ch. VII, § 6). The results of the theory appear in his
uncompromising distinction of ἐνέργεια from process—of
conduct from art, of the flash of philosophic insight from
the laborious process of learning which leads the metaphysician to it, and from his subsequent descent of the
Scala Universi, which is made possible by its light.[1] If
the doctrine is pressed to its logical conclusion, a fresh
form will be required for every phase—every moment,
indeed—of development between birth and maturity
within each species. And, since Aristotle extends this
timeless ingenerable character to accidents, a fresh accident
will be required for every moment of secondary change.
Not only does nature become a mere plurality of unconnected forms, but each scientist will have a task to
pursue in his own sphere as hopeless as that of the
geometer who tries to build up a line out of points.

But we shall better appreciate the position which
Aristotle has reached when we witness its reaction upon
the status of dialectic.

(c) DIALECTIC

If there be a man who is both metaphysician and
scientist—a man in whom speculative wisdom (σοφία), the
virtue of the theoretical soul, is fully manifest[2]—then his
thought is one with the universe as it really is. And the

---

[1] The doctrine of the instantaneous actualisation of ἕξις (see p. 104)
is a corollary.

[2] Σοφία is described in EN 1141ᵃ18 ff. as " νοῦς combined with
scientific knowledge of the highest objects—scientific knowledge with
a head on " (*i.e.* not truncated but properly completed).

universe really is a descending scale of being, in which upon the really prior and more knowable hangs the really posterior and less knowable   But σοφία is only achieved by the slow labour of learning, and in the thinking of the learner—or, if we prefer the converse view of it, the exposition of his teacher—the real order of being is reversed.   In fact, " Prior and more knowable," says Aristotle, " are ambiguous terms, for there is a difference between what is prior and more knowable in the order of being and what is prior and more knowable to man. I mean that objects nearer to sense are prior and more knowable to man ; objects without qualification prior and more knowable are those further from sense " (An. Post. 71^{b}33 ff.).   Now since " Any instruction given or received by way of argument proceeds from pre-existent knowledge,"[1] it follows that, whether a man is learning from a master or from nature herself, he must start from the level of sense-perception.   Thus we have before us a distinction between (a) knowledge which is either immediate intuition or a discursive and deductive thinking, and knows the real as it is, or at least, in the latter case, so far as it is knowable ; and (b) thinking which is essentially a learning, a process by which knowledge comes to be in the individual, and in which the real order is reversed. This antithesis—as the history of thought has shown abundantly—is susceptible of very various interpretation. Aristotle himself does not elaborate it without ambiguity, but he does on the whole definitely assign knowing, so far as it is a learning, to the province of dialectic.

The *Topics* (the last book of the *Organon*), in which dialectic is discussed, is an early work.   In writing it Aristotle is carrying on the Socratic and early-Platonic tradition by attacking the Sophists.[2]   He is trying to

---

[1] The opening words of An. Post.

[2] This is more particularly true of the *De Sophisticis Eleuchis*, which forms a sort of appendix to the main body of the *Topics*.

substitute an instrument—an *Organon*—of general culture
for the Sophistic educational method, which seemed to
him to teach little more than the use of logical fallacy for
the purpose of making the worse cause appear the better.
Later in life he lost direct interest in general culture,
and the *Analytics*, which he wrote to aid the specialist,
supersede in importance this propaedeutic for the dilettante.
But in some respects Aristotle's views on the function of
dialectic did not change. In the *Topics* the objects of
dialectic are given as three : (1) to provide intellectual
exercise ; (2) to teach you to meet a man in argument on
his own ground ; (3) to establish the first principles of the
several sciences, " for it is impossible to say anything
of the principles proper to the particular science in hand
by inference from them, seeing that the principles are
the *prius* of everything else. . . . Dialectic is a process
of criticism wherein lies the path to the principles of all
inquiries " (Top. 101ª37 ff.). This function of establishing
the principles of the special sciences and of metaphysics
is assigned to dialectic throughout Aristotle's works.
" Reasoning," he says, " is dialectical if it reasons from
opinions that are generally accepted . . . *i.e.* accepted by
all, or by the majority, or by the most notable of them—
the philosophers " (*ibid.* 100ª30 ff.). And as we read him
we can constantly observe Aristotle establishing his results
by the gradual development of a more comprehensive and
coherent theory through the criticism and modification
of other men's conflicting doctrines. In respect of its
method an Aristotelian treatise is a Platonic dialogue
stripped of its dramatic form and reduced to more or less
continuous lecture-notes.

Thus Aristotle's dialectic, like Plato's, is not a linear
process from pure particular to pure universal : its starting-
point is at once a particular and a confused universal, its
conclusion—at least in intention—a universal concrete
in essential differentiation. But though this dialectical

thinking may be the only way to learn and teach even the truths of metaphysic, it is not the thinking of the mature metaphysician. It is in fact below demonstration and not above it, for its " premiss " is opined and not known, and its " conclusion " is not logically proved. It terminates in the direct intuition of νοῦς, and the principle—the law of contradiction, e.g., or the definition of an infima species—is established but not proved. For as knowledge develops in the learner's soul—as, presumably, efficient reason actualises passive reason—the learner is climbing upward to the real starting-point of knowledge. His thought is moving from what is really consequent to what is really antecedent, and *causa cognoscendi* never in this dialectical movement coincides with *causa essendi*. His apprehension is, throughout, the opining of a connexion which lacks its true middle term. The scientist builds up a body of knowledge. He divides a genus into its infimae species, and defines each of these by considering what attributes are " severally of wider extent than the subject but collectively co-extensive with it : for this synthesis must be the substance of the thing."[1] To ascertain the genus he considers the common characters which specific groups of individuals possess, and selects what is common to these characters until a single generic character is reached—a process in which the use of division, though not logically cogent (cp. pp. 125 ff.), may help him. Faced at this point with a mass of species and properties confusedly connected within the genus, he hits by the quickness of his wit upon the middle terms which must fall within these gaps between substance and accident. Gradually the gaps close—become, as Aristotle puts it, " close-packed " —and suddenly all connexion is immediate. But these

---

[1] An. Post. 96ᵃ32. This view of substantive definition implies that the differentia is wider than the infima species (cp. p. 211), and it is cruder than Aristotle's usual conception of the differentia as that and that alone by which the genus is finally actualised as the infima species : cp. pp. 186-7, 197-8.

processes, which are in the main developments of ἐπαγωγή (cp. p. 211, note 3), are not logical proof, but the dialectical growth of individual thinking from its basis in sense—from that rough general whole which comprises a confused mass of particulars.[1]

So the problem of thought's twofold character—of its subjective and objective aspects (cp. p. 170)—is solved by a bold cleavage. We are offered the antithesis of (1) a perfectly true and impersonal thought, which has for its content the real as it is, or so far as it can be known ; and (2) a psychological process, a history of the individual soul. Plato had not—at least in the *Republic*—so divorced the learning and the knowing, the question and the answer, that in thought are inseparable ; but in Aristotle the chasm seems to be fundamental, for it follows from his doctrine of substance. It is but one instance of that severance of process from ἐνέργεια which leads him to take the atomic " now " as a " type and symbol of eternity." It also goes far towards explaining why he leaves the relation of passive and efficient reason in such obscurity. Efficient reason is the culmination of his psychology—of his treatment of thinking as adjectival to the individual. But individual thinking when perfected —when it is no more a learning—is bound on his own theory to become impersonal, and how efficient reason should at once constitute and transcend the individual thinker is beyond Aristotle's power to explain.

Yet the excluded moment of thought returns inevitably to confuse the antithesis. The premises of syllogism appear suddenly as material cause ; and conversely

---

[1] See Ph. I, 1. In this chapter of Ph. the presence of the universal *ab initio* in discovery and exposition is emphasised. Aristotle actually says : " It is a whole which is best known to sense-perception, and a generality is a kind of whole comprehending many things within it like parts." (In Greek the same word, καθόλου, stands for both " universal " and " general.") Usually the processes of learning and teaching are described as moving from particular to universal—no doubt from a wish to exhibit antithesis to a converse process of demonstration.

dialectic, it seems, has after all a partly logical nature, for syllogism in its weaker figures provides a form for dialectic.[1] Even ἐπαγωγή, if it is a complete " induction," can take shape as syllogistic argument (cp. An. Pr. II, 23). Division is now an aid to ἐπαγωγή,[2] now " a weak syllogism " (An. Pr. 46ᵃ33). *Naturam expellas furca.* . . . The dialectical movement of thought is always liable to reassert itself against Aristotle's linear conception. He cannot wholly desert the Socratic ideal which Plato, even if he abandoned it in later life, had developed in the *Republic*.

It remains for us to conclude this sketch of Aristotle's philosophy by attempting to strike some sort of balance between the conflicting tendencies which rend and yet enrich his thinking.

We have endeavoured to depict Aristotle's speculative achievement against its Platonic background, and Plato's successor came to divide and not to unify. Hence, as we watched him elaborate the detail of his system, inevitably he seemed to us to be laying emphasis upon difference rather than upon identity ; to be striving to give their full value and meaning to the parts even at the expense of the whole. We marked his association of perfection with definition and proportion, and so with limitation, and the severance of ἐνέργεια from process, which led him to contradict his own doctrine of the spatial point and the temporal " now." We saw the consequence of this in his conception of a substance which contains atomically its own whole nature within itself, unconditioned by accidents whose being is nothing but their inherence in substance ; and again in his hesitant doctrine of a real indeterminacy, and in his neglect of the hypothetical judgment. We

---

[1] Ἐπαγωγή and syllogism are given as the two forms of dialectical reasoning in Top. 105ᵃ11.

[2] Cp. the συναγωγή of Plato's *Phaedrus* ; pp. 57–8.

recognised a corresponding tendency to separate impossibly within cognitive activity (1) the flash of infallible intuition which grasps the fully real, (2) the discursive thinking which proceeds from that intuition by necessary logical development and yet leaves unmodified the self-evident truth which νοῦς apprehends, and, finally (3) the baser intuition by sense of the perceptible singular. We noted the seeming separation of God from the world, and of the divine in man from human personality. We observed within Aristotle's system as a whole the clash of the *Scala Universi*, the categories, and that residue of all-pervasive characters of the real which transcend the categories.

Yet even in his pursuit of distinction and difference we seldom failed to find in Aristotle some hint of the other side of the truth. Conduct that was opposed to art as pure ἐνέργεια to mere process, turned out, when contrasted with speculation, itself to be the pursuit of an end not fully immanent (p. 163). The substantial infima species, atomic as it seemed, still marked a stage upon a scale, and we found Aristotle indefatigable in tracing the analogical relations between the degrees of that scale. Indeterminacy, even if presupposed by the possibility of free will, was to him yet never a *vera causa* (p. 92, note 1). Against the diremption of cognitive activity we had to set the facts that Aristotle offers without comment and without sense of self-contradiction the premises of syllogism as an instance of the material cause, and that when he displays man's cognitive faculties in their order as phases of a unitary experience, he does his utmost to preserve continuity throughout the whole development from simple sense to thought. If he severs the divine spark in man from the hierarchy of human functions which should culminate in it, yet he himself tells us that νοῦς *is* the individual man. If we turn from detail to take a synoptic view, we find him fully aware that his own doctrine of causation—the mainspring of his speculation—demands that the divine perfection, which gives order and meaning to the universe, be immanent as well as transcendent. If Aristotle's God seem infinitely remote, we shall do well to remember that it was Spinoza and not Aristotle who said : " He who most truly loves God must not expect God to love him in return."

The problem in little or in large is eternal in philosophy. We may seem to find in Aristotle a conflict of partially discordant systems, and a certain insensibility to hints of a wider outlook in Plato. Yet it must be said that Plato's own attempt in the *Sophist* to build up a dialectic of partial definitions of the real as a whole was but inchoate, and that, indeed, any such effort is bound to fail, in so far as it is not the product of omniscience. And its failure can only find expression in the character of its moments, which are bound to fluctuate between abstract generality on the one hand, and the mere concreteness of the empirical on the other. It is not Aristotle's least achievement to have shown us that there can be no philosophy which, despite its intention, does not present a number of imperfectly harmonising systems.

APPENDIX

THE ARTS OF PERSUASION AND POETRY

(A) RHETORIC

" RHETORIC is an offshoot of dialectic and of the study of character which may properly be called politics " (Rh. 1356ª25 ff.). " In so far as anyone tries to construct either dialectic or rhetoric not as a knack but as a science, he will unconsciously destroy their nature by passing over, in his attempt to remodel them, into sciences of definite subject-matters, and not of mere words " (Rh. 1359ᵇ12 ff.). Aristotle's *Rhetoric* is consequently a purely practical manual for the orator. The work as we have it contains portions of more than one treatise, and the earliest part of it may have been written under the influence of Plato's *Phaedrus* against Isocrates, the spirit of whose successful school of oratory and general education was in some measure opposed to the more scientific ideal of the Academy. Aristotle emphasises the need of suitable argumentative forms—the "striking example" (παράδειγμα), which takes the place of genuine ἐπαγωγή, and the enthymeme, which is a syllogism with its major premiss omitted or its conclusion left to the audience to draw. But, if they are to persuade successfully, the political orator, the legal advocate, and the panegyrist must also appeal to the feelings. In describing oratorical device Aristotle displays some cynicism and a most unacademic knowledge of the world—he seems to be trying, and not unsuccessfully, to beat the sophists at their own game, and at the same time to show what a poor game it is. But his analyses of the emotions are profound, and pave the way for his ethic. He advocates a style clear, rhythmical, compact, and not aping the metre or diction of verse ; a style which he himself had in fact acquired largely from Isocrates, and uses with effect on the comparatively rare occasions when he does not spare words. The literary criticism with which he illustrates this part of the subject is blunt and practical rather than imaginative, but he never says a thing not worth saying.

(B) POETICS

Aristotle treats the fine arts no less than rhetoric or than the manual crafts as subordinate elements which subserve the moral life. In the *Poetics* he narrows the term ποιητική, which is normally equivalent to τέχνη (cp. p. 131, note 2), to cover a specially important group of τέχναι which comprises music and dancing as well as what we call poetry. What the precise purpose of poetry is, we are not told quite unambiguously. But Aristotle's theory develops against a Platonic background, and if we can measure his advance upon Plato, we may reach some answer to the question.

For Plato beauty and truth were hardly yet differentiated (cp. p. 63). He has no notion of aesthetic experience as in any sense autonomous. Hence his criterion of art is a moral one ; and for all the breadth and nobility with which he conceives the moral life, art plays within it but a humble rôle. His express doctrine—though he occasionally breaks through its limitations—is briefly this. The artist is a man who imitates in one medium or another the world of perceptible singulars, which itself " partakes in," or " imitates," the world of Forms. His function is duplication, and his best success is to create illusion. The poet, who with verse or music (which the Greeks but little dissociated) imitates human character, is therefore a mere pretender to knowledge which he has not got. The dramatic poet in particular plays perpetually at being other men, and by rousing the emotion of his hearers, while he lulls their critical faculty, he moulds them insensibly into the likeness of his puppets. At best, if his choice of models is a good one, his poems may serve to harmonise and make rhythmical the plastic imagination of youth, assimilating it to the rhythms and harmonies of nature, and colouring it with a pale reflex from the life of noble action in which the child cannot as yet take part The artist is, in short, a mere craftsman, and his craft is suspect. The poet's frenzy holds no vision of the truth, and it tends dangerously to deceit of self and others. Clear-sighted ardour belongs to philosophic thought alone.

Aristotle too bases poetry on imitation. But he begins characteristically by tracing its development from a primitive stage, and his final results differ greatly from Plato's. Though man's joy in disinterested sense-perception is an earnest of his desire for knowledge (cp. p. 17), he learns at first through his natural aptitude for imitation. The origin of the useful arts in the imitation of nature we have already seen (pp. 132 ff.), but the fine arts too, the end of which is especially pleasure, all derive from this imitative faculty ; for in recognising the relation of copy to original there is a pleasure over and above the pleasure we take in the copy as simply an object beautiful to look upon. This is shown by the fact that the realistic representation even of an object in itself painful to behold gives us pleasure. From imitation, and from an equally natural and fundamental sense of harmony and rhythm, sprang those rude improvisations in dance and song from which civilised poetry developed (Poet. 1448^{b}4–24).

Now though the fine arts exist especially to give pleasure, nothing, on Aristotle's own theory, can be said of pleasure save in terms of the activity which it graces (cp. p. 150). The pleasure, then, at this elementary stage belongs (*a*) to the activity of perceiving harmonious forms and rhythms, whereby the sensory-appetitive soul of the percipient, which receives the form of the object without its matter (cp p. 107), is made rhythmical and harmonised ; and (*b*) to an intellectual activity of recognition, which does not necessarily presuppose a pleasing original. The latter foreshadows the delight we take in the technique of the artist or the executant,[1] but Aristotle seems to mean also that the enjoyment consists in increasing our knowledge of the original under conditions which protect us from the irrelevant and disturbing emotions excited by direct con- templation. According to this account (*b*) implies more than mere reduplication : it is a new stage of reflective selection in which the desire to know gains fuller expression.

It seems possible to trace this development to higher levels. Plato had feared—perhaps himself experienced— the disintegrating effect on the artist himself and on the spectator of emotional self-assimilation to an imaginary character. Aristotle, though he says that the poet must be able to identify himself with his characters, and that for this " poetry requires a man with a special gift for it, or one with a touch of frenzy in him,"[2] ascribes to dramatic presentation a positive and valuable effect upon the feelings. He speaks of tragedy—to him the most important form of poetry—as " by means of pity and fear accomplishing its purgation of such emotions " (*ibid.* 1449[b]27). From references in the *Politics* to the especially purgative[3] effect upon excessive " enthusiasm " (mystic ecstasy) of certain musical performances, and also from the obviously medical phraseology, we may infer that the purpose of tragedy is to excite pity and fear so as to afford a safe outlet for surplus emotion which it is dangerous to confine. The suggestion is that this imaginative, and in one sense

---

[1] Cp. PA 645[a]11 ff., cited on pp. 261–2.
[2] Poet. 1455[a]32. He means, evidently, a man in whom φαντασία is highly, or even abnormally, developed.
[3] As opposed to moral or instructional : cp. Pol. 1341[b]32 ff.

secondary, emotion which Plato had failed to distinguish
from the emotions of " real " life, tends, unlike the latter,
to moderate " real " feeling, not to produce a habit of
excessive reaction. The artistic medium which the
dramatist interposes makes this difference : the purgation
is a purely pleasurable experience. But Aristotle could
never have offered a physiological account of human
experience save as a provisional description of matter
which subserves a higher end. The emotions are, after
all, " embodied " λόγος (cp. p 114, note 1), and we may
perhaps look for the developed meaning of poetry in a
famous but, unfortunately, isolated passage, which runs
thus : " The poet's function is to describe, not the thing
that happened, but a kind of thing that might happen,
i.e. what is possible as being probable or necessary. The
distinction between the historian and the poet is not in the
one writing prose and the other verse—you might put
the work of Herodotus into verse, and it would still be
history : it consists really in this, that the one describes
the thing that has occurred, and the other a kind of thing
that might occur. Hence poetry is something more
philosophic and of graver import than history, since its
statements are of the nature rather of universals, whereas
those of history are singulars " (Poet. 1451^{a}36–^{b}7). Now
to Aristotle the primary meaning of universality is necessary connexion and not generality.[1] Hence the implication
is, not that the figures of tragedy are types like the
Characters of Theophrastus or La Bruyère, but that when
we witness a dramatic representation we feel rationally,
because we then recognise the true connexions underlying
the apparent confusion of actual practical life, which the
annalistic historian can only record as a fragmentary
series of events. We exchange the bare fact for the
reasoned fact, and get a glimpse of what " real " life really
is. In the imaginative freedom of the theatre fact is

[1] See pp. 208 ff. and p. 219, note 1.

purged of its irrelevancies ; its unmeaning chasms are intelligibly bridged and its context made explicit.

Thus Aristotle seems almost to reverse the duplicative relation—to assert that art is really the *prius* of life. Yet there is here but the germ of genuine aesthetic theory. As a seer the poet still but apes the philosopher, and it is only to the philosophy of conduct that he contributes. Poetry is a practical art, though a nobler one than Plato had supposed. We take with us from the theatre neither a knowledge of things immutable nor an imaginative vision precious for its own sake. What we have learnt there will help us only to control and rationalise the blind impulses which lead us to wrongdoing in actual life. The universals we have learnt are but major premises for the practical syllogism.

Aristotle's discussion of literary forms is practical in character, but it seems at least not to contradict the aesthetic doctrine which we have hazardously reconstructed from scattered passages of the *Poetics*. The supreme form of poetry is tragedy, which uses all the three possible means of poetic "imitation," viz. rhythm, language, and melody. Tragedy is " the imitation of an action that is good and also complete in itself and of some magnitude " (Poet. 1449^{b}24–25), and we know already that its final cause is emotional purgation. The action must have a beginning, a middle, and an end—be, that is, an ordered whole (cp. p. 152). It must be long enough to interest and too short to fatigue.

Having thus generally defined the end which the dramatist must set before himself, Aristotle proceeds to analyse the constituent elements of tragedy which the tragedian has to realise.[1] Three of these are concerned with the object represented, viz. plot, character, and thought. Plot is the most important, the essence in fact

---

[1] Much as in EN I, he analyses happiness before explaining how it is to be achieved. The *Poetics* is a practical work.

of the play ; for plot is the primary form in which character is expressed, the activity in which the moral ἕξις issues. If plot and character are ideally combined, we shall not witness the bad man passing from misfortune to happiness, or even from happiness to misfortune ; nor again the good man passing from happiness to misfortune. For the first of these reversals is merely odious, and none of them excites tragic pity and fear. We shall be shown instead a hero " neither pre-eminently virtuous and just, nor one whose fate is due to vice and depravity, but a man whose fall is caused by some error of judgment[1]—a man, too, who is in the enjoyment of great repute and prosperity, *e.g.* Oedipus, Thyestes, and other such famous men " (*ibid.* 1453[a]7 ff.). " The plot must present an action which is one and whole, with its several incidents so closely connected that to transpose any one of them will dislocate and disjoin the whole."[2] It follows that the speech and action of the characters must be what they would necessarily or probably say or do : even if they behave inconsistently, they must do so consistently. Under the head of thought Aristotle considers only that expression of character in language which necessarily supplements its actualisation in plot, and he assigns this to the province of rhetoric.

Diction and melody are two lesser elements, connected

---

[1] Ἁμαρτία, a term usually signifying accidental and not immoral ignorance. Aristotle has in mind here his favourite tragedy, the *Oedipus Rex.* Yet he is merely trying to express the paradox that, in order to satisfy, tragedy must link destiny with character, and yet show it not wholly deserved. He knows well enough that the spring of tragedy is the never fully intelligible connexion of human happiness with " external goods." It is really irrelevant to his theory whether the historical cause of disaster is unavoidable ignorance or a moral fault, provided that the hero is not a wholly good man. Nor is the distinction a perfectly simple one. We feel that Lear is honestly deceived when he trusts Regan and Goneril, but that his misjudging of Kent and Cordelia springs from a blindness of the heart. Yet the man who would do the one would also do the other.

[2] Poet. 1451[a]31 ff. From this passage derives the " Unity of Action," one of the three famous rules for drama extracted from the *Poetics* by the critics of the *Renaissance* ; see p. 251.

Q

with the means of representation. Melody he does not discuss. Poetry, he says, should attain clearness and dignity by combining ordinary speech with unusual forms and with metaphor. The eye for an effective metaphor, is, in fact, a mark of genius and unteachable. And in devoting most space to illustrating that form of metaphor which depends upon analogy—as when old age is described as " Life's sunset "—he means, perhaps, to mark the manifestation within the poet's imaginative world of that hierarchic order of analogous stages which pervades the whole Aristotelian universe. The last and least important element in tragedy is spectacle.

He discusses also epic, to which he allows the peculiar merits of grandeur, variety of interest, and diversity of episode. But he rates it lower than tragedy which, with its greater equipment of means and its intenser unity of action, produces a more vivid and concentrated effect of pity and fear. A promise to speak of comedy is not fulfilled. The ridiculous is to Aristotle " a species of the ugly," and his remark that the characters of tragedy are meant to be better, those of comedy worse, than the men of the present day, only leaves us to wonder what the emotions are which laughter serves to purge.

PART III
THE VERDICT OF HISTORY

XI

THE HISTORY AND INFLUENCE OF ARISTOTELIANISM[1]

1. FROM THEOPHRASTUS TO THE DARK AGES

THE wisdom of Socrates was a prophecy ; Plato's philosophy was a vision half seen and half communicated, and his death an urgent challenge to make good his uncompleted conquest. But Aristotle's triumphant fulfilment of his inherited task was a climax from which the tide of speculation could only recede. We can trace through about two and a half centuries the names of his successors at the Lyceum, but each is a lesser and a dimmer figure than the one before. In Theophrastus survived some ember of Aristotle's universal genius, and for later generations his repute remained within a still measurable distance of his master's ; but Strato devoted himself almost entirely to natural science, and his brother Lyco, the fourth head of the school, seems to have been distinguished chiefly by an enthusiasm for adolescent education, and by an eloquence of speech which failed him sadly when he came to write.

Diogenes Laertius—an unreliable author—lists the works of Theophrastus and Strabo, but presumably the Aristotelian treatises remained the mainstay of the Lyceum curriculum. Strabo, Plutarch, and Athenaeus record inconsistent versions of a tale that Theophrastus left his

---

[1] Debts in this chapter which require special acknowledgment are to Sandys, *History of Classical Scholarship* ; Gilson, *La Philosophie au Moyen Age* ; Stocks, *Aristotelianism*.

own and Aristotle's works to his pupil Neleus, who removed them to Scepsis in the Troad. At Neleus' death his heirs hid them in a cellar for fear Eumenes II, who had become master of Scepsis, should covet them for the library of Pergamon, the rising literary rival of Alexandria. About 100 B.C. one Apellicon of Teos purchased and brought them back to Athens. But this dubious story becomes quite absurd if it means, as Strabo takes it to mean, that Neleus was allowed to remove MSS. which were unique, and that for one hundred and fifty years the Lyceum possessed no copy of the more important works of Aristotle and Theophrastus.

Towards the end of the first century B.C. Andronicus of Rhodes, the last-known head of the school, edited Aristotle's treatises, and his canon corresponds fairly closely with our *Corpus Aristotelicum*. In 86 B.C. Sulla sacked Athens and brought to Rome a mass of Aristotelian texts—according to Strabo he carried off Apellicon's library, which still contained the Scepsis MSS. There Tyrannion, a Peripatetic and the intimate of Cicero, worked on them, and he may possibly have collaborated with Andronicus.

Before this time the treatises were pretty certainly not in circulation outside the Lyceum, and Aristotle seems to have been known to the educated world chiefly through his dialogues (see pp. 254–5). But even the work of Tyrannion failed to inspire the leaders of the Roman literary Renaissance with any great enthusiasm for Aristotle's philosophy. Cicero is familiar with the dialogues, the *Rhetoric*, and the *Topics*, and he shows a vague knowledge of the ethical doctrine ; but the Romans lacked any metaphysical genius. They were interested in the moral teaching of Epicurus and of the contemporary Peripatetics, and the practical ethic of Stoicism became engrafted in the Roman character ; but the greater figures of Greek philosophy they admired and never understood. Horace, of course, knew the *Poetics*, but even the logical works attracted little attention until the fourth century. Towards the end of it the *Analytics* were at least twice translated into Latin, and Augustine, though Plato and the Neo-Platonists were his chief sources of pagan thought, had studied the *Categories*.

Augustine died at Hippo in 430, while the Vandals were besieging the city. Alaric had sacked Rome twenty years before, and by the middle of the century Attila, who had already spread terror and desolation in Persia and Eastern Europe, was threatening both the Empires. During the three centuries before Charlemagne scholarship decayed in the West and speculation ceased. Boethius (480–524) was the last Roman to possess a thorough knowledge of the language and literature of Greece, and some under-standing of Greek thought. He was by no means a dogmatic Christian, and his philosophy was eclectic. His *Philosophiae Consolatio* is a charming moral dialogue inter-spersed with attractive poems and drawing inspiration equally from Plato's *Timaeus*, from Aristotle, and from the Stoics. But for us he is significant because he was familiar with the *Organon*, and his translation of its first two books, and also his commentaries on them, survived to become the starting-point of medieval Aristotelianism.

Meanwhile in the Greek world the influence of the physical writings on the great physician Galen of Pergamon (131–201) is the only sign of any vital Aristotelian impulse. Erudition rather than originality was the characteristic of the Alexandrian age. Galen, a prolific and versatile writer, commented on the *Categories* and *Analytics*, and Averroes credits him with inventing the fourth figure of syllogism ; but the Aristotelian tradition was perpetuated by a series of more professional commentators, who expounded his works mainly at Alexandria and Athens, and later at Constantinople. The first name which we can trace is that of Aspasius, who flourished about A.D. 175 ;

we lack the links between him and Andronicus. But the tradition is traceable down to the fourteenth-century monk Sophonias, though the ninth, tenth, and thirteenth centuries are unrepresented. Far the best of these commentators is Alexander Aphrodisiensis, whose acute and methodical expositions are still of great value in themselves as well as for the light they throw on the text of Aristotle and on the history of Greek thought.[1] Porphyry (c. 233–301), the next name of importance, taught both in Athens and Rome. He was a pupil of Plotinus, who had developed and formulated in writing the doctrines of Neo-Platonism, the last legacy of Hellenic speculation. Neo-Platonism, though it absorbed something from the Aristotelian dialogues (see pp. 254–5), and drew also from some wholly un-Platonic sources, was in essence a religious and mystical interpretation of the theory of Forms. Hence Porphyry's Aristotelian studies were somewhat incidental—he was chiefly interested in the defence of paganism against Christianity—but his introduction to the *Categories*, which raises without solving a problem as to the status of universals, exerted through Boethius an important influence on medieval thought, and gave rise to the famous realist-nominalist controversy. Syrianus and Ammonius of Alexandria were also Neo-Platonists. The first Christian among the Greek commentators is the somewhat prolix and unhelpful Philoponus (c. 490–530).

In 529 Justinian closed the schools of Athens, and many of the evicted teachers, including the Aristotelian scholar Simplicius, sought the protection of the Persian king, Chosroes.[2] Through his intercession they were later allowed to settle in Alexandria. It was, however, from another source that the stream of Aristotelianism started on its strange course round the southern shore of the

---

[1] The extant commentary on Met. long attributed to Alexander, is genuine only to the end of Met. V.
[2] See Gibbon, *Decline and Fall*, Chap. XL, *sub. fin.*

Mediterranean. Themistius had expounded Aristotle at Constantinople soon after its foundation, and his tradition endured there for several hundred years. But far more important is the influence of this Byzantine Aristotelianism upon the Syrians and Arabs. Syriac versions of the treatises appear from the fifth to the twelfth century, and from centres such as Gandisapora the knowledge of Aristotle gradually percolated southward, until his works were translated from Syriac into Arabic during the reign (813-833) of Almanum, the son and successor of Harun-al-Raschid, Kalif of Bagdad. The chief Arab expositors of Aristotle were Alfarabi (d. 950), who had Neo-Platonic leanings ; the physician Avicenna, who accepted Aristotle with unreserved enthusiasm ; and Algazel (1059-1111), who opposed him on religious grounds.

The Arabs established themselves in Spain early in the eighth century, and by degrees the study of Aristotle spread westward in their path.

2. FROM ALCUIN TO AQUINAS

The rebirth of Aristotelianism in Europe determined the whole course of medieval and modern culture. We can reproduce only a few salient features from a complex and crowded panorama.

In the eighth century Charlemagne's efforts to reorganise education as he had reorganised the political situation, resulted in the establishment of schools throughout France, and the term "Scholastic" was first applied to the teachers in these schools. He was assisted by learned men of other countries, and the curriculum introduced by the most distinguished of them, Alcuin of York, consisted of the seven liberal arts. The two parts of this root from which European education was to ramify, were the *Trivium* (grammar, rhetoric, and dialectic), and the *Quadrivium* (arithmetic, geometry, astronomy, music, and, later, medicine). Philosophy and theology, which Alcuin regarded as crowning the seven preparatory stages of the arts, were also taught, but in close connexion at first with dialectic. The most important thinker of the Carolingian Renaissance was the brilliant Irishman, Joannes Scotus Erigena. Erigena felt no clash between faith and reason, and therefore no need to curb his speculative activity. His *De Divisione Naturae* draws upon the *Timaeus* (the only Platonic dialogue known in the Dark Ages) and on Augustine, but the main influence is that of Dionysius the Areopagite (*fl. c.* 500), a Christian Neo-Platonist. Thus Erigena sees the universe as a hierarchy of emanations created by God and destined to re-absorption in the divine nature. Yet Aristotle too contributes : the Forms are the first and highest stage of creation, but the ten categories are also structural elements in Erigena's rich but not wholly coherent system of created nature. Erigena, who had enough Greek to translate Dionysius, shows a knowledge also of the *De Interpretatione* in his vigorous self-defence against the theologians, to whom he seemed something of a pantheist.

Dialectic furnished the weapons for the ninth-century controversy concerning the reality of genera and species which Boethius had handed down unsolved, and Gerbert d'Aurillac, the sole distinguished scholar of the tenth century, the " leaden " age of the Norman invasions, may even have known the *Topics*.[1] In the next century the arts of the *Trivium* inspired its students with a veritable passion. In the absence of any new philosophic impulse dialectic developed into every sort of logic-chopping, and the dialecticians—Bérenger de Tours, for example—provoked theological thunders by trying their skill upon dogmas such as that of transubstantiation. In consequence philosophy became somewhat discredited, and the realist-nominalist controversy continued with but little regard

[1] So Gilson, *La Philosophie au Moyen Age*, p. 36.

to its metaphysical implications. On the other hand, whereas study of the *Timaeus* and the prevailing Neo-Platonist interpretation of the Forms had on the whole led the two preceding centuries to regard universals as real *ante res*, the influence of Aristotle's *Categories* now began to inspire a nominalist solution. Roscellinus, developing the doctrine of substance enunciated in that work (see pp. 178 ff.), argued from the reality of the singular individual to the merely nominal being of species and genera, which thus tended to become identified with the verbal names expressing them. Had Aristotle's *Metaphysics* been known at this time, the whole controversy might have proved more fruitful. Anselm, who died Archbishop of Canterbury in 1109, marks the moment of transition to Scholasticism in the narrower sense of the term. With his principle, *credo ut intelligam*, he mediates between the dialecticians and the theologians, and he reasserts realism against the nominalism of Roscellinus. But in elaborating his famous proofs of God's existence, which assume this realism, he broadened again the philosophic field, which had been contracted by the official ecclesiastical attitude to Erigena. His thought is Augustinian, but he prepares the way for Aquinas.

Arab Aristotelianism was flourishing in Spain by the beginning of the twelfth century. It contained Neo-Platonic and some native elements, and its devotees did not escape increasing conflict with theological authority. The greatest of them, Averroes (1126–1198), was banished for dissent from the orthodox faith of Islam in 1195, shortly before the Moorish dominion in Spain came to an end. But the Arabs possessed the bulk of Aristotle's treatises,[1] though only in translations from the Syriac version. The brilliant Abelard, who counted Aristotle the highest authority in dialectic, died in 1142, knowing

[1] But not the dialogues, which were lost irrecoverably before the Dark Ages.

only the *Categories, De Interpretatione,* and *Prior Analytics* ;
but the significant feature of the century is the gradual
filtration into Europe from about 1132 onwards of Latin
translations from the Arabic texts and commentaries,
the work largely of bilingual Spanish Jews. The remainder
of the *Organon* came first, and the *Metalogicus* of John of
Salisbury (1159) shows his acquaintance with the whole
of it. In conformity with the still persisting trend of current thought, he applies its teaching to the problem of
universals. He despairs of any solution, but he criticises
vigorously the narrow dialectical conception of logic which
belonged to his age.

The first Scholastic who knew all the treatises with their
Arab commentaries was Alexander of Hales (d. 1245),
and by the beginning of the thirteenth century this vast
influx of new material, positive and speculative, had set
Europe in a ferment of enthusiastic assimilation. But
with Aristotle came Averroes, and as a prophet at first
scarce distinguished from his master. And Averroes
interpreted Aristotle as maintaing the intelligence of the
aetherial spheres, the eternity of matter, the unity and
transcendence of the efficient reason, and the consequent
mortality of the individual soul. Hence the newly constituted University of Paris, now the fountain-head of
European culture and theologically under the close control
of the Papacy, forbade the reading of Aristotle's natural
science in 1205, and in 1215 explicitly banned the *Physics*
and *Metaphysics*. As late as 1263 Urban IV renewed this
prohibition, but the capture of Constantinople in 1204 by
the crusaders gave access to Greek MSS. of the treatises,
and the Church was enabled virtually to suspend judgment,
pending the investigation of this fresh evidence. Translations independent of Arab influence began to appear
(though slowly, owing to the general ignorance of Greek
in Europe), and in 1231 a commission was set up " to
expurgate errors from the text of Aristotle."

The two Dominicans, Albert the Great and his greater pupil, Thomas Aquinas, laboured—though unofficially—at this task. Neither knew much Greek,[1] but they reached an astonishingly clear understanding of Aristotle, and their interpretation was not that of Averroes.[2] The diverse trends of philosophic thought at this time, confused as they are by the jealousies of the various clerical orders, are hard to distinguish clearly ; but, roughly speaking, conservative Augustinianism is championed by the " seraphic " Franciscan, Bonaventura, and Averroism by the rather mysterious Siger of Brabant, both of whom taught largely at Paris. Meanwhile the Papacy awaited the issue, content with an occasional prohibition. In 1268 Aquinas was provoked to leave Italy for Paris. In debate and with his pen he crushed utterly the school of Siger. Two years later seventy propositions of Siger were condemned by the Bishop of Paris.

Aquinas' victory is commemorated by Traini's altarpiece at Pisa. He is there displayed with Averroes lying vanquished beneath his feet. On the saint's right hand Aristotle holds open his *Ethics*, on his left Plato his *Timaeus*. The whole of the allegory has some truth. Aquinas' philosophy, though its essence is a new Aristotelianism, contains Platonic elements, and is the subtle and really fresh synthesis of a great thinker. He offers his system to the world primarily as the truth, not simply as the correct interpretation of Aristotle, whom he professes to follow only " because few or no inconveniences follow from his views." For the astral intelligences Aquinas substitutes the angels. His theory of the creation seems to meet the conflict between the doctrine of eternal matter and the Book of Genesis by treating it as a question, if not *mal posée*, at least quite secondary. He points out

---

[1] Aquinas had special Latin translations made for him by William of Moerbeke.

[2] We have already seen that Aristotle's attitude is sometimes ambiguous enough to allow latitude in interpretation.

that creation is of the whole world and not of a part of it.
Secondly, creation is *ex nihilo*, but it is not a change
occurring in time, for time is only the measure of change
in the created world. Rather it is a relation (under which
category falls no form of change) of creature to creator,
which Aquinas calls now participation, now emanation,
but seems to think of as analogous to the inherence of
accident in substance. For he holds it not to be reciprocal :
God's nature is not in the least determined by the created
world which is related to him. When pressed, Aquinas
maintains creation in its essential nature to be a notion
compatible with regarding the world either as eternal or
as not eternal, but bows to the revealed truth of Genesis.
As regards personal immortality, he opposes alike the
Augustinian (ultimately Neo-Platonic) view of a soul
complete in itself and temporarily inhabiting a body, and
the Averroist doctrine. He holds with Aristotle that the
soul is the *forma informans* of the body, and that in
matter lies the principle of individuation. But, unlike
the form of lesser individual things, whose matter and
intelligible form are complementary and inseparable, the
soul is intelligent as well as intelligible. Hence soul differs
from soul, not as species from species, but yet substantially.
Nevertheless this difference is not a difference in essential
nature, but a difference of the " commensuration " which
fits each soul to its own individual body ; and the difference
so arising persists after death. He quotes in support
Avicenna's statement that the individuation and multi-
plication of souls depends on the body for its source, but
not for its end.[1] In effect he assimilates the human soul
to the angels, who are pure substances, rather than to the
materiate forms of the infra-human world, preferring to
locate the chasm in the developing series below man
rather than above him.

[1] See D'Arcy, *Thomas Aquinas*, p. 152—a book which I have found
most helpful.

We cannot pursue the effort of Aquinas to blend the Christian faith with Aristotelianism. Be it said that he develops the notion of " actus " and " potentia " subtly and fruitfully, and that, if he dances in chains, at least he moves with rhythm and vitality. It may, however, serve to show his continuity at once with Aristotle and with subsequent speculation, if we sketch shortly his theory of sense-perception and knowledge.

Aquinas' teaching develops from Aristotle's doctrine of the single actualisation of subject and object. In sense-perception the form without the matter of the sensible object is assimilated by the percipient, and that assimilation involves both a transient and an immanent activity : the object makes the percipient like itself, and the percipient thereby develops its own nature. Hence the percipient is both passive and active in perception, and the percept is at once the effect of the object and a phase in the development of the subject. The doctrine is not representational. The percipient does not compare percept and object, nor in any way infer object from percept so as to justify any distinction of percept as primary object, and sensible thing as secondary object, of perception : the percept is not that which is perceived but that " through which," or " in which " the object is perceived. In discursive thought the *intellectus agens* and the *intellectus passibilis*, which are to Aquinas inseparable moments of the rational soul which informs man's body, play a part analogous to the active and passive moments of sense-perception. The persisting percept becomes a *phantasma*, and this acts transiently upon the intellect, which *qua* passive is *per se* featureless, and likens it to itself. The intellect, in being likened to the *phantasma*, is informed by what may be called metaphorically a *species impressa*. But the mind does not know through or in *phantasmata*, and the *species impressa*, which informs the passive intellect, is more than mere impression by a *phantasma*.

By the illuminating action of the *intellectus agens*, which purifies it of particularities,[1] the phantasm is transformed and realised as an intelligible form. And this intelligible form, which informs the passive intellect, is also, *qua* product of the *intellectus agens*, a phase in the immanent activity of the intellect itself. It is therefore in this latter aspect a *species expressa*, a self-expression, or self-creation, of a mind whose essential nature is to know an object, and to know it by becoming it immaterially.

Again the doctrine is not representational. There is no inference from *species* to object. *Species* is that through and in which the object is known : " The intelligible *species* is that which is understood secondarily, but that which is understood primarily is the object, of which the intelligible *species* is the likeness."[2] The suggestion of succession in this quotation means that human knowing involves a reflective activity, which in sense is only rudimentary. We are always more or less aware of imperfect coincidence—of a difference between our concept and the object known through it ; and the criterion of truth[3] is conformity of concept to object. But explicit awareness of this difference—the critical, reflective, moment in knowing—presupposes and depends on direct apprehension of the object. By knowing its object mind comes to know the concept through and in which the object was grasped,[4] and in knowing its concept mind knows itself. The perfect self-knowledge of God, in which subject and object are undivided, is the norm which criticises and explains human knowledge.

This theory of knowledge, presupposing as it does both

---

[1] This function is often called by Aquinas " abstraction," but the term has now misleading associations.

[2] *Summa Theologiae*, I, q. 85.

[3] Truth is to Aquinas " Being *qua* known."

[4] It is by a further reflection directed upon the *phantasma* that mind grasps the individual singular.

an object acting transiently and an intellect immanently active, is usually given the name of realism.[1] And this same partial dualism, which assigns two imperfectly reconciled sources to knowledge, is of course not wholly absent in Aristotle. Had either thinker stressed more strongly the implication of the transient causal process, viz., that the object is actualised in being known just as the intellect is actualised in knowing, then something like Kant's position in his objective deduction of the categories might have been sooner reached. Descartes' idea with its dual *esse* as both mode of mind and image of object descends through Suarez from thirteenth-century Scholasticism. Descartes too conceives the intellect as an illuminant, and there are other inherited elements in his theory of knowledge, which remain unintelligible if he is regarded as the pioneer of a new speculative attitude without roots in the past. On the other hand, his stark opposition of mental and material substance,[2] set up in the interest of mathematical physics, sowed the seed of a representational theory of cognition, destined to be developed through Locke's empiricism, fatally damaged by Berkeley, and finally ruined by the scepticism of Hume. The implications of Descartes' discovery of the single subject in experience, which Descartes himself misread, could not be developed until Kant could set them side by side with Hume's results. Kant's doctrine of the transcendental unity of apperception (his heritage from Descartes) and of the categories, of which substance is only one, transforms and broadens the whole philosophic outlook. Yet his teaching (ambiguous as it is) that consciousness of objects and self-consciousness mutually condition one another, is linked through Descartes with the Aristotelian theory of knowledge, as Aquinas developed it, by a con-

[1] As opposed not to nominalism but to idealism.
[2] Descartes' erection of matter as substance marks the real difference between Cartesianism and all Aristotelian thought.

R

tinuity perhaps more real than that which (also through Descartes) connects Spinoza's notion of substance with Aristotle's.[1]

3. LATER SCHOLASTICISM

Aristotle had lent suppleness as well as precision to theological dogma, but he suffered in return the reaction of that rigidity which always befalls an official faith. His undeserved reward was a kind of secondary infallibility. As a direct vital impulse Aristotelianism died with Aquinas in 1272, and there seemed to survive only the dead hand of his authority. The basis of education was destined to remain unchanged in schools and universities for some centuries—the Inceptor in Arts at Paris swore in the fourteenth century to teach nothing inconsistent with Aristotle, and as late as 1624 that excitable and unexpected body, the Parliament of Paris, passed a decree threatening with death all who held or taught anything contrary to his doctrines. But after Aquinas the philosophy of Aristotle lived again once only—transmuted in the fabric of the *Divina Commedia*.

Yet even before the *Renaissance* the seed of a new freedom was germinating, and there are three great names which entitle this preceding period to be called transitional, and not the mere stagnant age of *a priori* dialectic and verbal hair-splitting which it appeared to the next generations.

Duns Scotus, the Subtle Doctor (d. 1308), offered the first serious challenge to Thomism on its own ground. His sympathies were Augustinian, and he tends to exalt faith far above reason ; to widen the sphere of theology, and to divorce it from philosophy. Regarding *a priori* deduction alone as cogent argument, he attacks the

[1] We may even justifiably regard the Spinozistic and Leibnizian notions of substance as alternative answers to the Aristotelian problem of immanence and transcendence.

Thomist proofs of God's existence, which are *a posteriori* and analogous to Aristotle's proof of the necessity of a prime mover. A violent realist,[1] he finds the principle of individuation solely in form and not in matter. It is his criticism of Aquinas rather than his constructive thought which is prophetic of a fresh era. In fact his dry and meticulous methods contributed largely to the almost burlesque conception of Scholasticism which the humanists of the Renaissance acquired, and epitomised by calling a blockhead impervious to the new learning a " dunce."

At Oxford, where Scotus taught, the threat of theological authority had been always more remote, and the Quadrivium more popular, than on the Continent. Partly for these reasons the physical works of Aristotle had given a strong and unchecked impetus to natural science. Roger Bacon (1214–1294), far more than Scotus, typifies the spirit of the university at this time. Though his combative temper and his studies in alchemy and astrology rendered him suspect to the orthodox, and gave him at a much later date the reputation of a charlatan, Bacon was an honest rebel and a true prophet. He knew Greek, and he was not anti-Aristotelian—in fact he held that Aristotle had perfected the philosophy of his time, and he complains that he is now ill-translated and read without understanding by all but Grosseteste, Bacon's own teacher. But Bacon's zeal for mathematics, and his even greater passion for scientific experiment, herald a new age of thought.

William of Ockham, the last of the great scholastics, died in 1347. He also was a product of Oxford. He opposed the teaching of Scotus with an extreme nominalism, regarding Aristotle's doctrine of categories as having a purely grammatical reference. For him the foundation of knowledge is intuitive apprehension of the individual

---

[1] As opposed to nominalist.

singular ; the universal concept is but a vague, confused, knowledge of particulars. In accordance with his maxim, *entia non sunt multiplicanda praeter necessitatem*—but certainly misunderstanding the doctrine of Aquinas—he denies the *intellectus agens* and the presence of any mediating *species* between the mind and its singular object. The act of intuiting the singular leaves no trace save a mere disposition of the intellect itself—an almost Humian expedient to account for the abstract general knowledge of singulars no longer present. This uncompromising nominalism forebodes a purely formal logic of validity, but Ockham's theory of knowledge shows his affinity with Roger Bacon,[1] and prepares the way for empiricism and for the inductive logic of Francis Bacon. Of how causal connexion is to be established by reference to empirical experience he writes in terms which seem prophetic of J. S. Mill's four inductive methods : *Hoc tamen non est ponendum sine necessitate, puta nisi per experientiam possit convinci, ita scilicet, quod ipso posito, alio destructo, sequitur effectus, vel quod ipso non posito, quocumque alio posito, non sequitur effectus.*

4. FROM THE RENAISSANCE TO THE EIGHTEENTH CENTURY

Constantinople was captured by the Turks in 1453, and the influx of classical MSS. into Europe, which had begun half a century earlier, increased fourfold. Another period of voracious assimilation began, and naturally enough the humanist scholars of the Renaissance turned to fresh fields, and applied their new knowledge of Greek rather to the study of authors hitherto unknown than to the works of Aristotle. The notable exception is the school

---

[1] His views had been partially anticipated in Paris by Durand de Saint-Pourçain and Pierre d'Auriole.

of Aristotelian interpretation at Padua, which lasted more than two centuries and culminated in the work of Zabarella (d. 1589) and his pupil Pacius. After the death of Aquinas, Averroism had revived somewhat even at Paris, and in Italy the repute of Averroes had suffered far less than in France. To Dante Averroes is " He who the great Comment made," and though St. Thomas is made the spokesman of theology, even Siger is " an immortal light." Among the Paduan interpreters, who included the famous Thomist, Caietan (1469-1534), the old controversy was pursued for two hundred years, although when Zabarella wrote the old bitterness had passed away. Zabarella is a vigorous and independent critic—perhaps the best commentator who ever set his mind at the service of another man—but he was a scholar, not an original philosopher. The complete understanding of Aristotle came too late. As Professor Stocks puts it : " As the real Aristotle at last came into view out of the mists of legend and tradition, the human spirit threw off his authority. The substance could not hold the empire which the shadow had won."[1]

Meanwhile the Aristotelian cosmos was falling to pieces. Though Paracelsus (1490-1541) by substituting his iatro-chemistry for alchemy, gave a saner turn to chemical studies, the four Aristotelian elements remained roughly the limit of analysis until the appearance of Boyle's *Sceptical Chemist* in 1661. But Copernicus had published his heliocentric theory in 1543, and though it was more than sixty years before Kepler proved planetary motion to be elliptical, his telescope and Galileo's were soon to pierce the illusion of the aetherial spheres.

Though Locke, who was born in 1632, found Scholasticism still dominant at Oxford—Aristotle still enjoyed some favour with the Protestant as well as the Roman divines—it was to the end of the seventeenth century the fashion to

---

[1] *Aristotelianism*, p. 133.

sneer at Aristotle.   The prevailing attitude is summed up
in Dryden's lines :

> " The longest tyranny that ever swayed
> Was that wherein our ancestors betrayed
> Their free-born reason to the Stagyrite,
> And made his torch their universal light." [1]

But the greater men of the two centuries which follow
the *Renaissance* do on the whole make the later schoolmen
rather than Aristotle the target of their scorn.   Francis
Bacon (1561–1629) was a vigorous opponent of syllogistic
logic ; but when he wrote : " As water will not ascend
higher than the level of the first springhead from whence
it descendeth, so knowledge derived from Aristotle, and
exempted from liberty of examination, will not rise again
higher than the knowledge of Aristotle,"[2] he may have
been partially conscious that his own spirit of empirical
inquiry was not wholly un-Aristotelian.   Hobbes, who
jibes constantly at Aristotle, had studied him deeply and
borrowed much.

With the dawn of the eighteenth century this very
reaction from Aristotle ceased to be a force.   Bayle merely
gossips about him.   Voltaire's much later article on him
in his *Dictionnaire Philosophique* contains almost as many
ludicrous errors as its brevity permits, but the author
confesses that he belongs to an age which does not understand Aristotle.   Berkeley can even regret that " In these
free-thinking times, many an empty head is shook at
Aristotle, as well as at the Holy Scriptures."

Kant canonised, in the very act of destroying it, the
deductive formal logic which the later schoolmen had
developed from the *Organon*, but emasculated by omitting
the doctrines of the *Posterior Analytics* ; and the teaching

---

[1] Epistle to Charleton, written about 1662 in the atmosphere created
by the founding of the Royal Society.

[2] *Advancement of Learning*, I, iv, 12.

of it in desiccated textbooks, more and more remote from the original, has persisted even to our own day in the universities of Europe, though its position in their curricula has become gradually insignificant, and it has long been breeding other types of formal logic, which have so far shown little promise of longevity. Only in one sphere— and one remote from the centre of his thought—did Aristotle remain a vital force. Throughout all these centuries the *Poetics* continued to exert an immense influence on literary practice. The Italian critics of the Renaissance took this orphan to their bosom, and the playwrights—particularly the seventeenth- and eighteenth-century French playwrights—made a creed of the three dramatic unities, which they believed (mistakenly as regards the unities of time and place) to be derived from it.[1] Dryden did not admire Aristotle save as a critic, but Pope in 1709 could write :

> " Not only nature did his laws obey,
> But fancy's boundless empire owned his sway."[2]

Though Tyrwhitt edited the *Poetics*, the great eighteenth-century scholars, such as Bentley, Porson, and Brunck, paid little attention to Aristotle. The work of bringing all the resources of scholarship to bear on the textual criticism and interpretation of his writings did not begin until the following century.

But the imagination of the scholar can only recreate a figure which with the lapsing years must grow smaller, if also more distinct. In 1879 Leo XIII stimulated the Roman Church to a fresh study of Thomas Aquinas, but the immediate witness to Aristotle's immortality is not the revival of Aristotelian scholarship but—as even the

---

[1] See note 2, p. 229. It must be added that the *Politics* was also much read during the Renaissance—witness Machiavelli's *Prince*—and still retained some influence during the seventeenth and eighteenth centuries.

[2] *Essay on Criticism* (1st ed. only).

central part of this book will have shown—the whole terminology of our intellectual self-expression, and even of our common speech. And that is but a symptom. There is a huge, almost impersonal, universality in Aristotle's thought, which makes it no less hard to select the appropriate epithet of praise than to find a real ποῦ στῶ for criticism. The seed of every speculative trend is in him. The concepts of energy in physics and of evolution in biology are now reshaped with startling frequency by the specialist ; but as little as the dialectic of Hegel could they, and all the divers phases of their interpretation, have originated in a world that had not for centuries thought in terms of form and matter, potency and act.[1]

---

[1] We are even threatened with a principle of indetermination, recalling a weakness in Aristotle's thought which he could not quite expel.

XII

MODERN ARISTOTELIAN STUDIES

THE chief feature of nineteenth-century work upon Aristotle was the attempt to combine philosophic knowledge and pure scholarship with historical sense. Most of it was done in Germany, and throughout the century historical interpretation[1] took the form rather of setting Aristotle in his place in a single great rhythm of speculative development than of examining in detail the philosophic history of his time. The groundwork of the period is represented (1) by the Berlin Academy's publication of Bekker's text of the *Corpus Aristotelicum*, begun in 1831 and crowned in 1870 by Bonitz's monumental Index, and (2) by the Berlin edition of the Greek Commentaries, completed in 1909. The highest peak of its achievement is Bonitz's edition of the *Metaphysics* ; a work of great insight and one free from *a priori* bias. The best complete exposition of Aristotle's thought which the latter part of the century produced is in Zeller's *Die Philosophie der Griechen*, II, 2.

Our own century has seen this interest in Aristotle sustained, and English scholars have played their part. Oxford has contributed a complete translation of the *Corpus* and standard commentaries on two or three of the treatises. These have been marked by some successful re-punctuation of the text (which calls for comparatively little verbal emendation), and by an increased attention to early Greek philosophy, to the Greek commentators, and to the *Renaissance* Aristotelians, such as Zabarella

---

[1] Inspired initially by Hegel, to whom, as to Aristotle, all philosophies seemed prophetic of his own.

and Pacius. But again the fresh impulse to Aristotelian studies has come from Germany. It has sprung from the desire to apply to Aristotle that more minute historical method which has already done service to the study of Plato. Though it had long been more or less clearly recognised that many of the treatises are composite, the scholastic view of the *Corpus* as containing a single homogeneous body of doctrine had persisted scarcely modified by five centuries of criticism, until it was challenged in 1912 by Professor Jaeger's *Studien zur Entstehungsgeschichte der Metaphysik des Aristoteles*. Professor Jaeger found it paradoxical that the notion of organic development, which Aristotle originated and used in order to relate himself to his predecessors, had never been applied to the forty years of its author's working life. He attempted accordingly to measure the gradual progress of Aristotle's thought by the degree of what is at once his reaction from and his development of Plato's teaching, and Jaeger's *Aristoteles* (1923) embodies the results of re-reading on this hypothesis some of the main treatises. I have written the central portion of this book on the assumption that it is possible to present a more or less consistent sketch at any rate of Aristotle's mature philosophy, but Jaeger's reconstruction is clearly destined to be influential. And even if it does not force us to revolutionise our conception of Aristotle, we shall find it singularly instructive. On the other hand, Professor Jaeger and his pupils have still plenty of work to do, and we have scarcely space here for either a fair exposition or a fair criticism of the work already done.

For many centuries after his death the dialogues of Aristotle were as famous as his treatises. To the general public they were, in fact, much more familiar. But when medieval Europe recovered the bulk of the treatises the dialogues had disappeared, and they survive for us only in quotations, which come often—and significantly—from

Neo-Platonist writers. Cicero praises their golden style, and they were evidently more simple and popular in character than the treatises. They are probably the object of Aristotle's occasional references to " the exoteric discourses." Professor Jaeger has now shown quite conclusively that they belong mainly to Aristotle's Academic period ; that, though they are less completely dramatised —the author himself sometimes conducts the discussion— many of them moot the same problems as Plato's dialogues, the titles of which they often repeat ;[1] finally, that the doctrine which most of them teach is purely Platonic. The *Eudemus* or *De Anima*, written about 354 B.C., exists in fragments long enough to show a close connexion with Plato's *Phaedo*, and proves the immortality of the soul by almost identical arguments.[2] The theory of Forms is by implication accepted whole-heartedly, and given a purely transcendent interpretation : the soul longs for death as for release from life and return to its true home. From the fragments of the *Eudemus* and of the *Protrepticus*, an exhortation to the philosophic life addressed to Themiso of Cyprus, Jaeger constructs a convincing picture of the young Aristotle steeped in the religious, almost mystical, spirit of his master, and almost out-Platonising Plato in his pessimistic contempt for this mortal life. He detects a hint of the mature Aristotle in the rigorous logical form of the argument, but he concludes to an early and wholly Platonic stage of Aristotle's thought.

On the other hand, the *De Philosophia*, as Jaeger reconstructs it from its fragments, is a dialogue published shortly after Plato's death. It embodies Aristotle's first criticisms of his master, but its strong religious feeling and the close connexion in it of astronomy with theology stamp it as spiritually a product of the late Academy.

---

[1] *Menexenus, Symposium, Politicus, Sophistes*, are titles of Aristotelian dialogues.

[2] See, however, p. 46, note 1.

Much of it recalls the *Epinomis*, and it had a marked influence on Hellenism and, later, on Neo-Platonism. The first of its three books was a critical history of philosophy from the earliest times, probably influenced by the Magian doctrine of world-periods. Platonism perhaps appeared as the culmination of a six-thousand-year period and as the rebirth of Zarathustra's teaching.[1] The second book contained a criticism of the Forms ; the third offered in the form of a cosmological theology Aristotle's first exposition of his own philosophy. To Plato's four elements Aristotle now adds the aether, but his main divergence from Plato is this :—With the disappearance of the Forms the visible heavens gain a new divinity : the world is not, as the *Timaeus* had taught, created, but ingenerable as well as indestructible. Though the movement of the planets is attributed—Platonically—to the volition of an indwelling soul, yet from a statement of Cicero (*De Nat. Deor.*, I, 13) that Aristotle in this dialogue sometimes regards God as a being who rules and preserves the world's *replicatione quadam*, Jaeger deduces that Aristotle—perhaps inspired by a suggestion in Plato's *Laws*, 898e—had already introduced the Prime Mover to explain the movement of the first heaven. A passage cited by Simplicius— " Where there is a better there is also a best. Since, then, among the things that are, one thing is better than another, therefore there is too something which is best. And that should be God "—shows Aristotle's conception of a hierarchy of forms already developed, and contains the germ of many subsequent proofs of the existence of God.

The *Corpus* of Aristotle's treatises, as we possess it, probably does not differ greatly from Andronicus' edition in the first century B.C. The terse and elliptical style of the writings indicates that they are for the most part lecture notes not intended for the general public, but they seldom dwindle to the mere jottings upon which the fluent

[1] Cp. p. 92, note 1.

lecturer relies. Usually the text is continuous enough to be intelligible to anyone familiar with the main Aristotelian doctrines. Probably they not only formed the basis for the lectures of Aristotle and of his subordinate teachers, but were also written with an eye to making some sort of permanent record within the school. Again, the order of our *Corpus*—the propaedeutic logical works, the natural sciences in order of concreteness from physics to psychology and biology, ethics and politics for the mature student, and finally rhetoric and poetics for the specialist in the practical life—may very well reflect roughly the order of the Lyceum curriculum. So much is at least probable, but, despite frequent cross-reference between the treatises, often a single one of them seems to comprise sections from different courses of lectures, which sometimes repeat one another, and fails to constitute an organic whole. Only upon internal evidence can we attempt to decide how far the composition of materials in a given treatise is Aristotle's own, how far it is due to Andronicus or to any previous editor.[1] Now tradition has assigned the treatises *en bloc* to the period of Aristotle's teaching activity at the Lyceum ; but even at Assos Aristotle probably had an audience large enough to lecture to, and Jaeger detects in them strata which represent roughly two separable stages of his life and of his intellectual development—347 to 334, and 334 to 322.

This theory is based primarily on an analysis of the *Metaphysics*[2]—the signal instance, as its title suggests,[3] of a composite treatise. To the first stage of Aristotle's metaphysical development belong Met. I, III, IV, VI, Chap. i, XII (less Chap. 8), and XIII 1086ª21–XIV end. The

[1] There seems in fact to be no evidence of editing before Andronicus.

[2] What follows in the text is simply an attempt to present the views advanced by Jaeger and a complementary theory of Aristotle's logical development put forward by his pupil, Solmsen. Save in an occasional footnote I neither endorse nor criticise until p. 268.

[3] See note 1, p. 192

history of philosophy which fills Met. I is developed from *De Philosophia* I, and it presupposes the fourfold causal analysis and the doctrines of matter and form, change, potentiality and actuality, appealing to the *Physics* for their justification. We can therefore infer that at least Ph. I–VI also belong to this period, and that probably these doctrines had already appeared in De Phil. The criticism of Platonism corresponding to De Phil. II, which appears in Met. I, and in a more extended form in XIII 1086ª21–XIV end, is marked by the use of the first person plural to introduce Platonic arguments ; thus showing that Aristotle still speaks as a Platonist among Platonists. Book III, in which this use of the first person also appears, formulates fifteen problems. The first four concern the possibility and scope of first philosophy. The fifth asks whether there are any non-sensible substances, and, if so, of how many kinds. This and the remaining problems, which further develop it, still betoken a Platonic outlook. Aristotle asks whether the first principles of things are one in kind and number, the same for sensible and non-sensible things. Are they the genera, the species, or the singular individuals ? Are being and unity, the mathematicals, and the Forms, substances ? Are the first principles potential or actual ? Are they, finally, universal or individual ? In short, Aristotle has abandoned the Forms, but is still searching for a non-sensible substance as the subject-matter of first philosophy. This is proclaimed by IV and VI, Ch. 1, to be God, and first philosophy is equated with theology. This stratum of Met. is marked by the assumption that non-sensible substance is wholly transcendent, and the sensible world that which is essentially opaque to genuine knowledge.

Book V is a philosophical lexicon, probably early in date. II and XI seem to be the notes of a pupil—II on some general lectures on theoretical science ; XI, Chs. 1–8 on an earlier phase of Bks. I, III, and IV; the remainder on a portion of Ph.

To the last period of Aristotle's life belong the rest of VI, VII, VIII, IX, X, and XIII, 1–9 1086ª20. Of these VI 2–end discusses the various senses of " being " as a preface to the treatment of substance in VII–IX, which were written as a separate treatise but inserted by Aristotle[1] to precede the discussion of non-sensible substance. X, on unity and being, was also added late. XIII, 1–9, criticise Platonism, but the tone is harsher and the first person appears no more. The criticism of Plato's original Forms is here repeated from its earlier formulation, but the main point of attack is now the mathematical development of the theory by Speusippus and Xenocrates. In particular Xenocrates, once Aristotle's companion at Assos, but now official head of the Academy, receives a much severer treatment than in XIV.

A significant difference between the two strata is this. The discussion of sensible substance is at first always relegated to physics, and emphasis is laid on the necessity of non-sensible substance to save us from the notion of a universe where all is flux. But in VII–IX the treatment of sensible substance is assumed to be an integral part of first philosophy, being said in VII 1037ª14 to belong only " in a sense " to physics. In VII Aristotle concludes (see p. 187) that the infima species is the substance *par excellence* of the perceptible world, a substance immanent but ingenerable.

The theology of the first period is contained in XII, although this book does not belong to the main plan of Met. It is in fact a compressed, sometimes almost unintelligibly curt, statement of the whole of Aristotle's philosophy, which yet rises at its climax to a sublimity which Aristotle never parallels in his extant works.

---

[1] There is no external evidence that Aristotle himself put together the *Metaphysics*.

Chapters 1–5 discuss sensible substance, and might seem to be a *précis* of VII–IX ; but here again sensible substance is said to be the province of physics. Passages in the later chapters are obviously based on passages in XIV. The cosmology of Cael. I and II also belongs to this period, and those books contain passages which from their style and manner may be confidently assumed as actual quotations from De Phil.[1] The later treatment of supra-sensible substance does not appear in Met., but XII, Ch. 8—an awkward insertion which breaks the discussion—formulates a new cosmology, increasing the number of first movers to account for planetary movement in deference to the astronomical calculations of Callippus (see pp. 84–5).

The characteristic of this second period—that of Aristotle's activity at the Lyceum—is his complete absorption in natural science and all other realms of detailed research. The perceptible world of change is not so totally opaque to knowledge as it had seemed to the younger Aristotle. He seeks a substance immanent and not transcendent The infimae species, ingenerable and real, appear as fixed islands in the ocean of sensible flux. These patient toil can elicit, and Aristotle now devotes all his energies to the pursuit of the materiate form in every department of experience which admits of minute empirical investigation. The accumulation of observed fact, which this demanded, was not possible until the Lyceum was founded. To this time, then, belong the psycho-physical teaching of An. I and II, which scarcely suits the older and more Platonic doctrine, as Jaeger supposes it to be, of νοῦς in An. III, and also the biological treatises. The latter probably include the work of colleagues ; for collaborative research, guided by one master-mind, is the mark of this period.

[1] Yet, as Jaeger points out, they exhibit side by side the attribution of planetary movement to soul (see p. 90), and a physical doctrine of rotation as the *natural* movement of aether. The inconsistency might perhaps be thought a sign of transition.

More *a priori* physical writings, such as GC, are likely to be early, but the elaborate last book of Ph. on the Prime Mover is probably a late product.[1]

To illustrate Aristotle's outlook at this time Jaeger quotes PA I, 5 : " Of things constituted by nature some are ungenerated, imperishable, and eternal, while others are subject to generation and decay. The former are precious and divine, but less accessible to human speculation. The evidence that might throw light on them, and on the problems which we long to solve respecting them, is furnished but scantily by sense-perception ; whereas respecting perishable plants and animals, growing up among them as we do, we have abundant information, and ample data may be collected concerning all their various kinds, if we are willing to take sufficient pains. Both realms have their own charm. The scanty conceptions to which we can attain of things divine give us, because of the precious nature of such knowledge, more pleasure than all our knowledge of the world in which we live, just as a casual half glimpse of persons that we love is more delightful than an accurate view of other things, whatever their number and dimensions. On the other hand, in certitude and completeness our knowledge of terrestrial things has the advantage. Moreover, their greater nearness and affinity to us somewhat balances the loftier interest of the heavenly things that are the objects of first philosophy. Of the latter we have already treated, so far as our conjectures could reach. Hence it remains for us to treat of animals, omitting, so far as we can, no member of the kingdom, noble or ignoble. For if some have no graces to charm the sense, yet even these, by disclosing to intellectual perception the craftsmanship of nature, give vast pleasure to all who can recognise the causes, and are inclined to philosophy. Indeed, it would

---

[1] I do not feel certain that an unbiassed reader would think GC more *a priori* than Ph. VIII.

S

be strange if mimic representations of them were attractive, because they disclose the skill of the painter or sculptor, and the original natural objects were not a more interesting spectacle, to all at any rate who have eyes to discern their causes. We must therefore not recoil with childish aversion from the examination of the humbler animals. In every creation of nature there is something marvellous : and as Heraclitus, when the strangers who came to visit him found him warming himself at the furnace in the kitchen and hesitated to go in, is said to have bidden them not fear to enter, as even in that kitchen gods were present, so we should venture on the study of every kind of animal without distaste ; for each and all will reveal to us something natural and beautiful. Absence of chance and conduciveness of everything to an end are found in nature's works in the highest degree, and the end for which they have been constituted or have come to be takes the place of beauty. Moreover, if any man thinks the investigation of the rest of the animal kingdom an unworthy task, he must likewise condemn the study of man. For no one can look at the constituents of the human organism —blood, flesh, bone, vessels, and the like—without much repugnance. Accordingly, when any one of the parts or structures is under discussion, we must bear in mind that it is not its matter to which attention is being directed or which is the purpose of the discussion, but its relation to the total form—just as the true object of architecture is not bricks, mortar, and timber, but the house." To Jaeger this passage betokens Aristotle's farewell to theology, and the close of a movement from the " otherworldliness " of his Platonic youth to an intense preoccupation with special science, which develops against a background of metaphysical agnosticism.

The ethical and political writings are analysed by Jaeger in conformity with this view. The first and purely Platonic stage of Aristotle's ethical teaching he recon-

structs from the fragments of the *Protrepticus*. Here, as
in the *Republic*, the highest human virtue is attainable
only by those who have travelled the long road of a
philosophic education, and risen to contemplation of the
Forms illuminated by the Form of the Good. The Form
of the Good is the ultimate and consciously grasped norm
of their conduct : at this stage the distinction of φρόνησις
and σοφία, practical and speculative wisdom, has not
emerged. The ethics of the second and third stage have
to be discovered from the three ethical treatises of our
Corpus. Since the *Magna Moralia* is, in Jaeger's view, a
later Peripatetic compilation,[1] the problem is confined
to EE and EN. In the *Corpus* EE I–III covers the ground
of EN I–IV, and follows it closely. EE IV covers
EN VIII and IX on friendship. EE V covers the latter
part of EN X on the speculative life, but with marked
differences. Most MSS. of EE state at the end of EE III
that the next three books are identical with EN V–VIII,
and accordingly number Books IV and V as VII and VIII.
Jaeger solves the problem by rejecting the old ascription
of EE to Eudemus of Rhodes, and regarding it as portions
of Aristotle's ethical course as he delivered it during his
absence from Athens. EN, on the other hand, represents
the mature ethic of the Lyceum period. In EE, as in
EN I, 6, the Forms are attacked, and the Form of the
Good somewhat scornfully rejected as too remote for
human conduct to take as its ideal, even if it did not in
any case involve a metaphysically monstrous blurring
of categorial distinctions (see note 2, p. 181). But in EE
the norm and the inspiration of conduct is God : " To
serve and to contemplate God " is the end of human
life (1249ᵇ20). Aristotle is still clinging to a position very
different from that of EN, where speculative and practical

---

[1] Von Arnim, who, like Jaeger, measures Aristotle's development in
terms of his relation to Plato, but often reaches very different results,
regards MM as the work of Aristotle and the earliest of the three ethical
treatises. Jaeger's view seems more probable.

wisdom are totally divorced, and in EE he uses the term
φρόνησις, as he had used it in the *Protrepticus*, with much
the same meaning as it bears in Plato's *Philebus*. There
it signifies theoretical insight into the Forms, viewed as
the factor of intelligence in the best life for man (see p. 63) :
in EE the only change is that the divine nature replaces
the Form of the Good. Yet Aristotle seems to hesitate.
Though he holds that speculation is of value to the
statesman, he warns his hearers against abstract *a priori*
discussions on ethics, which ignore the facts of life. He
is already moving towards the position of EN, in which
the norm and ultimate guiding ideal of conduct is the
fully developed good agent, whose practical nature has
reached its full human consummation : the ideal citizen
and statesman. It is true that in EN Aristotle is troubled
somewhat as to the ultimate source of that ideal of goodness which is at once the τέλος and the essential nature
of the practically wise man, and that in EN X speculative
activity is still the ideal life for the few. But in EN X,
it seems to Jaeger, the religious emotion, which persists
in EE from Aristotle's Platonic period, has grown cold.
The divorce within man's self of human and divine makes
an insuperable problem from which Aristotle turns his
face away to the empirical world.

In the political writings different periods of composition
are particularly evident. The Platonic stage is given us
by a fragment of the *Protrepticus* : " No good and perfect
law-giver, perhaps, in giving laws to a city, or governing
it as a statesman, looks to the practice of other men, or
to constitutions such as the Spartan or Cretan, or any
other, as his pattern. For the copy of what is not ideally
good cannot itself be ideally good : the copy of what is
not of a divine and permanent nature cannot be immortal
and permanent." Other fragments proclaim the supreme
accuracy of the political art, and the outlook is clearly
that of Plato's *Republic*. As in the first stage of the ethics,

speculation and practice go hand in hand, and the ideal Utopia is the true *prius* of political thinking.

The two later stages can be traced in our obviously composite *Politics*. The last paragraph of EN forms a transition to politics proper : " Our predecessors have left the subject of legislation to us unexamined ; it is perhaps best, therefore, that we should ourselves study it, and in general study the question of the constitution, in order to complete to the best of our ability our philosophy of human nature. First, then, if anything has been said well in detail by earlier thinkers, let us try to review it ; then in the light of the constitutions we have collected let us study what sorts of influence preserve and destroy states, and what sorts preserve and destroy the particular kinds of constitution, and to what causes it is due that some are well and others ill administered. When these have been studied we shall perhaps be more likely to see with a comprehensive view, which constitution is best, and how each must be ordered, and what laws and customs it must use, if it is to be at its best." When we look to see how this promise is fulfilled, we find in Pol. VII and VIII (the two last books) an account of the ideal state and of ideal education. Though practice and speculation are here already more sharply divided than in EE—the ideal ruler is not to be a philosopher—yet the influence of the *Laws*, in which Plato brings the Utopian vision of the *Republic* nearer to fact, is everywhere present, and Aristotle proceeds by criticism further in the direction of common sense. The political atmosphere of Assos can be detected in some passages. Book II gives an account of previous ideal commonwealths and of the best existent states. It contains Aristotle's famous comment on the *Republic* (see p. 158) and a criticism of the *Laws*. Book III discusses the citizen and civic virtue as such, and the classification of constitutions. The scale of good constitutions and their perversions (see p. 161), which derives from the *Politicus*, marks the Platonic character of the thought, and the book ends with an obvious forward reference to VII, which is repeated in the first words of the latter. Jaeger accordingly groups these four books— II, III, VII, and VIII—as representing Aristotle's first course of lectures on politics, maintaining that the references in them to the *Ethics* are all to EE and not to EN. On the other hand, IV–VI are written in a different vein, and are never referred to by the first group. They discuss the inferior forms of constitution. Although IV refers back to the scale of constitutions in III, yet the ideal state is now " only an aspiration," and does not really function as a norm. Aristotle distinguishes in IV a vast variety of actual constitutions ; and oligarchy and democracy, though still referred to as " perversions," appear in fact as the immanent materiate forms of the contemporary political world. " Polity," the worst of the good constitutions, in which democracy and oligarchy are fused, is the best practical ideal which Aristotle has to offer. V, on the causes and cure of revolutions, is dated by a reference to the murder of Philip of Macedon (336). VI concerns the proper organisation of oligarchies and democracies. Both are written solely for the practical statesman. These three books are marked by acute and mature insight, and by a mass of historical information which clearly belongs to the second Athenian period. They are probably based on the collection of one hundred and fifty-eight constitutions which is known to have been compiled at the Lyceum.[1] Jaeger infers that Aristotle inserted IV–VI at Athens, in order to give a more concrete filling to the programme sketched at the end of EN, but that he fails really to unify the whole course, and leaves the *Politics* " Janus-faced." Book I, on the definition and

---

[1] Aristotle's *Constitution of Athens* alone survives. The historical part of the *Poetics* presupposes, according to Jaeger, a corresponding literary research, and the miscellaneous pseudo-Aristotelian *Problems* is another such compilation.

structure of the state and on household economy—the
fundamental relations of master and slave, husband and
wife, parent and child—he regards as an introduction
added with IV–VI, partly because it refers forward for a
discussion of the family to the criticism of the *Republic*
in II.[1]

For the work of Professor Jaeger's pupils we have space
only for a brief mention of Herr Solmsen's results in the
sphere of Aristotle's logical works.[2] In close connexion
with an analysis of different strata in the *Rhetoric*, he
argues that the dialectical *Topics* is an early Academic
work, completed at the latest by 343–2. The conception
of the perfect basic syllogism of scientific demonstration
belongs, he thinks, to the period of Aristotle's absence
from Athens, and derives from the mathematical procedure
of the understanding in the *Republic* (see p. 211). The
exposition of it in An. Post. I (see pp. 208 ff.) presupposes
that An. Pr. has contained a general treatment of the
inferior figures and moods of syllogism, of which the
basic demonstrative syllogism in " Barbara " is the norm—
much as the ideal state, which is set forth in Pol. VII and
VIII, assumes a previous discussion of inferior and existent
constitutions. But the actual contents of our An. Pr. are
later. Though Aristotle in An. Pr. still does lip-service to
the perfect basic syllogism as the form to which the other
figures require conversion, the conception of reasoning in
An. Pr. is in fact much wider and looser than the doctrine
of Post. An. I permits. To meet the needs of special
science, logic has been made less strict and more flexible.
It has become abstract and " conceptualised " : its
premises (ἀρχαί) have become mere definitions, which

---

[1] It is odd, on this account of the *Politics*, that whereas VII shows a
detailed knowledge of the *Laws*, the account of it in II is most inaccurate.
Professor E. Barker, in a recent paper, has suggested that II was composed at Pella, when Aristotle's memory of the *Laws* was dimmer. At
least this may be true of II 6. Book I has a composite appearance, and
is not easy to place.

[2] *Die Entwicklung der Aristotelischen Logik und Rhetorik*, Berlin, 1929.

no longer reflect real counterparts, as do the ἀρχαί of
An. Post. I. In fact the later elaboration of An. Pr.,
which is what we possess, corresponds closely to our
Pol. IV–VI, where the inferior constitutions gain a prominence not really consistent with the homage still paid to
the ideal state. An. Post. II is also mainly of later origin.
The *Categories*, which is not discussed, would presumably
be ascribed, as by Jaeger, to the scientific activity of the
Lyceum after Aristotle's death.[1]

And now to pass a summary and all too dogmatic
verdict on the two separate questions which arise from
this new analysis of Aristotle's writings : (*a*) the various
dates of their composition, and (*b*) the degree of change
in philosophic outlook deducible when the first question
is settled.

It can be said at once that Jaeger's conclusions as to
the contents and philosophic significance of the dialogues,
and as to their intimate connexion with the earlier phases
of Aristotle's life, are highly probable—although it must
be added that Zeller had already inclined to see in them
a Platonic stage of thought.[2] But the problem with regard
to the treatises is a harder one. (*a*) Jaeger's hypothesis
assumes that any given passage of an Aristotelian treatise,
which does not seem to fit its context, must—if its presence
there is due to Aristotle himself—be either a survival
which escaped revision, or a later addition inserted to
avoid the labour of re-writing. This kind of assumption
has proved a dangerous weapon in the hands of many

---

[1] The elementary character of this work (see note 1, p. 178) makes it
very hard to date. That " In the Lyceum " occurs in it as an example
of place, is no proof (as Jaeger imagines, cp. *Aristoteles*, p. 45, note)
that the work is late—the Lyceum was a haunt of Socrates. It is not
easy to conceive Aristotle or his immediate successors rejecting the
results of Met. VII in favour of its crude teaching, but it is perhaps
safer to base on it no conclusions as to Aristotle's development. The
same may be said of Int., which is also ignored by Solmsen.

[2] *Aristotle and the Earlier Peripatetics* (the English translation of
Phil. der Gr., II, 2), p. 8.

scholars, but in this case it has been used with moderation. On the whole the results of the analyses are at least plausible, and the dates of composition suggested for the treatises, or portions of treatises, discussed, are not improbable.

(b) Jaeger has undoubtedly established the fact of development in Aristotle's mature philosophy, and, as in the case of many other important discoveries, we are left wondering why it had not been made long before.[1] But that Aristotle's whole outlook suffered a revolutionary change is much harder to believe. Doubtless he practically created the natural sciences as such, and doubtless his colleagues at the Lyceum also devoted much time to their pursuit. But the metaphysical fragment of Theophrastus affords no evidence that the speculative enthusiasm of the school was on the wane at Aristotle's death. Nor need we suppose that Aristotle did not acquire his interest in empirical observation until he was fifty. Alexander's Asiatic expedition may have widened his knowledge of the habits of the elephant, but his biological works refer with significant frequence to the fauna of Assos and Mitylene.[2] Moreover, the basic syllogism of An. Post. I, which Solmsen attributes to Aristotle's middle period, is in effect constructed to express a real counterpart in the realm of *nature*. It was no doubt in the first instance taken over from mathematics, but it depends on the distinction from immutable substance of essential accidents which express capacities of *change* (see note 1, p 199). Despite the markedly mathematical atmosphere of An. Post. I, the somewhat unsatisfactory fusion of mathematical and physical method has already there taken place : already the first figure is said to be the vehicle of demonstration in " practically all the sciences which

[1] There are hints of it in Case's article on Aristotle in the *Encyc. Brit.*, 1910. Case regarded EE as an earlier version of EN.
[2] See Ross, *Aristotle*, pp. 3–4.

investigate causes " (79ª20). And the rigorous distinction
of substance from accident is still present in An. Pr. ;
e.g. 43ᵇ6–8. The more flexible logic of the latter treatise
was more probably created to meet the increasing need
for expressing *provisional* formulations of scientific truth.
Aristotle is conscious of the constant coming to light of
fresh species, but he does not question their nature as
real substances.[1] He is still far from the divorce of thought
and things which creates a purely formal logic, and it is
a mistake to minimise in An. Pr. the doctrine of conversion
to the first figure. Again, the treatment of sensible
substance within first philosophy, which Jaeger finds so
significant, may show that Aristotle felt the increasing
importance of empirical science ; but already in the
earlier strata of Met., as Jaeger admits, the results of
physics are presupposed and used by first philosophy.
There does not really seem to be any great change in
Aristotle's attitude here. Jaeger seems, too, to hold that
Aristotle himself deliberately retained different strata in
his courses on first philosophy, psychology, and politics.
The only evidence of complete re-writing is the substitution
for EE of EN, which certainly does exhibit a changed
view of practical intelligence.[2] At all events Aristotle
himself was not conscious of violent self-contradiction.

Nor is it legitimate to argue that because Aristotle felt
the pressing need to encourage and methodise empirical
investigation, he therefore became in respect of first
philosophy a regretful agnostic. In the passage of PA
cited above Aristotle is really contrasting with biology
not the theology of Met. XII, 6, 7, and 10, but cosmical
speculation about the aetherial spheres. The exact con-

---

[1] In Met. X, 9, which Jaeger regards as late, the sharp distinction
of substance and accident is even maintained by the rather startling
exclusion of male and female from the essence of man; cp. note 1, p. 102.

[2] This change of view accounts for the undeniable discrepancy in
Pol. It is in the sphere of the *theoretical* sciences that Jaeger's hypothesis
fails to convince.

nexion within first philosophy between theology and the science of the aether is always ambiguous in Aristotle (cp. p 88, and note 2, p. 195), but that he is thinking in the passage quoted by Jaeger from PA of eternal *sensible* substance is clear from his statement that the evidence from sense-perception is scanty. But of this fact Aristotle was well aware when he wrote Cael. II (see p 90), and it did not prevent him from using the mathematics of Callippus at a much later date to " save the appearances." Jaeger proves definitely that the increased number of unmoved movers is a late doctrine, scarcely hinted at even in Ph. VIII, and that Chap. 10 is an insertion in Met. XII (*Aristoteles* III, Chap. 3) ; but it does not follow that Aristotle, who felt himself bound to take account of Callippus' work, would not have attempted to fit in the new unmoved movers as a grade in the *Scala Universi* intermediate between the Prime Mover and the world of nature. That he failed to do so is clear from objections raised by Theophrastus (*Metaphysics* II, 7, 8), but the very fact that Theophrastus points to the contradiction produced by the new doctrine suggests that Aristotle would have reconciled it if he could, and that he had no intention of sacrificing the *Scala Universi* on the altar of a new faith in empirical truth. No doubt, when he re-wrote his ethical lectures Aristotle had changed his conception of practical wisdom, but it is not a quite unprejudiced eye that sees in EN X a wavering in his conviction that the life of speculation—the full consciousness of union with God in philosophic thought—is man's highest happiness. Nor is it easy to think that those Scholastics who acclaimed their own close kinship with Aristotle's theology, embraced in fact no more than its author's discarded faith.

A more just conclusion from the evidence—which we have in any case to thank Professor Jaeger for setting out so brilliantly—would seem to be this. With the accumulation of observed fact, the results of *a priori* speculation and of empirical inquiry clashed acutely in the middle of the fourth century, as they were bound to clash then and in all successive ages. But Aristotle's solution of the problem was not to cast off theology and to embrace a purely formal logic of validity.[1] The compromise which he reached was a more or less pluralistic system, a *Scala Universi* which offered a place to individual materiate forms. And Aristotle reached this solution early in his career, and, though he developed it, never abandoned it. The difficulties involved in his pluralism are great (see pp. 214–5 ff.), but the materiate form could have meant nothing to him without the notion of pure form, upon which his whole doctrine of form and matter depends. It is less likely that he simply lost grip upon one side of the question, and became a disillusioned empiricist, than that from the day he left the Academy, if not earlier, he strove always after reconciliation.

Professor Jaeger's position presents a further difficulty. In the first part of this book we often enough found Plato in two minds ; but Jaeger tends to assume a fixed and definite Platonic position as the starting-point of Aristotle's reaction. In respect of those dialogues which were closely modelled on Platonic originals this assumption does not greatly vitiate his argument, but in respect of the treatises it does. Though Aristotle is an uncompromising antagonist of the Forms, he never expounds the Platonic theory quite unambiguously,[2] and it is not impossible that under the impulse of his reaction from Plato he believed his own problem newer than it was. To Jaeger the equating in

---

[1] We need not deny that the growth of empirical science has often tended to formalise logic—witness medieval nominalism (see Chap. XI §§ 2 and 3) and modern mathematical logic. But there is not sufficient evidence to show that Aristotle ever forgot that the antithesis of *a priori* thinking and empirical observation is always a relative one.

[2] Jaeger appears to accept the untenable and surely antiquated view (which is certainly not suggested by Aristotle) that Plato first thought of the Form as a re-ified, or substantiated, concept ; see above, pp. 34 ff.

Met. VI 1 of theology with the study of being *qua* being
(see pp. 192 ff.) is prophetic of the transition to the new
formulation of metaphysic, based on analysis of the meanings of " being," which begins in the later VI 2 ; and he
sees in the attempt to unite the notions of this science
of immovable being as (*a*) universal, and (*b*) prior to the
other sciences,[1] a late and unsuccessful harmonising insertion.[2] But the problem of immanence and transcendence—the effort to conceive the fully real as at once
the whole and the culmination of a hierarchy—is eternal
(cp. p. 222). This antinomy lies beneath the conflicting
logical tendencies of Plato's *Sophist*, and it appears already
in the *Republic*—reflected microcosmically—when Plato
likens the definitive rational part of man's soul to the
figure of a man concealed within the image of the whole
man (see p. 46). The essence of that Platonic simile
re-emerges, divested of metaphor, in the discrepancy—
which is due to no mere difference of date—between the
psycho-physics of An. I and II and the hesitant doctrine
of νοῦς in An. III.[3] And we find it again, writ large, in
the last chapter of Met. XII, where Aristotle asks whether
the presence of the good in the universe is analogous to the
discipline of an army or to its general (see p. 172). Not
only St. Thomas, but Descartes, Berkeley, Leibniz, Spinoza,
Kant, and Hegel—all the masters, in fact, who represent
more than a one-sided reaction to their predecessors—
struggled to solve it ; and though each of them stamped
it with the form of his own genius, it remains with us still.

Professor Jaeger's brilliant researches will still be fertile
when the weight of emphasis becomes again normally
distributed, but they do not compel us to modify greatly
our outline sketch of Aristotle's system. Plato's pupil is

---

[1] Met. VI, 1026a30 ; cp. p. 193.
[2] *Aristoteles*, pp. 266 ff.
[3] A doctrine, incidentally, common to An. III and EN X ; see on this
point and others connected with Jaeger's position, Burnet, *Aristotle*, in
Proceedings of the British Academy, Vol. XI.

of the company of the great philosophers who have never forgotten that " all time and all Being " is their province. Were he not, his teaching would be no true development of Plato's ; no form for the sake of which Platonism could be shown to have existed.

BRIEF BIBLIOGRAPHY

I. GENERAL

Aristotelis Opera. Berlin, 1831–70. Text ed. I. Bekker, Fragments ed. V. Rose ; Index (Vol V) by Bonitz.
Teubner texts of all treatises except Cat., Int., An. Pr., An. Post., GA.
Oxford Translation, 1908–31, ed. J. A. Smith and W. D. Ross.
Commentaria in Aristotelem Graeca. Berlin, 1882–1909, with *Supplementum Aristotelicum,* 1882–1903.
G. GROTE. *Aristotle.* Ed. 3. London, 1883.
E. ZELLER, *Die Philosophie der Griechen,* II, 2. Ed. 4 (Anastatic). Berlin, 1921. Eng. Tr. London, 1897.
R. ADAMSON. *The Development of Greek Philosophy.* Edinburgh and London, 1908.
H. SIEBECK. *Aristoteles.* Ed. 4. Stuttgart, 1922.
W. D. ROSS. *Aristotle.* Ed. 2. London, 1930.
W. JAEGER. *Aristoteles.* Berlin, 1923.
J. L. STOCKS. *Aristotelianism.* New York, 1925.

II. SPECIAL

Logic

Organon : text, Lat. tr. and comm., J. Pacius. Frankfort, 1597.
Organon : text and comm., T. Waitz. Leipzig, 1844–6.
An. Post. : Lat. tr. and comm., J. Zabarella. Venice, 1582, etc.
J. ZABARELLA, *Opera Logica.* Venice, 1578, etc.
H. MAIER. *Syllogistik des Aristoteles.* Tübingen, 1896–1900.
F. SOLMSEN. *Entwicklung der Aristotelichen Logik und Rhetorik.* Berlin, 1929.

Natural Science

Physica : text, Lat. tr. and comm., J. Pacius. Frankfort, 1596, etc.
Physica : Lat. tr. and comm., J. Zabarella. Venice, 1600.

Cael., GC, Meteor. (De Mundo), Parva Naturalia : text, Lat.
tr. and notes, J. Pacius. Frankfort, 1601.
GC, Meteor. : Lat. tr. and comm., J. Zabarella. Frankfort, 1600.
GC : text and comm., H. H. Joachim. Oxford, 1922.
J. ZABARELLA. *De Rebus Naturalibus.* Cologne, 1590, etc.
A. MANSION. *Introduction à la Physique Aristotélicienne.*
Louvain and Paris, 1913.
HA : text, Germ. tr. and comm., Aubert and Wimmer.
Leipzig, 1868.
GA : text, Germ. tr. and comm., Aubert and Wimmer.
Leipzig, 1860.
De Anima : text, Lat. tr. and comm., J. Pacius. Frankfort,
1596, etc.
De Anima : Lat. tr. and comm., J. Zabarella. Venice, 1605,
etc.
De Anima : text, French tr. and comm., G. Rodier. Paris,
1900.
De Anima : text, tr. and comm., R. D. Hicks. Cambridge, 1907.
Sen. and Mem : text, tr. and comm., G. R. T. Ross. Cam-
bridge, 1906.
J. I. BEARE. *Greek Theories of Elementary Cognition from
Alcmaeon to Aristotle.* Oxford, 1906.

Metaphysics

Met. : text and comm., H. Bonitz. Bonn, 1848–9.
Met. : trans., H. Bonitz. Berlin, 1890.
Met. : text and comm., W. D. Ross. Oxford, 1924.
L. ROBIN. *Théorie Platonicienne des Idées et des Nombres
d'après Aristote.* Paris, 1908.
W. JAEGER. *Studien zur Entstehungsgeschichte der Metaphysik
des Aristoteles.* Berlin, 1912.
F. RAVAISSON. *Essai sur la Métaphysique d'Aristote.* Ed. 2.
Paris, 1913.
J. STENZEL. *Zahl und Gestalt bei Platon und Aristoteles.*
Leipzig, 1924.

Practical Science

EN : text, Bywater. Oxford, 1890.
EN : comm., J. A. Stewart. Oxford, 1892.
EN : text and comm., J. Burnet. London, 1900.
EE : text, Lat. tr. and comm., A. Fritzsche. Ratisbon, 1851.
H. VON ARNIM, *Die drei aristotelischen Ethiken.* Vienna, 1924.

Pol. : text and comm., W. L. Newman. Oxford, 1887–1902.

Pol. : Bks. I–III, VII, VIII, text and comm., F. Susemihl and R. D. Hicks. London, 1894.

E. BARKER. *Political Thought of Plato and Aristotle.* London, 1906.

Rh. : text and comm., E. M. Cope and J. E. Sandys. Cambridge, 1877.

Rh. : trans., R. C. Jebb. Cambridge, 1909.

Poet. : text, Lat. tr. and comm., T. Tyrwhitt. Oxford, 1794.

Poet. : text, tr. and comm., I. Bywater. Oxford, 1909.

INDEX

This Index is intended to supplement, not to cover, the Table of Contents.

PRINTED BY J. AND J. GRAY, EDINBURGH